Religion in the Medieval West

Bernard Hamilton

Reader in Medieval History, University of Nottingham

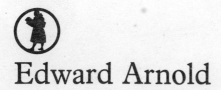

Edward Arnold

© Bernard Hamilton 1986

First published in Great Britain 1986 by
Edward Arnold (Publishers) Ltd, 41 Bedford Square, London WC1B 3DQ

Edward Arnold (Australia) Pty Ltd, 80 Waverley Road, Caulfield East,
  Victoria 3145, Australia

Edward Arnold, 3 East Read Street, Baltimore, Maryland 21202, USA

British Library Cataloguing in Publication Data

Hamilton, Bernard
    Religion in the medieval West.
    1. Church history——Middle Ages, 600–1500
    2. Europe——Church history
    I. Title
    274   BR728.2

ISBN 0-7131-6461-1

Text set in 10/11 pt Plantin Compugraphic
by Colset Private Limited, Singapore
Made and printed in Great Britain by Richard Clay Ltd, Bungay, Suffolk.

Contents

Acknowledgements

Although I have no doubt that this book has many faults these do not result from any lack of expert help and advice but from my incapacity to use it well. I owe much of my understanding of medieval religion to the guidance which I have received from two of the great masters of western spirituality: the late Dom David Knowles, who assisted in the supervision of my post-graduate research, and Father Jean Leclercq, who throughout my adult life has always been ready to advise me and to share freely the wealth of his erudition. In learning to appreciate relations between the Western Church and the Churches of the East I am indebted to the initial training which I received from Professor J.M. Hussey and, in more recent years, to the regular discussions which I have enjoyed with Mr George Every. In writing this book I have been helped in many ways by the kind advice of Professor Rosalind Hill, and I should also like particularly to acknowledge the intellectual stimulus given by Mr R.I. Moore about the problems of medieval heresy. Mr A. Murray has helped me to understand the nature of doubt in the Middle Ages and has kindly allowed me to cite a passage from an unpublished paper. Yet perhaps my greatest thanks are due to my pupils who by their contributions to tutorials and seminars during the past twenty-five years have greatly increased my understanding of medieval religion.

I should like to thank the staff of the following libraries in which I have worked while collecting materials for this book: the British Library, the Bodleian Library, Dr Williams's Library, the University of London Library, and the Library of the School of Oriental and African Studies of the University of London. I should particularly like to thank Mr Peter Hoare and the staff of the Library of the University of Nottingham, where the greater part of the work was carried out, for their invariable courtesy and assistance.

My colleagues in the History Department of the University of Nottingham, Robin Storey, Antonia Gransden, Jan Titow and Michael Jones, deserve my special thanks because they have been willing to undertake additional teaching in order to leave me free time in which to write this book. I should also like to thank the staff of Edward Arnold for their sympathetic attitude to the problems and delays which beset academic writing.

All these friends and colleagues, however great their help, have been able to escape from medieval religion at will, but such has not been the lot of my unfortunate family, and I should like to thank Janet, my wife, and Sarah and Alice, my daughters, for bearing with me so patiently and good-humouredly during the long period which it took me to complete this manuscript. I should like to thank Alice for the help she has given me in correcting the proofs, and Janet deserves special thanks for meticulously proof-reading the typescript, including the index, thus leading me to think that I can answer King Solomon's rhetorical question: 'Mulier fortis quis inveniet?'.

Bernard Hamilton
Nottingham, 1986

Introduction

Religion occupies a very central place in medieval history but one with which many students, coming to the period for the first time, are singularly ill equipped to deal. Books which are written about the medieval church, or even about popular religion at that time, almost all assume a knowledge of the fundamental beliefs of the Christian faith and the organization and worship of the Christian church which many students no longer have. This is a relatively recent problem and largely a consequence of the silent revolution in schools which has transformed Religious Education into some form of Community Ethics. This creates a difficulty for those of us who teach medieval history, for whereas one can tell a student to look up a technical ecclesiastical term like 'dalmatic' or 'tithe' in a standard work of reference, concepts like the Incarnation, Original Sin, Holy Orders, and Purgatory cannot be summarily dealt with in the same way. It is difficult to explain fully what is meant by them without seeming to give a short course in Christian doctrine, which most historians are rightly reluctant to do, but it is not easy to find simple, written accounts to which students may be referred. For simple books about religion have two salient characteristics: they are intended to be persuasive as well as informative; and they are more interested in the present state of the churches than in their historical development.

A second point which needs emphasizing when teaching medieval religious history is that religion, like all other ranges of human activity and experience, constantly changes. This does not necessarily imply any relativism in matters of principle, merely a difference in ways of understanding and applying them. Because Catholicism was the dominant faith in the medieval west students often tend, naturally enough, to think of it in terms of modern Catholic societies such as those of Poland and Ireland, and transpose that kind of well-instructed religious fervour, which was the product of the Counter-Reformation, to medieval society. In fact, as I hope to show, a more accurate analogy would be with some modern South American countries, like Peru or Ecuador, where the population is almost entirely Catholic, but the general degree of instruction, practice and commitment is low.

The third point which needs to be made when dealing with the medieval Christian west is that the word 'religion' did not have the same connotation then. In our own society religious commitment is a matter of personal choice and religion itself an essentially private concern. Students seldom realize how unusual a situation this is, seen in historical perspective, and are confused when they find that in medieval society there was no necessary correlation between belief and commitment. I shall try to examine Christianity in the wider context of

1

a world view, and to explain how in the Middle Ages no distinction was made between religious knowledge and any other kind of knowledge. In such a society there was no necessary connection, as there is assumed to be in our own, between belief in a religious explanation of the universe and personal piety.

The first part of this work deals with the institutional church, the faith which it taught and the means which it used to instruct lay people in it. The second part examines the extent to which the laity understood and practised that faith, and the ways in which lay piety took different forms. Nevertheless, the book is called *Religion in the Medieval West*, not *Christianity in the Medieval West*, for the west was not monolithically Christian then although it is often represented as being so. There were, for example, always communities of Jews in the west and of Muslims too in many frontier regions, while in the later Middle Ages the west gained some knowledge of Buddhism and of the other religions of Asia. The alternatives which those faiths presented to orthodox belief held an attraction for a few people in any generation. From *c.*1000 there were always some dissenters in the west, who in the thirteenth century numbered many thousands, and at other times were reduced to a few hundred, but they never died out and the Protestant Reformation of the sixteenth century inherited a model of religious pluralism and did not invent it. It might have been expected that in a society in which religion was so important a force some people might, in protest, have transferred their allegiance from God to the devil. I have discussed the evidence relating to this, but I venture to disagree with some of the popes who reigned then: I think that there were no Satanists in the Middle Ages, no doubt because people realistically supposed that the prince of darkness only had hell in his gift and were not tempted by the offer.

I end the book with a discussion of the religious difficulties faced by medieval Christians. It is often wrongly supposed that they had none, because their society was homogeneous and shielded them from contrary opinions. As I have tried to show in earlier chapters, the medieval west was not sealed off from all contacts with other religious and philosophical systems; while doubts of all kinds are fundamental human reactions to any kind of certainty.

The chronological limits of this book extend roughly from *c.*500, when Roman rule finally collapsed in western Europe, to the eve of the Protestant Reformation, after which it is impossible to write about Europe as a religious entity.

I had difficulty in deciding which translations to use when citing Biblical or liturgical texts. Since this book is designed largely for people who are not familiar with the Bible or the liturgy, and since no single translation of either is now commonly used in the English-speaking world, I have decided to cite the Bible in the Authorized Version of 1611 and the medieval liturgy where possible in the translations made by Cranmer for the 1549 Prayer Book. Medieval churchmen, of course, read the Bible in the Latin text of the Vulgate, and, in cases where that text differs on points of substance from the Authorized Version, I have amended the passages to give the Vulgate sense. I have also substituted modern words at a few points in the liturgical translations where I think that the older version might confuse my readers (e.g. I have substituted 'Holy Spirit' for 'Holy Ghost' in the Nicene Creed).

I can claim little originality in writing most of this work which, except in a few rather limited areas, is based on my reading of the research undertaken by other scholars. Nevertheless, a work of this kind has not, to my knowledge, been written before, and my experience suggests that there is a need of something of the kind. In one way only it is like the Rule of St Benedict: it is a little book designed for beginners, who, having with its help mastered the basic principles of the beliefs and practices of the medieval west, may then proceed to read with more profit the learned works of other historians listed in the bibliography.

Part I

The Western Church

1
The Emergence of Christian Europe

The church in the Roman Empire

While Roman imperial power collapsed throughout western Europe in the course of the fifth century the established religion of the empire continued to thrive. This was the Catholic church and its period of ascendancy in the Roman state had been very brief. For almost 300 years the imperial authorities had refused to recognize Christianity as a lawful religion and during that time the church was subjected to sporadic, and, on occasions, severe persecution. This ended in 312 when the emperor Constantine the Great granted Christians legal toleration. At that time there were as many Christian churches as there are now, but the largest and best organized of them called itself the Catholic, or universal, church, and it was this church which Constantine patronized and into which he was received on his death-bed. Catholicism became the religion of the court and the church received fiscal and legal privileges from Constantine and his successors, together with huge endowments. Theodosius I (379–95) made it the official religion of the Roman state.

The church's experience of Roman authority left it with an ambivalent attitude towards secular rulers. Three centuries of persecution could not lightly be set aside and even the conversion of Constantine did not guarantee complete security. Some of his successors took the wrong side in doctrinal disputes, while the emperor Julian (360–3), although brought up as a Christian, apostatized from the faith and sought to deprive the church of its privileged status. Throughout the medieval centuries the church remained conscious of its unique responsibility to act as guardian of the Christian revelation and to prevent kings from usurping its spiritual powers. This attitude was a source of much conflict between church and state, although it was also arguably a source of vitality to the church, since it prevented it from sinking into an Erastian torpor.

Theodosius' establishment of the church did not result in the mass conversion of all his subjects to the Catholic faith. The practice of pagan cults was made illegal, but that enactment proved impossible to enforce, and in any case the church was opposed to forced conversions. From its earliest days Christianity in the western empire had been based chiefly in the cities. During the fourth century the church gained many new adherents who followed the example of the court, but it still remained predominantly urban, whereas the majority of people in the late empire, as in all pre-industrial societies, were peasants. The evangelization of the countryside depended on the creation of a Christian landowning class who would encourage the clergy to minister to their tenants and this was far from being achieved by the late fourth century. In some areas, like central Italy, the Rhône valley, southern Spain and north Africa, Christians formed a majority of the population, but elsewhere they were at best a privileged and growing minority. The establishment of the church did not in itself change this.

The barbarian invasions

In less than a generation after its establishment the church was faced by a new challenge as the western provinces of the empire began to be overrun by barbarian tribes of Germanic origin. Although the invaders did not in most cases seek to destroy the empire, which they greatly admired, they nevertheless created conditions of life which made the survival of imperial structures of government impossible. In the course of the fifth century Roman imperial power in the west faded and in its place there grew up a number of independent, barbarian kingdoms. The eastern provinces were less affected by these developments. Christian Roman emperors continued to reign in Constantinople until the Ottoman conquest of 1453 and it would be possible to describe their state as the medieval Roman empire and their church as the eastern Catholic church. Historians do not use these terms, but customarily speak of the Byzantine empire and the Orthodox church when referring to the eastern Mediterranean after *c*.500. This terminology has the merit of emphasizing the different ways in which the two halves of the Roman empire evolved, for Byzantium was the Greek name for Constantinople and Greek came to be the official language of the eastern empire and the liturgical language of the Orthodox church. A different kind of Christian civilization developed there from that found in the medieval west.

The establishment of barbarian kingdoms in the west marked the beginning of the Middle Ages. The Catholic church survived the collapse of Roman power and preserved certain features of classical civilization in the newly evolving society. Three of those features were of great importance. First, the church inherited from Rome a concept of universality; as western Europe became politically fragmented the church kept alive an awareness of a wider community, that of Christendom, which embraced all its members. Secondly, the church's organization had been closely adapted to the secular organization of the late empire: these structures were not merely preserved, but were also extended during the Middle Ages to newly converted regions beyond the former imperial frontiers, and this type of organization, which transcended political divisions, was a concrete expression of the church's belief in universality. Thirdly, the church preserved the Latin language. Latin had been the official language of the Roman empire and the one which all educated people in the western provinces knew well. It performed much the same function of facilitating communication between peoples of different linguistic groups as English does in modern India. It was therefore the language which the church used in its public worship and it continued to use it after the empire had fallen. Thus throughout the medieval centuries, as the vernacular languages of modern Europe came to be formed, Latin remained the *lingua franca* of churchmen and of educated people. This had important consequences for western civilization as well as for religion: the Latin learning of the ancient world remained accessible to scholars, while the exchange of ideas was greatly facilitated by the existence of a single learned language in which all men, irrespective of their racial origins, could express themselves.

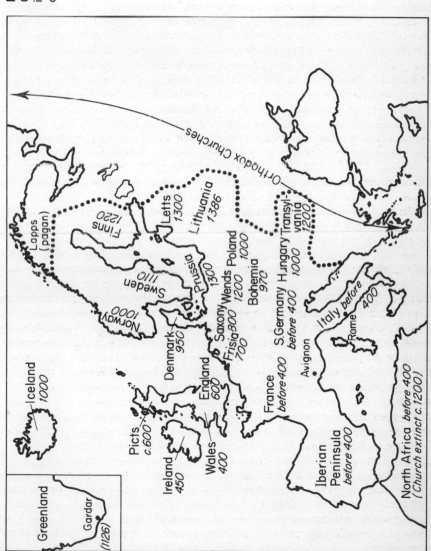

Map 1 The expansion of Catholic Europe. Dates indicate approximate time of conversion.

Orthodox Churches

Greenland
Gardar
(1126)

Iceland
1000

Lapps
(pagan)

Norway
1000

Sweden
1110

Finns
1220

Letts
1300

Lithuania
1386

Prussia
1300

Denmark
950

Saxony
800

Wends
1200

Poland
1000

Bohemia
970

Picts
c.600

Ireland
450

Wales
400

England
600

Frisia
700

France
before 400

S.Germany
before 400

Hungary
1000

Transyl-
vania
1200

Avignon

Italy before
400

Rome

Iberian
Peninsula
before 400

North Africa before 400
(Church extinct c.1200)

The barbarians who settled in Italy, southern France, Spain and north Africa in the fifth century had an aristocracy who were already Christian when they entered the empire, although many of the common people may still have been pagan. Unfortunately for the Catholic hierarchy, these barbarians had been converted to the wrong kind of Christianity. They were Arians, who believed that Christ, though divine, was inferior to God the Father. Arianism had caused deep divisions in the church during the fourth century until it was declared heretical by a General Council in 381, but before that time some of the German tribes beyond the imperial frontiers had been converted by Arian missionaries. When those tribes settled in the empire, they established Arian churches in their kingdoms, which had their own clergy and used a vernacular liturgy. The Catholic church in the fifth century was therefore faced in some parts of the west by the dual problem of a largely pagan rural population and an heretical, ruling warrior-class.

Conversion of the barbarians

The Germanic invaders of northern Europe were pagan. The Franks, who conquered most of northern and central Gaul, tolerated the Catholic church, but a different situation obtained in the neighbouring province of Britain, the only part of the western empire to offer sustained resistance to the barbarians. During the long wars of the fifth and sixth centuries organized Christianity collapsed in those areas occupied by the Anglo-Saxons, although the church survived in the western parts of Britain controlled by the Celts.

A less resilient institution than the Catholic church of the fifth century might have been demoralized by the turn events had taken, but it is an index of the church's vitality that it was, on the contrary, stimulated by the challenges which the new situation presented. Thus the chronicler Prosper of Aquitaine records how, when barbarian immigration was at its height, pope Celestine I (423–32) sent Palladius as bishop to the Irish. This was the first serious attempt by the Catholic authorities to evangelize the pagans of northern Europe living beyond the imperial frontiers. The experiment was successful, for Palladius' work was continued by St Patrick and by *c*.500 the Catholic church was firmly established in Ireland. This was of great importance for the future of Catholicism, since it proved that the church was capable of adapting its structures to the needs of a society in which there were no cities. During the sixth century Irish missionaries, working out of Iona under the leadership of St Columba (†597), succeeded in converting the Picts of the Scottish highlands, another non-urban people living beyond the old, imperial frontier.

Meanwhile the church was also experiencing success in the lands where it had long been established. In 496 Clovis, king of the Franks, who had conquered much of the former province of Gaul, was baptized a Catholic. His people followed his example and the Frankish kingdom was henceforth viewed with special favour by the papacy as the first of the barbarian states to receive the Catholic faith. A century later pope Gregory the Great sent a mission headed by the monk Augustine to the pagan king of Kent, Ethelbert. The king was baptized and Augustine consecrated to the see of Canterbury, and during the next 100 years the numerous pagan kings of the Anglo-Saxons were converted by the joint, if not always harmonious, endeavours of Augustine's successors and of Irish missionaries trained in the Celtic tradition. A uniform system of church government was introduced in England, transcending the political divisions of the heptarchy, by the godly, learned and long-lived archbishop of Canterbury, Theodore of Tarsus (668–89), a Byzantine Greek, who may justly be called the founder of the English church. Thus by 700 the whole of the British Isles had been converted to the Catholic faith, for although the Celtic churches of Ireland, Wales and Scotland differed in organization and discipline from the rest of Catholic Christendom (see chapter 2), they did not differ in belief.

The Arianism of southern Europe collapsed for a variety of reasons during the centuries which witnessed the spread of Catholicism in the north. In north Africa and Italy Arianism was suppressed by the military intervention of the emperor Justinian I (527–65) who restored those provinces to direct rule from Constantinople. The Visigothic kings of Spain abjured their Arianism in 589, while the Arian Lombards, who had conquered much of northern and central Italy after Justinian's death, were finally converted to Catholicism after the death of king Grimoald in 671. The end of Arianism is significant not simply because it marked the triumph of a particular theology of the Holy Trinity, but also because it ensured the emergence of a single church in medieval western Europe. This was to be important for the shaping of a new and distinctive civilization in the west as well as in the religious formation of Europe.

The other, smaller Christian sects which had existed in western Europe in the fourth century gradually withered away during the period of barbarian settlement, until by 700 the Catholic church was unchallenged. By that time it had succeeded in evangelizing most, though not all, of the rural population living within the old imperial frontiers, so that the former Roman provinces of the west had become at least nominally Christian.

The challenge of Islam

As the challenge posed by Arianism ended, the church was faced by a new threat from the south. The prophet Mahomet (570–632) united the peoples of Arabia under his leadership in obedience to a new religious revelation. The religion which he founded was Islam, and in the century following his death the Arabs conquered an empire which extended from the Indus valley to the Atlantic. In the western Mediterranean they conquered north Africa in the late seventh century and by 718 had annexed Spain, with the exception of a small Christian enclave in the Basque provinces and Galicia. This did not lead to the extinction of Catholicism in Muslim-held areas. The Muslims tolerated Christians and allowed them freedom of worship, although they subjected them to certain civil disabilities. There was no policy of forced conversion in Islam, although during the centuries of Muslim rule there were many voluntary conversions among the Christian community. Throughout the early Middle Ages a Catholic hierarchy survived in Muslim Spain and north Africa and maintained a fitful contact with the rest of the church. Christians living under Muslim rule in Spain were known as Mozarabs, but this name does not signify any break with the Catholic tradition: they held the same faith as the rest of the Christian west and remained in communion with the church there.

The Arab empire formed a barrier to Catholic expansion in southern Europe. While prepared to tolerate members of other faiths who were monotheists,

Islamic rulers refused to permit attempts to convert Muslims. It was an offence punishable by death in Islamic states to criticize the Muslim faith, and similarly it was a capital offence for a Muslim to renounce Islam and become a Christian. The Islamic world thus provided opportunities for martyrdom but not for fruitful missionary activity. This meant that after 700 the church could not expand to the south and had to concentrate its missionary endeavours on the pagan peoples to the north and east.

The conversion of Germany

The major part in the initial stages of this work was undertaken by the Anglo-Saxons. From the late seventh century they inaugurated a period of intense missionary activity directed chiefly to the Low Countries, and central and southern Germany. Having received their own faith partly from Rome, the missionaries worked in close conjunction with the papacy. The Frankish rulers claimed authority over many of the territories in which the Anglo-Saxons worked and gave them their support, and in this way, particularly through the influence of St Boniface of Exeter (†757), the close links between the Frankish crown and Rome, which had been established under Clovis, were renewed by his Carolingian successors. When Frankish rule was extended to Saxony by the conquests of Charlemagne (768–814), the population was forcibly converted, despite the protests of enlightened churchmen. This policy was completely at variance with the practice of the western church in the early Middle Ages, but, as a result of it, Germany as far east as the Elbe became part of Catholic Christendom.

The conversion of Scandinavia and central Europe

Christian expansion was halted in the ninth century by a new wave of barbarian invasions. First Viking raiders from Scandinavia began to attack the coastal areas and river systems of northern Europe. These raids lasted throughout the ninth century and caused widespread devastation, particularly in the British Isles, northern and western France, the Low Countries and northern Germany. Pagan Vikings settled and founded independent states in some areas where Christianity was firmly established, notably eastern England, the area around Dublin in Ireland and the duchy of Normandy.

Just as the Viking raids were becoming less intense, the pagan Magyars crossed the Carpathians in 895 and settled in the plains of Hungary. They were skilled horsemen and conducted annual raids throughout much of central and southern Europe, reaching as far afield as Burgundy and Rome, before their attacks were finally halted by the defeat which Otto I of Germany inflicted on them at the Lechfeld in 955. There were few areas of the Christian west which were not raided either by the Vikings or by the Magyars and the institutional church suffered much damage because the raiders singled out great churches and monasteries which housed liturgical vessels made of precious metals.

Christianity was by this time too well established in the west to be seriously threatened by pagan raiders, or even by pagan settlement, and, as in the fifth century, the church responded to this new challenge by undertaking missionary activity. The pagan Vikings who settled in the west, despite their proclivity to loot shrines, were not hostile to Christianity in principle. Many of them married

Christian girls and the children of these mixed marriages came in the course of the tenth century to accept the Catholic faith. Since the Viking settlers preserved strong links with their homelands, their conversion afforded the church opportunities of spreading the faith in Scandinavia. This was a slow process, for whereas Denmark became predominantly Christian in the second half of the tenth century and Norway in the reign of St Olaf (1016–29), Sweden remained largely pagan until the mid-twelfth century, while Finland did not accept Christianity formally until the end of that century. The Christian Vikings spread their faith in the lands which they had discovered and settled in the north Atlantic. Iceland was converted in 1000 and in 1126 the first Catholic bishop took up residence at Garda in western Greenland to care for the Viking colonists there.

The tenth and early eleventh centuries might be described as the golden age in the expansion of the medieval western church, for missions were at work in central Europe simultaneously with those in the Viking lands. After a number of false starts the church was finally established in Bohemia with the appointment of a bishop of Prague in 972; while the rulers of Poland accepted Christianity and a new province of the church was set up there in 1000. Arguably the greatest triumph of the church was to convert the Magyars. Their ruler, Waik, was baptized a Catholic in 996 and became St Stephen 'the first-crowned', the first Christian king of Hungary, and during his reign a Catholic hierarchy was established in his country.

Christian reconquest in the south

Thus by *c*.1050 much of central and northern Europe had been converted to Christianity and this had been achieved mainly through peaceful missionary activity. The next phase of Catholic expansion took the form of military conquest. This began in the eleventh century when Sardinia, Sicily and Malta were reconquered from the Muslims. At the same time the Christian rulers of northern Spain began the wars of reconquest which ended only with the fall of Granada in 1492, when the whole Iberian peninsula was restored to Christian rule. These wars were an expression of the same social and religious factors which gave rise to the crusading movement, to which they are closely related. In the view of the Catholic hierarchy the purpose of wars against Islam was not to force Muslims to become Christians, but to replace Islamic by Christian rulers who would protect the church and allow it to evangelize their non-Christian subjects peacefully. This policy was followed: the Catholic church was re-established in all the conquered regions and the Mozarabic church of Muslim Spain was reintegrated with the rest of western Christendom, but Muslims were granted religious toleration and forced conversions were forbidden. Indeed, in Spain, though not elsewhere, attempts at evangelization were so half-hearted that sizable Muslim enclaves were still to be found in the Christian kingdoms at the end of the fifteenth century. (See chapter 15.)

The western powers failed to make any lasting conquests in north Africa, but their frequent attacks on the coastal cities led to a growth of intolerance among the Muslim population for the native Christian communities there. By the early thirteenth century organized Catholicism in north Africa had come to an end, although a few isolated Christian villages survived for another hundred years.

Expansion in the Baltic

Christian expansion in the central Middle Ages was not confined to the Mediterranean. In 1146 Eugenius III allowed the Second Crusade to be preached against the pagan Wends, living to the east of the Elbe, as well as against the Muslims of Spain and the Holy Land. The area between the Elbe and the Oder had briefly been brought under German rule by the Ottonian emperors in the tenth century but had subsequently regained its independence. The Second Crusade initiated a period of German conquest and settlement in that region, accompanied by the imposition of Catholicism on the native population. During the thirteenth century, chiefly through the work of the Teutonic Knights, a military religious Order (see chapter 3), East Prussia, Latvia and Esthonia were conquered and converted to Catholicism. In all these Baltic areas pagans who refused to become Christian were baptized at the point of the sword, and the papacy, while deploring this policy, reluctantly conceded that most of those baptisms were valid. The Teutonic Knights failed in their attempt to conquer Lithuania, which was a large kingdom comprising much of what is now western Russia and the Ukraine. It remained pagan until 1386 when its ruler, Ladislas Jagiello, married the heiress to the Polish throne and was baptized, thus enabling Catholic missionaries to work freely among his people.

Further opportunities for Catholic evangelization in eastern Europe were limited. Missionaries from Constantinople had, in the ninth and tenth centuries, converted Bulgaria, Serbia and Russia to the Orthodox church. At the western end of the religious frontier between Catholics and Orthodox, Bosnia, in what is now northern Yugoslavia, became nominally Catholic, and Croatia, which had strong links with Italy, was very firmly Catholic, while all the lands to the south remained Orthodox. In the modern state of Romania, the northern province of Transylvania was converted to Catholicism in the twelfth century through Hungarian influence, while the remaining provinces of Moldavia and Wallachia embraced the Orthodox faith. By 1400 there were no pagan enclaves left in Europe, except among the Lapps, who lived in Scandinavia to the north of the Arctic circle. Christianity extended from the Atlantic seaboard to the Volga, but the dividing line within that area between the Orthodox and Catholic churches was not simply a religious one, for it separated two distinct civilizations, each of which was given cohesion by an established church.

When considering the western church in the medieval centuries it is necessary to remember that it had spread at a very uneven rate. Although it is customary to speak of the Christian west at that time as a unity, the concept needs to be treated cautiously. Throughout the Middle Ages there was a great difference between those lands where Christianity had been established for centuries and those which had been newly converted: thus in 1500 Lithuania had been Christian for only a century, whereas in England the faith had been established for 900 years, while in cities like Rome and Lyons the church had existed for 1400 years or more. It is therefore essential, when considering evidence about medieval western religion, to reflect whether it relates to a newly converted region in which church organization was slight and paganism a living tradition, or to an area which had been Christian for centuries.

2
The Church in Society

The word church was used in the Middle Ages in two senses: in the broader sense it referred to all baptized Catholics and was virtually coextensive with western society, but in a narrower sense it referred to an institution recognized at law, with the right to hold property and legislate for its members, in which authority was vested in the clergy. They were divided into two groups. The regular clergy, who lived under a rule (Latin *regula*), were monks or members of religious orders and will be discussed in chapter 3. This chapter is concerned with the secular clergy, those who lived in the world and were engaged in active ministry. Ordinary church members, who held no special office, were known as the laity, which means 'the people [of God]'. The institutional church not only regulated the religious life of lay people but also influenced western society in a variety of other ways and these need to be considered because they formed an important part of the impact which Christianity made on western Europe during the Middle Ages.

The ecclesiastical hierarchy

The most important members of the clergy were the bishops, who were regarded as the successors of the apostles whom Christ had appointed to rule over the church. From the earliest times bishops had normally lived in cities and exercised authority over all Christians in the surrounding region: the bishop's city was his see, and the area which he ruled his diocese. A more complex ecclesiastical structure developed by the fourth century, which was closely modelled on the imperial administration. In the late empire the basic unit of local government was the city (*civitas*); cities were grouped together to form provinces; and groups of provinces formed vicariates. In the church the basic unit was the diocese ruled by a bishop; dioceses were grouped together to form church provinces presided over by archbishops; and provinces were grouped under the direction of metropolitan archbishops, or primates. Above the metropolitans were the patriarchs of Rome, Constantinople, Antioch, Alexandria and Jerusalem, each of whom had authority over the metropolitans in his patriarchate. Archbishops, metropolitans and patriarchs were all in bishop's orders, and each had his own diocese, but they possessed greater dignity and authority than their fellow bishops.

The papacy before 1050

Rome was the only patriarchal see in the western church. Its bishop is normally called the pope (meaning father), and that title will be used throughout this book, although until the eleventh century when it was reserved to the Roman see, it could be used of any bishop. The pope, as successor of St Peter, claimed powers which were different from those of other bishops, and these will be discussed in chapter 4. The present chapter is concerned solely with his role in church government. Although his relations with the eastern patriarchs were often stormy (see chapter 16), his position as chief bishop in the western church was, with rare exceptions, not contested throughout the Middle Ages.

The role of the institutional church in western society underwent a great change in the eleventh century chiefly as a result of a revolution in papal leadership. Before that time the pope had been revered as successor of St Peter, guardian of the apostolic shrines in Rome and chief bishop in the western church. Until 751, when the Byzantines lost control of central Italy, the popes were political subjects of the eastern emperors. Pope Stephen II (752–7) laid claim to the former Byzantine territories, which became the States of the Church. This claim was justified by the Donation of Constantine, a document forged in the papal chancery in the later eighth century, which purported to be the grant of jurisdiction over all the lands of the west made to pope Sylvester I by Constantine the Great when he moved his capital to Constantinople. It represented a symbolic truth in that the Catholic church had indeed preserved many of the ideals of imperial Rome in the barbarian west since the fifth century. Stephen II called in Pepin, king of the Franks, to protect the papacy against the Lombards and he and his successors guaranteed papal sovereignty in the States of the Church. In 800 Leo III crowned Pepin's son, Charlemagne, as emperor of the west, and although this was merely a recognition of Charlemagne's political power, the pope's claim to confer the imperial title derived from the Donation of Constantine. But the popes made little further use of their alleged temporal powers before the eleventh century, although it was accepted that only the pope could crown the western emperor. The theory which governed relations between church and state in the early Middle Ages was that of the two swords enunciated by pope Gelasius I (492–6). The swords symbolized supreme spiritual power, conferred on the pope by God, and supreme temporal power, conferred on the emperor by God: since each power was sovereign in its own sphere problems only arose in determining the boundaries of the two jurisdictions.

Papal elections were regulated by the decree of 769 which stated that the pope should be chosen by the clergy and people of Rome from among the priests and deacons of the city. In practice this meant that the Roman nobility controlled the appointment unless the western emperor intervened. Papal administration was rudimentary: the pope's librarian and archivist acted as his private secretary, and there were seven lay officials who ran the papal chancery and treasury and dealt with civil law cases in the city of Rome. The pope's chief religious advisers were the cardinals: they were the seven bishops whose sees were nearest to Rome, the twenty-five priests of the main city churches and the seven deacons attached to the pope's household. The papal revenues came almost entirely from the landed endowments of the Roman church and from certain dues paid by the inhabitants of the Papal States.

Most of the early medieval popes were Roman clergy with little experience of a wider world and few resources to enable them to intervene in its affairs had they wished to do so. There were popes, like Gregory I (590–604) and Nicholas I (858–67), who had considerable influence throughout Christendom, but they were exceptional. Nevertheless, all popes had some degree of influence in the western church, because certain powers belonged to the pope alone. He was the final court of appeal in ecclesiastical cases; his permission was needed to set up a new province in the church; he alone could remove an archbishop from office or exempt clergy from the jurisdiction of their bishop. The pope could make written rulings, known as decretals, which were binding on the whole church, appoint legates to represent him in any part of the church, and summon a General Council. Because the pope possessed these prerogatives his power was felt throughout the western church, but it was exercised only occasionally, not routinely. His most important function was to be a focus of Catholic unity, and this was symbolized from the ninth century by the requirement that every newly elected archbishop should visit Rome to be invested with a *pallium*, a woollen scarf which he should wear when officiating as a sign that he was in communion with the Roman see. This rule came to be taken seriously: Harold II of England refused to be crowned by archbishop Stigand of Canterbury in 1066 because he had not been granted a *pallium*.

Bishops in the early Middle Ages

So long as papal authority remained weak real power in the church rested with the bishops. A bishop was assisted in his diocese by lesser clergy whom he ordained and who exercised delegated authority on his behalf. There were seven grades of holy orders in the medieval church: those of janitors, lectors, exorcists, acolytes, subdeacons, deacons and priests, but only priests had a significant role in church organization. The other six orders were an archaic survival from the early church when a wider range of ministry had existed: they continued to be conferred as a preliminary to priestly ordination, and there were always some men who remained permanently in one of the minor orders. Although they were recognized as clergy, such men were only empowered to carry out minor functions in the church, whereas a priest could perform all the functions necessary for the routine conduct of church life and was, in effect, the bishop's delegate in the local community.

The bishop had his throne in a cathedral, which was administered by a chapter of canons, who were normally priests and were in charge of public worship there. Other churches in the diocese were founded in a piecemeal way, by lay or ecclesiastical patrons who paid the building costs and provided stipends for the priests who served them. In some areas, where churches were few, minsters were founded, which were served by a group of clergy responsible for ministering to a large district. But by c.1000 churches had been established in all major areas of settlement throughout most of northern Europe apart from newly converted regions. This made possible the growth of a parish system. Each diocese was divided into parishes in each of which a priest had cure of souls. In southern Europe, where the church had been established longer, a full parish system developed rather more slowly, but the result was much the same throughout western Europe, in that by the eleventh century everybody living in a town or village had a local church. It remained true, of course, throughout the Middle Ages, that people living in isolated farmsteads and small hamlets often had to travel long distances to the nearest church.

Clergy and laity in the early Middle Ages

Even in the early Middle Ages bishops were set apart from lay people. They were forbidden to marry and although they enjoyed the same legal and social status as noblemen they were not allowed to fight. They were also exempt from secular jurisdiction: a bishop accused of a criminal offence was tried by his fellow bishops. The lesser clergy were not so clearly differentiated from the laity. Although a decretal of 386 forbade the marriage of priests and deacons this was widely disregarded. Lower clergy, like their bishops, were exempt from military service, but their judicial position was not clearly defined. All clergy accused of criminal offences were tried by secular courts and, if found guilty, sent to their bishop to be unfrocked, that is, deprived of clerical status. In some kingdoms the punishment of convicted clergy was left to the bishop's discretion, but in others it was imposed by the secular courts.

The church enjoyed some degree of autonomy in the early Middle Ages. An archbishop had the right to convene synods of the bishops in his province which had powers to enact ecclesiastical laws binding on the laity as well as the clergy. In addition each bishop had a court which had powers to deal with ecclesiastical offences committed by both clergy and lay people. Church courts could only impose ecclesiastical penalties, such as excommunication or various forms of penance. The power of church courts was weakened by the absence of an authoritative code of canon law in the western church: each province had its own collection of church laws, and considerable variation existed between them.

The institutional church was centrally involved in the secular activities of society. Bishops and abbots received considerable grants of land from kings and noblemen, which gave them political and economic power in all the kingdoms of the west. In addition the clergy's virtual monopoly of literacy in the early Middle Ages made them indispensable to rulers in the work of administration. Throughout those centuries bishops and abbots sat in royal councils, were influential in drafting secular law-codes and took a major part in affairs of state.

To the peasants who lived on the estates of the church the bishop or abbot was not merely ecclesiastical superior but also secular landlord. If the peasants were serfs the ecclesiastical landlord had jurisdiction over them, and this was extended in some cases to free peasants also when central government broke down in parts of Europe during the Viking invasions. Since clergy were forbidden to pronounce sentences involving death or mutilation for criminal offences, as the secular law-codes often required, the task of presiding over criminal justice for church tenants was delegated by them to laymen known as advocates.

During the ninth and tenth centuries churchmen frequently became involved in military organization. In pre-Carolingian times lands were normally given unconditionally to the church, but from the ninth century a number of conditions began to attach to such grants. Some donors specified only that certain prayers should be said for the benefactor, but others imposed military obligations. Churchmen who held lands in this kind of feudal tenure were not required to fight, but they had to provide and marshal a specified number of troops for the donor's service.

Not all dioceses were well-endowed, while some parishes had no landed endowments. This led the church to introduce a religious tax, the tithe, modelled on Old Testament enactments. Initially payments were voluntary, but by the tenth century tithe had become a legal requirement throughout the west. It was payable by all Christians unless, as was the case with some religious orders, they were exempted by the pope. It consisted of the payment of a tenth of all major grain crops, the greater tithe, and a tenth of other produce, like fruit and poultry, the lesser tithe. Theoretically tithe should have been paid on all sources of income, but this enactment was seldom enforced because non-agrarian income proved difficult to assess. In theory a proportion of the tithe should have been paid to the bishop in poor dioceses and the rest used for the support of the parish clergy, but in practice it was received by the patron of the living. Parish churches had been founded in some cases by bishops or abbots, but in the majority of cases by laymen. The founder reserved the right to nominate the priest and normally claimed the tithe: if he was a layman this was known as lay impropriation of tithe. The patron, whether a layman or a senior churchman, kept most of the tithe and only granted a proportion to the parish priest, sometimes only the lesser tithe. Tithe was the only tax regularly levied in most western countries throughout the Middle Ages and compared with modern rates of taxation it was not harsh, but it must have proved burdensome to those of the peasantry who lived at subsistence level. Moreover it did not achieve its purpose, since the chief beneficiaries were lay landowners, not the parish clergy.

Lay control of the church, 900–1050

Lay impropriation of tithe was a symptom of a wider problem which the church faced in the post-Viking age. In the years 900–1050 throughout most of the west the church passed under lay control. In areas like England or Germany, where there was a strong monarchy, lay control meant royal control. Devout rulers often made exemplary church appointments and endowed the church lavishly, but others despoiled the church and appointed unsuitable men to high office. In areas where royal power was weak, like France and parts of Italy, the situation was much worse, for church lands were sequestered by rapacious noblemen who often conferred bishoprics and abbacies on men who did not take holy orders, but drew the revenues of their benefices while styling themselves bishop-elect or abbot-elect. Moreover, the sale of church offices by lay patrons became common: this was denounced as simony by the devout, the sin of Simon Magus who had tried to buy the Holy Spirit from the Apostles (Acts, 8, 9–24). The appointment of unsuitable bishops led to a decline in observance among the lower clergy, who in some places ceased to perform their religious duties.

The extent of these abuses created a desire for reform among devout laymen, monastic reformers (see chapter 3) and canon lawyers, but these isolated groups made only a limited impact until they were given cohesion by the papacy. This occurred in 1046 when the emperor Henry III ended the dominance of the Roman nobility at the papal court and began to nominate popes with reforming ideals.

The political consequences of papal reform

When Henry III died in 1056 the papal reformers were still seeking to achieve their aims by working in harmony with secular princes. They were soon super-seded by radical reformers, led by the future pope Gregory VII (1073–85), who believed that abuses could only be eradicated by freeing the clergy completely from lay control. Gregory VII considered himself a conservative who was merely seeking to restore the good order which had formerly existed in the church, but in fact he was a radical who attempted to revolutionize the traditional pattern of relations between church and state. He abandoned the Gelasian theory of the two swords and claimed that both temporal and spiritual authority were granted to the pope by God, and that the pope delegated temporal authority to lay rulers but reserved the right to define how it should be used and therefore had the power to depose those who refused to use it in the right way. His successors never formally relinquished these claims, which were re-stated in more extreme forms by canon lawyers, but the reality was very different.

The papacy itself did become independent from lay control. In 1059 the right of electing the pope was vested in the Roman cardinals alone and all lay parti-cipation was excluded. The cardinals ceased to be exclusively Roman and were recruited from all over the west. They delegated their ecclesiastical duties in Roman churches to deputies, and while some, who were usually bishops, spent most of their time in their country of origin, others became full-time admini-strators in the Roman curia and the pope's chief advisers. By broadening membership of the college popes became better informed about world affairs, while the cardinals began to choose popes of different nationalities, so that the papacy ceased to be a Roman monopoly. The popes could only remain indepen-dent of lay control by preserving their sovereignty in the States of the Church. This involved them in wars, lasting intermittently from 1075 to 1268, with the other rulers of Italy, the western emperors who ruled the north and the kings of Sicily who ruled the south. The papacy was victorious in these struggles and did not become politically subject to any lay power.

Papal attempts to end lay control of all senior church appointments met with less success. This policy was vigorously resisted by all western rulers since it struck at an important base of their power, and the dispute was ended by a series of concordats which the papacy made with those rulers in the early twelfth century. It was agreed that the forms of free elections should be observed in the appointment of bishops and abbots, but that the ruler should be represented and an appeal might be lodged to Rome if the election were conducted uncanonically. Bishops and abbots should continue to do homage to lay rulers for their feudal lands and perform the customary services for them. Thus secular influence was not eliminated, since kings continued to have a decisive voice in the appointment of senior churchmen, but the right of appeal reduced the likelihood of scandalous appointments being made. Twelfth-century bishops were, on the whole, more suited to senior office in the church than their unreformed predecessors had been.

During its prolonged and often bitter disputes with lay rulers the papacy became a major political force. Since its military resources were negligible the Holy See had to rely chiefly on diplomatic skills, and the employment of legates in an age when no state had resident ambassadors in other countries gave the popes an advantage in this regard. The papacy formed political alliances against rulers who threatened their Italian interests, and exploited weaknesses within the feudal monarchies. Vassals were bound to their kings by oaths of homage and by dis-pensing them from those oaths the popes were able to unleash civil war in feudal states.

It is not a coincidence that the first crusade was preached in 1095 when the struggle between the papacy and temporal rulers was at its height, for the crusade was an affirmation of the pope's claim to supreme temporal as well as spiritual power. The crusade had revolutionary implications for a feudal society: knights who took the cross withdrew their services from their lords for an indefinite length of time to serve in the holy war under papal leadership, while serfs who joined the crusade became free men. The success of the first crusade in recapturing Jerusalem guaranteed the survival of crusading as an integral part of papal policy throughout the Middle Ages. The crusade proved a flexible weapon, for it was later directed against the Moors in Spain, the pagans in the Baltic, the schismatic Greeks, western rulers who were sympathetic to heresy and Catholic princes whom the pope had excommunicated. In the crusade the papacy had found a method of calling on the knighthood of the west to defend the church against both internal and external enemies.

The ecclesiastical consequences of papal reform

The reformed papacy came to exercise greater control over the institutional church, partly through the regular appointment of legates to represent the pope at a regional level and partly through the enforcement of a uniform code of canon law. The twelfth century witnessed a great revival of learning in western Europe, and one example of this was the growth of a school of canon lawyers at Bologna, led by Gratian who systematized the heterogeneous laws of the church and produced in *c.*1150 a coherent corpus, the *Decretum*. This made it possible to train canon lawyers in a uniform way and to provide the church courts throughout the west with a standard text of church laws, which could be updated as new laws were enacted.

The new code of canon law made the distinction between clergy and laity more clear-cut than it had previously been. Strenuous attempts were made to enforce the law of priestly celibacy, and from the twelfth century priests were not allowed to contract legal marriages. This set them apart from the laity, for although priestly concubinage remained common, priests' children were bastards and could not inherit property and priests' mistresses had no social status. Clergy were also further distinguished as a class by being exempted from the jurisdiction of secular courts. Clergy accused of criminal offences were tried in the church courts which could not impose sentences of death or mutilation. Those convicted of serious offences would normally be unfrocked, which would render them liable to prosecution in the secular courts for any subsequent offence, but this did not lessen the resentment which lay people justifiably felt about the double standard which existed in the punishments inflicted on clergy and laymen who had committed the same crimes. The problem was compounded by the fact that benefit of clergy extended not only to those in minor orders but even to tonsured clerks. It was customary for those who intended to take holy orders to be tonsured by a bishop, and such men could claim clerical status even if they were not subsequently ordained. This privilege extended to a wide group of men: most university students in the Middle Ages, for example, received the tonsure, but they, and those who had received any of the four lowest orders, remained free to marry and to pursue lay careers, so that only their clerical privilege distinguished them from laymen.

As a result of the growth of canon law, church courts came to exercise a much greater degree of control over lay people from the twelfth century. Marriage law and testamentary law, which dealt with the making and execution of wills, were administered by the church courts which thus came to occupy a central place in the lives of the propertied classes. In addition church courts became responsible for the enforcement of public morality and religious observance. This involved matters like prostitution, illegitimate births and blasphemous behaviour during divine worship, and such cases were heard in the courts of archdeacons, the legal advisers of bishops. The strictness with which such laws were enforced varied a great deal in accordance with the diligence of the archdeacon and the readiness of lay witnesses to give evidence.

The laity were, of course, also affected by the establishment of the Inquisition by pope Gregory IX in 1233 to investigate cases of heresy. This will be considered in more detail in chapter 18, but it should be noted here that the Inquisition's importance has been greatly exaggerated. It only operated in certain parts of Europe (there was no Inquisition in England, or Castile, for example), it was vigorous only between c.1255 and 1325, and it was more concerned about reconciling heretics to the church than about handing them over to the secular authorities for punishment. Nevertheless, it is a further example of the way in which lay people became more subject to the judicial authority of the church in the later Middle Ages.

Canon law emphasized the importance of the papal office and the implications of this affected all levels of society. Certain sins, such as the murder of a bishop, were reserved to the pope, that is, only the pope could grant absolution in such cases; similarly only the pope was empowered to grant dispensations from some canon law enactments, for example from impediments to marriage; and Rome was the final court of appeal in all ecclesiastical cases. The Roman curia increased tenfold in size between 1050 and 1350 because of the volume of business with which it had to deal. A large curial staff meant increased papal expenditure, as did the regular dispatch of legatine missions and the wars and international diplomacy in which the papacy engaged. Traditional sources of revenue proved insufficient and the history of the western church from c.1300 to the end of the Middle Ages was centrally affected by papal efforts to remain solvent.

Papal finances in the late Middle Ages

This phase of papal history opened with a quarrel between pope Boniface VIII and Philip IV of France about the king's right to tax the clergy. It was conducted with all the rhetoric of earlier quarrels about the relation between temporal and spiritual power, but the subject of contention was money and this is indicative of the preoccupations of both governments: how to meet the rising costs of a centralized administration. Boniface found that the traditional spiritual sanctions, which had served his predecessors well in their quarrels with feudal monarchs, did not work in the context of an embryonic nation-state like fourteenth-century France, where power was vested in salaried officials, dependent on the king's goodwill, not in feudal vassals bound to the king by oaths of homage.

Boniface's successors profited from his experience and became more willing to compromise with heads of state. Throughout much of the fourteenth century the popes lived at Avignon, where they enjoyed a peace which they seldom found in Rome, and were able to overhaul their machinery of government. As a result papal revenues increased enormously. Judicial profits grew largely as a result of popular demand, for it became common to refer cases to the curia in the first instance since no appeal was possible from a papal decision and therefore less time was wasted in litigation. But the chief source of increased revenue came from the extension of papal provisions. Provision was the system whereby the pope reserved the right to appoint, or provide to, certain benefices, and during the fourteenth century all senior church appointments as well as many minor ones were made subject to provision. Provision was a financial device: candidates continued to be appointed in the traditional way, many of them by lay rulers, but papal ratification was necessary before they could take up office. This involved the payment of fees for letters of appointment and the successful candidate was also required to pay a third of his first year's income to the pope if his benefice was worth more than 100 florins a year and his entire first year's income if the benefice was worth less. These payments were known as annates and were in effect a tax on all the senior clergy.

Heads of state were willing to allow the popes to receive large sums of money in this way from their subjects provided that they were allowed to tax the clergy themselves. Nevertheless, there was an imbalance in the system, for the popes received money from the provincial churches every year but only allowed kings to tax their clergy occasionally. This system changed in the fifteenth century when papal authority was weakened by attempts to make General Councils a regular feature of church government (see chapter 4). Popes then became willing to make concessions to western rulers in order to gain their support against the conciliarists. Those concessions were embodied in a series of concordats in which the popes agreed to restrict their right to provide to benefices in particular countries, and allowed rulers to make appointments instead.

As a result papal income declined. Various measures were taken to make good the loss: the sale of curial offices and of indulgences (see chapter 13) and the increased grant of dispensations were among the more profitable. But the papacy's greatest financial asset was the States of the Church and in the later fifteenth century popes sought to enforce their authority more strictly in those States and to collect their revenues in full. Inevitably this policy led to wars with neighbouring states over boundary disputes, but these conflicts could not be considered wars of principle, like those which popes had fought in the twelfth and thirteenth centuries. Popes like Julius II (1503–12) were concerned to acquire new provinces, not to secure the political independence of the Holy See, which was not at risk. The popes of the early sixteenth century were widely censured for behaving like secular princes and, of course, their financial problems remained unsolved because war involved them in additional expenditure.

The decline in episcopal authority after 1300

The most notable characteristic of the late medieval church is a weakening of the powers of bishops within their dioceses. This was a direct consequence of the centralization of ecclesiastical power in the Roman curia. Whereas bishops had formerly had authority over all the clergy in their dioceses, this was no longer true by 1500. Successive popes had granted exemptions from episcopal authority to the religious orders and had made them directly responsible to the Holy See (see chapter 3), and since many of those orders held the right of presentation to parish churches this weakened the bishops' authority over the parish clergy. Moreover, the growth of papal provisions weakened the bishops' powers of patronage, while the centralization of judicial business in the curia weakened the powers of the bishops' courts.

The calibre of parish clergy arguably declined as a result of papal centralization of power: certainly it showed no improvement. The eleventh- and twelfth-century reformers had persuaded many lay patrons to surrender their tithes to the church, but such grants had normally been made to a bishop or a religious community and rarely to the parish priest. The tithes were usually retained by their new holders, so that the parish clergy were in most cases no better paid than they had previously been. Some parishes, particularly town parishes, had substantial endowments and did not rely on tithe, but many of these became subject to papal provision. In many of those cases the priest appointed was non-resident and drew the stipend while paying a fee to a curate to carry out his duties. Many of the best livings were held in plurality by bishops or curial officials.

The clergy who were willing to serve in poor country parishes or to act as vicars for the non-resident incumbents of rich city churches were usually the least gifted members of their profession. They were often poorly educated and tended to be rapacious about the exaction of minor fees because they were badly paid. Yet it was such men who came to have cure of souls in many parishes. This is not, of course, the whole picture: there were also devout and well-educated parish priests who performed their duties diligently, but the abuses of non-residence and pluralism were sufficiently widespread to be a cause of complaint in most parts of the western church.

Moreover, there was by the end of the Middle Ages a general feeling of pessimism about the possibility of finding remedies for these evils. Many bishops did not reside in their sees and made no attempt to discipline their clergy, while even reform-minded bishops who sought to enforce residence on their clergy and to suppress pluralism were thwarted by the ease with which dispensations could be obtained from the papal court. Even a General Council of the church could find no solution. The Fifth Lateran Council sat from 1512–17 with the specific mandate of reforming the church, yet all its enactments proved ineffective because it was possible to obtain dispensations from them.

Nevertheless, although the popes were criticized because of their territorial ambitions in Italy, although bishops had fewer ecclesiastical powers than in earlier centuries and although the parish clergy were, as a class, held in low esteem by the laity, the church remained a powerful force in society in the early sixteenth century. It was still the greatest single landowner in Europe. In most countries clergy continued to take an important part in all levels of secular administration, and when, from the thirteenth century onwards, parliaments were called to advise the crown in many western states, the clergy were represented in them as a separate estate. At the very end of the Middle Ages churchmen held positions of great political power in some states, for example cardinal Ximenes in Castile and cardinal Wolsey in England. Moreover, the papacy, while unable to compete on equal terms as a political power with the nation-states of Europe, still remained an important force in international diplomacy.

The institutional church continued to make a considerable impact on the secular activities of lay people. All the rural population paid tithe to support it, while canon law, administered by the church courts, affected everybody because it regulated marriage, the making of wills and public morality. In addition a high proportion of the rural population were tenants of the church. On the whole church discipline was less strictly enforced in the late Middle Ages than it had been in the twelfth and thirteenth centuries because dispensations from all kinds of obligation were granted far more readily than they had previously been. The laity clearly welcomed this as is evident from the large volume of applications which reached the curia each year. The most common lay grievances were not that the church was too powerful, or that it used its power oppressively, but that the clergy enjoyed a privileged status at law and that there was too wide a disparity between the wealth of the church and the standards of service provided by the clergy at parish level. Yet those grievances were tempered in some measure by the fact that the clergy were not a closed caste: they were recruited from the laity and in the late Middle Ages were drawn from a remarkably wide social spectrum. The clergy were both privileged and numerous and their kin benefited from their patronage. In some degree this allayed discontent about clerical abuses, since it was not merely the clergy who profited from them.

3
Monasteries and Religious Orders

Monastic origins

Monasticism originated as an expression of popular piety in early fourth-century Egypt and spread from there to the rest of the church. Although few of the early monks were ordained they were treated as clergy in western Europe and were collectively described as regular clergy, those who lived in accordance with a *regula*, or rule. In time monasticism came to be an integral part of the institutional church, but it retained its spontaneity and was never completely systematized. Thus whereas the ecclesiastical hierarchy was established uniformly throughout the Catholic world, monasteries were founded in a random fashion. Monasticism developed very differently in the west, but monks there remained conscious of their origins and looked back to the Desert Fathers of fourth-century Egypt as the true exemplars of the religious life.

Monks had the same aim as all other Christians, to fulfil Christ's injunction, 'Be ye therefore perfect, even as your Father which is in heaven is perfect' (Matt.,5,48). Monks sought to achieve this by renouncing all worldly ties in order to devote themselves entirely to God, following the example of the apostles, who said to Christ, 'Lo, we have left all and followed thee' (Luke, 18, 28). When they were professed they took three vows, poverty, which entailed the renunciation of all personal property, chastity, which meant abstaining from all sexual acts, and obedience to the abbot and the monastic rule. They did not regard the things which they renounced as sinful: property, marriage and self-determination were lawful for other Christians, but were incompatible with the religious vocations of the monastic clergy.

From the earliest times a distinction was made between two kinds of monastic vocation, the eremitical and the coenobitic. Those called to the eremitical life lived as solitaries, or hermits, and will be considered in chapter 19; this chapter is concerned solely with coenobites, those who lived in a community (from Greek *koinos bios*, common life). In origin each community was autonomous and adopted a particular written rule of life. All monasteries were governed by an abbot, or father, who was elected by the community and held office for life. Monastic rules, while differing considerably in matters of detail, all made provision for three main types of activity, which are usually referred to by their Latin names. The most important was the *Opus Dei*, the work of God, which entailed the recitation of set prayers by the entire community meeting in chapel eight times during each twenty-four hour period. These services were known collectively as the Divine Office. (See chapter 5). Part of each day was set aside for *Lectio*

Divina, or spiritual study, and this could be used either for reading and writing religious texts, or for private prayer and meditation. But in early monasticism the greater part of each day was spent in *Opus Manuum,* or manual labour. This was viewed as a religious activity, for St Benedict taught that 'to work is to pray' (*laborare est orare*), but it was also an essential part of monastic life, because the communities aimed, as far as was possible, to be self-supporting.

There was at first a danger that monasteries would develop independently of the ecclesiastical hierarchy and come to form a church within the church. This was averted by appointing the bishop visitor, or supervisor, of all monasteries within his diocese. This gave him powers to ensure that the rule was being observed in those houses and to hear complaints from the brethren about the conduct of the abbot. The bishop became responsible for the enthronement of a new abbot and had the power to dispense monks from their vows. Abbots usually presented one or more of the brethren to the bishop to be ordained as priests, so that they could be chaplains to the community and celebrate the eucharist on Sundays and holy days.

Western monasticism before 900

The earliest western monasteries, founded by men like St Martin of Tours (†397) and John Cassian (†435), observed rules of life which were strongly influenced by eastern monasticism, which placed great emphasis on bodily mortification. As all successful athletes know, regular training is a precondition of success, and the early monks, who called themselves 'Christ's athletes', sought through physical mortification to make their bodies obedient to their wills.

A less harsh form of monasticism was introduced to the west by the influence of the Rule of St Benedict. There is now general agreement among scholars that St Benedict of Nursia (†c.550) adapted the anonymous *Regula Magistri,* written in the early sixth century, but gave it a distinctive character, based on his own experience as an abbot. The Benedictine Rule differed in aim from those of earlier monastic legislators. Whereas the great abbots of Egypt and their imitators had sought to train their monks for the spiritual Olympics, St Benedict was content to produce a respectable local team. The distinguishing characteristics of his Rule are common sense and moderation: it envisages a community which is run like a well ordered household rather than like a highly disciplined regiment. For example, the brethren are allowed a certain latitude in arriving late for the night-office, because it is recognized that some people find it more difficult to wake up than others. St Benedict introduced one important innovation in monastic profession: his monks were required to take a fourth vow, that of stability in the house in which they were professed. This meant that a monk remained in one community throughout his life unless he was seconded to other duties by an ecclesiastical superior. This was intended to eliminate the disruption of community life caused by restless monks who kept moving from one monastery to another.

When Benedict died his Rule was observed only at Monte-Cassino, near Capua, which he had founded. Later in the sixth century it spread to Rome, and Augustine, whom Gregory I sent to convert the Anglo-Saxons, was a Benedictine. The Rule was adopted in many of the monasteries founded in Anglo-Saxon England and was introduced in the Frankish kingdom in the eighth century by English missionaries (see chapter 1). In the ninth century it was favoured by the

Carolingian emperors, particularly through the influence of St Benedict of Aniane, the religious adviser of Louis the Pious (814–40). Nevertheless, until the tenth century older forms of monastic observance coexisted with the Benedictine Rule in all parts of western Europe.

The social function of monasteries

All the monasteries in the early Middle Ages, whatever rule they followed, recruited brethren in three main ways. Some boys were presented to monasteries by their parents at the age of seven, were trained in the religious life and took vows when they were adult. These child oblates were highly valued by communities with good choirs because they could sing treble. No concessions were made to them and they were expected to take part in the night office as well as in daytime services. Most monks entered monasteries as young men and were professed after serving a year's noviciate, but there were also some late vocations. Some men joined in middle life after their wives had died, while some elderly married couples separated in order to take religious vows and to end their lives as members of different communities. Consequently most monasteries had some brethren who had experience of the outside world.

Monasteries varied a great deal in size and permanence. Some attracted few vocations, while others had several hundred professed brethren; some were abandoned after a few years, while others, like St Gallen in Swabia which was founded in the eighth century, survive to the present day. Yet despite the vicissitudes of individual communities, the monastic ideal became an established part of the Catholic tradition. Monasteries were uniquely well suited to survival in the early medieval world in which existing social and political structures were disintegrating, for they were self-supporting communities, large enough to possess their own specialist craftsmen.

They had an important role in the new barbarian kingdoms. The peoples of western Europe were all eventually converted to Catholicism, but during the early Middle Ages there was a dichotomy between the Christian ideals to which they theoretically subscribed and the still largely pagan values which determined their day-to-day conduct. In that society the monasteries were almost the only communities in which Christian values were put into practice in everyday life, and arguably the monks' greatest contribution to the religious development of the west was to bear witness to the practice of the Christian life in a barbarous society. Of course, standards of monastic observance were very uneven, but there were always some houses in which the rule was enforced strictly. During the early Middle Ages it was generally accepted that society was divided by occupation into three main groups: peasants who worked the land, warriors who defended it, and clergy who prayed for society as a whole. The prayers of monks were particularly valued because they recited the eightfold office by day and by night without intermission. Monks also became involved in the work of active ministry: they played an important part in the evangelization of northern Europe and often assumed pastoral care for lay people living near their communities in the centuries before a parish system had developed.

The rise of western monasticism coincided with the collapse of the Roman system of secular education. Most monasteries ran schools to teach novices how to recite the Latin office and, although the standard of education which many of them provided was very elementary, some communities became centres of learning. This affected the evolution of western society in a number of ways. Large monastic libraries had texts not only of theological works but also of the Latin classics: the oldest surviving exemplars of most of those works were copied in western monasteries in the early Middle Ages and, had this not been so, little classical Latin writing would now be preserved. Most of the important writers and scholars in western Europe in the period 500–1000 were monks. Kings who needed literate administrators in those years relied very largely on the services of men trained in the monastic schools.

Monasteries also affected society in more direct ways. It was quite common for monks to be recalled to the world to become bishops and archbishops, positions which usually led to some degree of political involvement (see chapter 2). Moreover, younger sons of noble families were sometimes trained as monks but recalled to the world before they had been professed because of the death of an elder brother. Such *milites literati*, knights able to read and write Latin, were able to use their training in a secular environment.

The effects of monastic wealth

Thus monasticism, which had its origins in a desire to withdraw from the world, became once more integrated with society as a whole. Inevitably this produced considerable changes in monastic life. Monasteries acquired property commensurate with their new social status, for it was a paradox that although all monks were vowed to personal poverty no parallel restriction applied to monastic communities as corporate bodies. All monasteries needed some land on which to grow their own food, but in the early Middle Ages most houses accumulated additional lands through private benefactions while some received huge endowments from kings and great noblemen.

This growth in wealth led to a change in the social composition of communities. Whereas in the sixth century any man of free birth could be professed, by the ninth century monks in great monasteries were almost exclusively of noble birth, because a rich monastery afforded a respectable career to younger sons of good family who had no prospect of inheriting land. The sons of free peasants might still gain admission to small monasteries, but they seldom rose to important office in them. Between the ninth and the thirteenth centuries a high proportion of the western peasantry were serfs and they were not allowed by law to become monks because they were tied to the land. Serfs on monastic estates might be employed as monastery servants, as might some poor free men. Servants shared in some measure in the life of the community, and they were not free to marry as long as they remained in monastic service, but they received no training in the spiritual life. In the eleventh century it was recognized that some of them might have a monastic vocation and they were allowed to take vows and to be enrolled as lay brethren in some houses. The lay brethren had their own rule of life, recited a much shortened and simplified form of the Divine Office and performed manual work.

The fully professed brethren became known as choir-monks because their chief duty was to recite the Divine Office. Since they employed servants and possessed estates which were worked by tenants, they had no need to perform manual labour, although some observant communities, mindful of their rule, continued to do some occasional, ritual weeding. The Divine Office, which in earlier times had been said, began to be set to elaborate chants and occupied a considerable part of each day. From the ninth century onwards a high proportion of monks were ordained as priests and the eucharist was celebrated daily in the monasteries. The choir-monks were still required to spend part of each day in study and meditation, but most of them had a good deal of time to spare when they had fulfilled their religious duties. Some of them spent that time in administrative tasks, which ownership of property breeds, while others performed specialist tasks which could not be delegated to servants, such as copying and illuminating manuscripts, producing liturgical metalwork and caring for sick brethren. Abbots who were great landowners often became important political figures. Many of these duties took the brethren away from the monastery, and in great houses there can have been relatively few occasions when the entire community was present in choir.

That was the situation in monasteries which attempted to observe their rule in changing social circumstances, but in some houses there was a decline in the standards of observance, although this only became an acute problem during the Viking and Magyar invasions of the ninth and tenth centuries. In many places monastic life was severely disrupted by these raiders, and in areas where royal authority was weak the monasteries came to be controlled by lay patrons. This had consequences similar to those which affected the secular clergy (see chapter 2): the office of abbot was sometimes put up for sale, and in many cases was held by men who had no interest in the religious life, did not take monastic vows, but drew the revenues of their office while living as laymen. Since obedience to the abbot was at the heart of monastic observance good order collapsed in houses with non-resident abbots or abbots who lacked religious training. The monks of the great Lombard abbey of Farfa in the reign of abbot Campo (936–62) divided the monastic estates between them, took wives, lived in private houses and totally neglected their religious duties. This was an extreme, but by no means unique example of the kind of monastic corruption which was prevalent at that time.

Monastic reform movements, c.900–1200

Devout people in different parts of the west sought to restore strict observance in some communities. During the tenth century the West Saxon kings of England and the Ottonian emperors in Germany founded well endowed monasteries and appointed reforming abbots to rule them. In Lorraine St John of Gorze founded a community in 939 whose strict observance of the Rule of St Benedict was adopted by many neighbouring houses. The most influential reform was that inaugurated at Cluny in Burgundy, founded in 909 by duke William III of Aquitaine who renounced all patronal rights and placed the house directly under the protection of the pope. Cluny was blessed with a series of exceptionally able and long-lived abbots: Sts Maiolus, Odilo and Hugh ruled consecutively for 160 years (949–1109). They founded new monasteries and were called in to reform existing ones, and many of these were given to Cluny by their patrons. They became daughter-houses, administered by priors who were responsible to the abbot of Cluny, and in this way the Cluniac order came into existence. This was the first religious order in the western church, for all earlier monasteries had been self-governing. All Cluniac houses were free from lay control and had no ecclesiastical superior except the pope. Cluny acquired daughter-houses throughout France, as well as in Lombardy, Christian Spain and Norman England. Cluniac ideals were also introduced in Germany by St William of Hirsau (†1091) but the houses which he reformed were not affiliated to the order.

All the reformed monasteries of the post-Viking age adopted the Rule of St Benedict and older monastic rules died out, except in Celtic areas where they persisted until the twelfth century. The reformers, however, did not agree in their interpretation of the Benedictine rule. The Cluniacs emphasized the importance of the eucharist and the Divine Office, which they performed with a degree of ritual and elaboration previously unknown in the western church, whereas some reformers, like St Romuald (†1027), believed that the rule was designed primarily to train hermits. This led to a revival of eremitical observance among western monks which culminated in the foundation of the Carthusian order in the late eleventh century (see chapter 19).

Other reformers believed that manual labour should form an important part of Benedictine observance. St John of Gorze favoured this interpretation, but it was fully implemented by the Cistercian order, founded in 1098 by St Robert of Molesme. The Cistercians are sometimes called white monks, to distinguish them from most other Benedictines who wore black habits. The early Cistercians settled in remote places, spent much of the day in manual labour, used simple forms of worship and were characterized by their great austerity of life. They became immensely popular and by 1200 had 530 houses, situated in all parts of the west. Like the Cluniacs they were exempt from all ecclesiastical authority except that of the pope.

New types of monastic life

Until the eleventh century western monasticism had in intention remained faithful to the ideals of the Desert Fathers, being primarily directed towards the renunciation of the world and the cultivation of a life of prayer, but from c.1050 a diversification of the monastic ideal is observable. Communities of Austin Canons were formed in the second half of the eleventh century, who adopted a rule attributed to St Augustine (†431). This could be interpreted more flexibly than other monastic rules, and so while some of the canons lived a traditional monastic life, others engaged in pastoral work. The rule was also adopted by some chapters of cathedral canons whose chief duty was to conduct public worship.

In 1113 the order of St John of Jerusalem was founded to care for the sick and destitute in the newly conquered capital of the crusading kingdom. It rapidly spread throughout the west and, although it later developed a military wing which has attracted more attention from historians, the order never neglected its charitable duties. It founded hospitals in other parts of the Crusader States and in the west, devoted a substantial part of its revenues to the care of the sick and poor and trained some brethren exclusively for charitable work. This order was the largest and most successful among many which were founded in the later Middle Ages to care for the suffering.

In 1128 pope Honorius II licensed the Knights Templar, the earliest military order. The brethren took the three traditional monastic vows, but their chief function was to fight the infidel and defend the Holy Land rather than to pray, although they were bound to recite the Divine Office in chapel when they were not engaged in military duties. The order was divided into knights of noble birth, sergeants of common birth, and priests who served as chaplains, and was ruled by an elected Master, responsible to the pope. The order and its lands were exempt from episcopal jurisdiction and it afforded an attractive alternative career to young men who were destined by their families for the church but had no taste for conventional forms of priestly and religious life. It rapidly spread to most parts of western Europe, where it inspired the growth of other, similar orders: those of Calatrava, Alcantara and Santiago were founded by the Christian kings of Spain in the second half of the twelfth century to help them in their wars against the Moors, and the Teutonic order was founded in 1198 for German knights. Although initially founded to defend the Holy Land the Teutonic order's chief centre of activity shifted to the eastern Baltic in the thirteenth century (see chapter 1). Unlike earlier monks, the members of military orders did not make their profession to a particular community but to the order itself, since they were required to serve wherever their superiors determined.

The work of the friars

The military orders gave institutional form to the crusading ideal which had become an important part of western European life in the twelfth century, but society was also changing in other ways at that time. There was a growth of urbanization, particularly in southern Europe, and in southern France and Lombardy this was accompanied by serious outbreaks of heresy. New religious orders came into being in response to these challenges, the most important being those founded by St Francis of Assisi (†1226) and St Dominic Guzman (†1222).

St Francis's order of Friars Minor, or little brothers, was licensed by Innocent III in 1210. It is commonly called the Franciscan order, and in the Middle Ages its members were known as greyfriars from the colour of their habits, whereas modern Franciscans dress in brown. St Francis was concerned to tell lay people about the life and teachings of Christ as set out in the Gospels and to minister to those in need. The chief hallmarks of his order were simplicity and poverty. Though not opposed in principle to learning, St Francis set no store by it among his friars, and he made poverty an absolute rule, forbidding the order to receive endowments of any kind. The early Franciscans lived in small wooden huts and owned nothing except the tunics and sandals which they wore. Because they were totally dependent on charity for their daily necessities they were known as mendicants, a dignified term for beggars.

St Francis was revered by his contemporaries as a man who in his life imitated Christ more closely than any other Christian in the post-apostolic age. He attracted large numbers of adherents through his personal sanctity and the refreshing simplicity of his teaching, but his success caused many problems to the church authorities, even though they sympathized with his ideals, because he was averse from imposing rules on his order. The papacy forced the Franciscans to accept a structure: the order was divided into provinces and placed under the authority of a superior, who had the typically Franciscan title of Minister General, or servant of all men, and was directly responsible to the pope.

The order of Friars Preacher founded by St Dominic, whose members were known as Dominicans or blackfriars, had a quite different purpose. Dominic was concerned to combat heresy by training preachers to instruct the laity in the

Catholic faith, which the parish clergy were, for the most part, too ill-educated to do. A high proportion of Dominicans were priested and the chief activities of the order were study and pastoral care. From their inception they founded priories in the main university cities of western Europe and drew into membership some of the most intelligent men of the age. Like the Franciscans, the Dominicans were organized in provinces and were ruled by a General who was responsible to the pope. The order was exempt from all ecclesiastical authority except that of the papacy. Dominicans owned priories, since they needed conditions in which they could study, but, like the Franciscans, they refused endowments and relied an almsgiving for their support, for St Dominic believed that lay people were attracted to heresy partly because of the apostolic poverty of heretical preachers which contrasted markedly with the wealth of the established church (see chapter 18).

After St Francis's death in 1226 his order abandoned his ideal of absolute poverty. They were allowed to build friaries and to establish houses of study, and they founded communities in university cities and produced some eminent scholars. Many members of the order became priests, which in St Francis's lifetime had not been the custom. The order was granted privileges which its founder had steadfastly refused: it was exempted from the authority of bishops and its members were licensed to preach in any diocese without the bishop's permission.

The mendicant orders were immensely popular and by 1300 there were few towns of any size in western Europe which did not have at least one community of friars. Other, lesser orders of friars were founded, the most important of which was the Carmelite order. This had originated as an order of hermits (see chapter 19), but it was reorganized in the thirteenth century as a mendicant order, charged with the work of ministering to the laity, and its members were known as whitefriars.

Unlike the older monasteries, which had become the virtual monopoly of the rich, the mendicant orders attracted vocations from all social classes. Like the members of the military orders, the friars joined an order, not a particular community, and pledged themselves to serve wherever their superiors ordered them to go. This mobility enabled them to undertake a wide range of work, as will be apparent in later chapters of this book.

Convents of nuns

This chapter has so far been concerned exclusively with the religious life among men, but from the earliest days of monasticism there had been women who became nuns. They did not occupy so important a place in the life of the medieval church as they do in that of most modern Catholic countries partly because there were far fewer of them. Throughout the Middle Ages there were about twenty times as many men who had taken religious vows as there were women. Nuns took the three monastic vows and lived in convents ruled by abbesses, elected by their communities for life. They used a form of one of the rules drawn up for monks and they organized their time in very similar ways. Nuns recited the Divine Office themselves, but, because women could not be ordained, each convent had to engage a chaplain to celebrate the eucharist. He had no authority in the community, but was subject to the abbess who paid his stipend. Most rules specified that nuns should be enclosed, that is, they should not leave the convent without the permission of the bishop or, in the case of exempt houses, of the pope, but this regulation was often not enforced at all strictly.

Most of the new religious orders founded in the central Middle Ages had some female communities, except for the purely military orders. The order of St John of Jerusalem, which undertook charitable as well as military duties, had communities of nuns who helped to nurse women patients. Women were also admitted to the mendicant orders, but they were allowed no share in the work of active ministry. Dominican nuns were excluded from such work because they could not become priests and they lived in enclosed convents devoting their lives entirely to prayer. A similar disparity need not have existed in the Franciscan order, since most of the early brethren were not priests and the charitable work which they performed was equally suited to women. Indeed, St Clare (†1253), who was one of St Francis's most fervent disciples, wished to join him in the work of active ministry. This wish met with overwhelming disapproval, not only from the church authorities, but also from society at large, and St Clare reluctantly founded a separate order of Franciscans for women, known as the Poor Clares. The rule which they followed was one of the most austere among all those observed by religious communities in the Catholic church: they were allowed no endowments but had to subsist entirely on almsgiving; they observed strict enclosure, and devoted their lives to prayer and to manual labour.

Nuns did not always occupy a secondary place to men in religious orders. In the Celtic church in the early Middle Ages some double monasteries were founded, one for monks and the other for nuns, which were built on adjacent sites and in which the abbess had authority over both communities. This system was introduced into Anglo-Saxon England in the seventh century by Celtic missionaries, but died out in the ninth century during the Viking invasions. A similar pattern was revived in France by Robert of Arbrissel (†1117), founder of the order of Fontevrault, although it is not known whether he was influenced by earlier Celtic models. St Gilbert of Sempringham (†1189) founded a similar order in England, and although it never spread elsewhere it proved popular, for there were twenty-five Gilbertine houses in England at the time of the dissolution of the monasteries. In the double monasteries of both these orders supreme authority was vested in the abbess.

Every abbess had authority over her convent and its lands and in the case of great, royal foundations this office conferred considerable economic and political power. An abbess might delegate much of the routine work of administration to lay officials, but they were her servants and final decisions rested with her and with the choir-nuns who formed the chapter which advised her. Some convents were exempted from the bishop's jurisdiction and in such cases the abbess had no religious superior except the pope. No medieval laywomen enjoyed powers equal to those of the abbesses of great, exempt convents, except some queens who were regents for minor heirs, while, after the Reformation, women living in Protestant countries rarely enjoyed comparable authority until the nineteenth century unless they were queens-regnant.

Convents were also important because they were the only centres of female education throughout much of the Middle Ages. Secular schools and most universities only admitted male students, and, although some noblewomen were taught by private tutors, this was exceptional. All convents needed to teach their novices to recite the Divine Office and, although great variation existed in the standard of education which they provided, some convents did become centres of learning. Whereas learned men were by no means all monks in the Middle Ages, with a very few exceptions learned women were nuns. Some nuns were very learned indeed: St Hildegarde of Bingen, abbess of Rupertsberg (†1179), for example, wrote treatises on the liberal arts, the natural sciences and mystical theology, as well as composing music which is still performed today.

The Religious Orders in the later Middle Ages

After 1350 there was a marked decline in most forms of the religious life in western Europe. The new orders, founded in the eleventh and twelfth centuries, had long since lost their fervour, and even the newer mendicant orders became lax in their observance. The Dominicans did not rescind the prohibition of endowments contained in their rule until 1464, but they allowed individual friars to receive stipends for ministering to lay people, which inexorably caused a decline of austerity in the order as a whole. The Franciscans allowed endowments to be given to the papacy for the benefit of their order, from which they could draw the revenues. This led to a split in the order between the Spirituals, who wished to adhere to St Francis's ideals, and the Conventuals who were content with the new dispensation. The Spirituals were driven to take up an extreme position about the virtue of poverty and were condemned as heretical in the early fourteenth century (see chapter 18). In the later fourteenth century a reforming group of Franciscans, known as the Observants, sought to restore the primitive rule of 1223, which had governed the order in St Francis's later years, and this was adopted in some houses. Indeed, this reforming movement had a wider influence, in that Observant groups subsequently developed in other orders of friars during the later Middle Ages, inspired by similar ideals.

Nevertheless, although the religious orders did not lack some zealous members after 1350, and although the Carthusians maintained their austere standards throughout the later Middle Ages (see chapter 19), in general there was a marked decline in monastic observance. No major, new religious orders were founded, few new monasteries were built and there was a decline in the number of vocations to existing communities. Many of the great abbeys of western Europe only had a few professed members by 1500 and this, in part, accounts for a change of life-style among the brethren. The other chief cause of change resulted from the appointment of non-resident abbots, who drew the revenues of their office but delegated their duties to priors who lacked their authority. This problem was caused partly by the extension of papal provisions and also by the ease with which dispensations were granted to pluralist and non-resident clergy (see chapter 2).

There were some scandalous cases of communities in which the rule was totally disregarded and where religious duties were neglected, but it was more common for monks and nuns to infringe the rule in lesser ways in order to lead more comfortable lives. Thus dormitories were often divided up into private rooms; communities ceased to eat together and each member had private meals served in his own room; each received some share of the revenues of the house as a *peculium*, or spending money, and began to acquire personal possessions. They began to wear jewellery and to add unauthorized trimmings to their habits; to entertain lay visitors and to go out more often into lay society. Yet they continued to perform their religious duties and to sing the daily eightfold office, so that their self-indulgence did not cause grave scandal except to the puritanically minded.

Despite their decline in fervour and in numbers the members of the religious orders continued to occupy an important place in western society at the close of the Middle Ages. The monasteries were still great landowners and were therefore landlords to a substantial section of the agrarian population. In addition, many monasteries held the right of presentation to parishes situated on their estates, while many of the urban parishes were run by the mendicant orders. Many of the important shrines of western Europe were in monastic control (see chapter 13), so that, in various capacities, most lay people had some degree of contact with the regular clergy. Their chief function remained what it had been for the previous thousand years, the offering of perpetual prayer to God by day and by night on behalf of all Christians. This was an integral part of the religious experience of the medieval west, an expression of the importance which that society attached to the worship of God.

4
The Faith of the Church

What was meant by 'faith'

The Catholic church in the Middle Ages claimed to hold and teach the faith which it had received from the apostles. By this was meant not only the facts about Christ's life and teachings but also the way in which the apostles had interpreted their significance. It was accepted that the revelation given by Christ had ended with his life on earth and that God would reveal nothing new to men, but it was also believed that, under the guidance of the Holy Spirit, each generation of Christians would come to understand their faith more fully, for Christ had said, 'When he, the Spirit of truth, is come, he will guide you into all truth' (John, 16, 13). The faith was therefore conceived as being a living tradition of belief, preserved by a community united in religious practice, which was capable of receiving fresh insights into the meaning of Christ's revelation. It followed from this that the faith could not in its entirety be encapsulated in a series of verbal formularies. Even the Bible, which possessed a unique authority as a source of revelation, could not be understood in isolation from the tradition of Christian experience of which it formed part (see chapter 6).

When various explanations were advanced about some part of the received tradition, it became necessary to decide which of them was correct. In this way some parts of Christian belief came to be defined in precise, verbal terms, intended to exclude erroneous interpretations, and all members of the church were required to subscribe to those definitions. But it must be emphasized that the entire body of belief was not defined in that way, because there was no need to define teachings which were uncontroversial, and that Catholics in the Middle Ages were required to accept the faith of the church in its entirety and not merely to assent to those articles of belief which had been precisely defined.

General Councils of the church

Authority to define the church's doctrine was not vested in theologians, even though they had a specialized knowledge of Christian teaching, but in the bishops who were regarded as the successors of the apostles and therefore as the guardians of the apostolic faith. From the early fourth century final authority was exercised by General, or Oecumenical, Councils, which all bishops had the right to attend. In the fifth century it was agreed that in order for such councils to be truly representative of the whole church, the patriarchs of Rome, Constantinople, Antioch, Alexandria and Jerusalem should be present at them either in person or by proxy. The number of bishops attending such councils varied considerably, but it was agreed that, provided their right of free discussion had been respected, their decisions were binding on the whole church. The Catholic church of the west recognized seven councils of this kind: Nicaea I (325), Constantinople I (381), Ephesus (431), Chalcedon (451), Constantinople II (553), Constantinople III (680–1), and Nicaea II (787).

After 787 increasing tensions between Rome and the eastern patriarchates, which later hardened into a religious schism (see chapter 16), precluded the assembly of General Councils representing all the churches of east and west. The popes then assumed responsibility for convening General Councils, most of which were attended solely by western clergy, because the eastern patriarchs seldom sent representatives. Ten General Councils of this kind were recognized by the western church: Lateran I (1123), Lateran II (1139), Lateran III (1179), Lateran IV (1215), Lyons I (1245), Lyons II (1274), Vienne (1311–12), Constance (1414–18) (although some doubt existed about the canonical status of the early sessions of that council), Ferrara/Florence (1438–9) and Lateran V (1512–17). The decisions of all these councils were binding on the western church.

The nature of papal authority

It may surprise some readers, familiar with modern Catholicism, that the right to define doctrine was vested in a General Council rather than in the pope alone, and some consideration must therefore be given to the nature of papal authority in the Middle Ages. The pope was recognized as possessing powers which were different from those of other bishops. He enjoyed a certain degree of prestige as bishop of the former imperial capital, and that undoubtedly influenced the growth of papal claims to universal, temporal sovereignty which were examined in chapter 2. But it was also acknowledged by all the churches of east and west that the pope was the successor of St Peter, who had been first bishop of Rome and was buried in the Vatican basilica. St Peter occupies a special place in the Gospel narratives because of Christ's solemn charge to him. He had previously been called Simon, but Christ gave him a new name, Peter, the rock:

> Thou art Peter, and upon this rock I will build my church; and the gates of hell shall not prevail against it. And I will give unto thee the keys of the kingdom of heaven: and whatsoever thou shalt bind on earth shall be bound in heaven: and whatsoever thou shalt loose on earth shall be loosed in heaven (Matt., 16, 18–19).

The pope, as successor of St Peter, was recognized as enjoying primacy of honour by the churches of east and west, but in the western church he was credited with far wider powers. His headship of the church was undisputed and therefore Catholics were defined as those who were in communion with the pope. The popes themselves did not make extravagant claims to spiritual authority. This is true even of pope Boniface VIII who in his bull *Unam Sanctam* of 1302 declared that obedience to the pope was necessary to salvation, for as Knowles has pointed out, when stripped of its rhetoric, this bull merely reasserts the traditional belief that Christ had founded his church as the guaranteed means of salvation for all men and had placed St Peter at its head. It is true that canon lawyers made far greater claims on behalf of the papacy, and went so far as to affirm that *papa omnia potest*, or 'the pope can do all things'. Yet canon lawyers, while influencing general opinion, were not theologians, still less were they bishops. They had no authority to define the doctrine of the church.

The power of the keys, exercised by the pope as the successor of St Peter, was considered to relate to the church's power to absolve sins, and will be examined later in this chapter. As head of the church the pope claimed the right to condemn false teaching, and there was no appeal from his decisions about what constituted heresy, but such rulings were merely declaratory, being authoritative statements about what the church's true teachings were. Medieval popes did not make definitions of doctrine binding on the whole church without consulting their fellow-bishops assembled in a General Council. Nevertheless, no council could make authoritative pronouncements about doctrine unless the pope was represented at it and ratified its decisions, and this was true even of the councils held in conjunction with the eastern patriarchs before 787. In that sense the pope was the final arbiter of doctrine in the western church.

Although groups of dissenters broke with Rome at various times, papal authority was only once challenged by a large body of Catholic opinion during the Middle Ages. In the late fourteenth century the church was divided by a schism between rival popes which lasted for almost forty years. A General Council met at Constance to restore church unity in 1414 and secured the abdication of one claimant and the deposition of his rivals. Before a new pope was elected the council enacted the decree *Sacrosancta* in 1415, which affirmed that a General Council derived its authority directly from Christ and was superior to the pope. In 1417, by the decree *Frequens,* the council enacted that General Councils should be summoned at regular intervals, usually of ten years, to share in the work of church government. Only then was Martin V elected pope.

The decree *Sacrosancta* was rescinded by Pius II in 1460 in the bull *Execrabilis,* in which he declared that it was heretical to exalt the authority of a General Council above that of the pope. This ruling provoked no widespread protest, for it was merely reaffirming the tradition of the western church whereby the pope had to be represented at a General Council and to ratify its acts. No medieval pope had ever overruled a General Council, but decisions had always been reached by agreement between pope and council. The attempt at Constance to subordinate the pope to a council was certainly innovatory and had been made at a time when the Roman see was vacant. The decree *Frequens* fell into desuetude, but it was not rescinded because there was nothing contrary to tradition in the concept that the pope should regularly consult as wide a spectrum of Catholic opinion as possible.

The Nicene Creed

The medieval church accepted the doctrinal definitions made by General Councils in the fourth and fifth centuries. These were epitomized in the Nicene Creed, which was attributed to the council of Nicaea of 325, although it was not drawn up in its final form until about a century later. It occupied an important place in the life of the western church, since during the Middle Ages it was recited at the eucharist on Sundays and great feast days as a general profession of faith. The text never varied:

> I believe in one God the Father almighty, maker of heaven and earth, and of all things visible and invisible: and in one Lord Jesus Christ, the only begotten son of God,

begotten of his father before all ages: God of God, light of light, very God of very God, begotten not made, being of one substance with the father, through whom all things were made; who for us men and for our salvation came down from heaven; and was incarnate by the Holy Spirit of the Virgin Mary; and was made man; and was crucified also for us under Pontius Pilate. He suffered and was buried. And the third day he rose again according to the scriptures, and ascended into heaven, and sitteth on the right hand of the Father; and he shall come again in glory to judge both the living and the dead, whose kingdom shall have no end. And I believe in the Holy Spirit, the Lord and giver of life, who proceedeth from the Father [and the Son],* who with the Father and the Son together is worshipped and glorified, who spake by the prophets. And I believe in one holy, catholic and apostolic church. I acknowledge one baptism for the remission of sins, and I await the resurrection of the dead and the life of the world to come. Amen.

This creed is not intended to be self-explanatory. It is designed for use by people who have been fully instructed in the faith and understand the assumptions on which it is based and the facts to which it alludes. The fundamental assumption is belief in the Holy Trinity, one God in three Persons, God the Father, God the Son and God the Holy Spirit. St Patrick is said to have used the three-leafed clover to explain this central mystery of the Christian faith to the pagan Irish, likening the godhead to the three leaves which spring from a central stem, each distinct, yet each part of an organic whole.

God the Father, assisted by the Son and the Holy Spirit, was assumed to be the sole creative principle. The creed distinguishes between the visible creation, meaning by this the material universe, and the invisible creation, which included heaven, the dwelling-place of the angels who served God, and hell, the dwelling place of the fallen angels who, led by Lucifer, had rebelled against God. More will be said about the invisible creation later in this work, but two points should be noted here. First, heaven and hell were not conceived as having physical locations outside the visible universe, but as being spiritual states, with no location in space or time. Secondly Lucifer (known after his revolt as Satan, 'the adversary'), and the fallen angels, although the proximate cause of evil in the physical universe, were held to have been created good and to have become evil through abusing their free will. The ultimate origin of evil was a problem with which medieval theologians had to wrestle (see chapter 20).

The Nicene creed presupposes knowledge of the Christian view of man's fall. Man had been created perfect and had lived in harmony with God until, tempted by Satan, he sinned, that is he sundered himself from God by using his free will to oppose the will of God. As a result of this man's relationship to the whole created order became flawed. To restore man to perfection, God the Son became man as Jesus of Nazareth: this event is known as the Incarnation, and it could only have occurred in the way that it did because Jesus' mother, Mary, agreed to do God's will. When told that she had been chosen to bear God's son, she replied: 'Behold the handmaid of the Lord, be it unto me according to thy word' (Luke, 1,38). Mary, while still a virgin, conceived Jesus through the agency of the Holy Spirit. Thus the Incarnation, which was at the centre of the whole history of creation, was made possible by the cooperation between God and a human being, Mary. Jesus was the second Person of the Trinity, but he received from his mother not only a human body, but also a full human nature. In order to affirm

---

*The phrase in brackets was added unilaterally by the western church and rejected by the eastern churches (see chapter 16).

the church's belief in his full humanity, which some Christians found difficult to accept, the council of Ephesus in 431 gave Mary the title of Mother of God (Greek *Theotokos*). The council was not seeking to deify Mary but, on the contrary, wished to emphasize that God the Son had been born in the normal way of a human mother. Yet the title indicates the reverence in which the fifth-century church held Mary, a reverence which was to grow in depth during the Middle Ages.

Jesus was called Christ, 'the anointed one', because the church believed that he had fulfilled the Jewish prophecies about the Messiah, the anointed ruler whom God would send to save his people. While he lived on earth Jesus taught men about the nature of God and about their own true nature and trained the apostles to continue his work. He was crucified in the reign of the emperor Tiberius (14–37 AD), while Pontius Pilate was governor of Judaea, and his death was understood by his followers to be a voluntary sacrifice which reconciled men to God. For this reason the cross became the central Christian symbol.

Jesus died because he was truly human, but he rose from the dead on the third day following because he was truly God. After manifesting himself for forty days to his followers, he returned to heaven, taking with him his human body and nature, an event symbolically described as the Ascension. The church believed that at the end of time he would return to earth in glory to preside at the Last Judgement, when all men who had ever lived would be summoned before him to give account of themselves.

Jesus had promised his followers that after his Ascension he would send the Holy Spirit, the third Person of the Trinity, to guide and strengthen them. The Holy Spirit was already at work in the world: he had inspired the prophets to prepare men for Christ's coming and had presided at his conception. Christ's followers received the gift of the Holy Spirit who became present within them to sanctify their lives. Thus the Incarnation of Christ enabled men to share in the divine life of the godhead and to grow in perfection as they had, at the creation, been given the capacity to do.

Christ's saving work was continued by the church which he had founded. He had commanded his followers to be baptized and the church believed that this rite was a vehicle of God's grace, which conferred the forgiveness of all sins and marked the beginning of a life of perfection. The church taught that men had immortal souls which, when they died, would go either to heaven or hell, but it also taught that men's bodies would be resurrected at the Last Judgement and transformed into spiritual bodies, just as the human body of Jesus had been at his resurrection. The belief grew up in the eastern churches in the late Roman period that Mary, the mother of Jesus, had been assumed body and soul into heaven, and this belief spread to the western church by the ninth century. It was doctrinally uncontroversial, for it was believed by everybody, on the authority of the Old Testament, that Enoch and Elijah had been taken up to heaven in bodily form, and that all people would in the end experience the same transformation.

The invocation of saints

The early General Councils of the Church, whose rulings were reflected in the Nicene creed, were chiefly concerned with defining the doctrines of the Trinity and the Incarnation, but the Second Council of Nicaea of 787 dealt with two different problems, the invocation of the saints and the veneration of religious images. The controversies which led to the summoning of this council arose in the eastern churches, but the pope was represented at it and its rulings were binding on the western church as well. It enacted that worship might be paid to the Trinity alone, but that saints and angels might receive reverence, and that, within those terms, religious veneration might be shown to likenesses (Greek *eikones*) of Christ, the angels and the saints without fear of idolatry, because all veneration shown to a likeness was received by the being whom it portrayed.

The works of the church Fathers

Definitions made by councils and formularies such as the Nicene creed represented only a part of the church's faith, because many beliefs, which were uncontroversial, were not defined. These unformulated parts of the faith were known from three main sources: the Bible, which was the revealed word of God, the forms of liturgical prayer used by the church (see chapter 5), and the works of the church Fathers, collectively known as patristic writings. The last category encompassed a very heterogeneous collection of religious works composed by men of orthodox belief in the early Christian centuries, and included theological treatises, religious poetry, sermons, histories, biographies and biblical commentaries. The western church preserved the writings of the Latin Fathers, together with those of such Greek Fathers as had been translated into Latin. Among the most widely read of the early Fathers were Tertullian, Origen, Augustine, Ambrose and Jerome. These works did not contain authoritative teaching, but were very influential in shaping medieval religious thought, partly because many of the authors were men of considerable intellectual capacity and originality of mind, but also because the writings bore witness to the way in which the church had understood its faith in the early centuries.

During the early Middle Ages a constant stream of new religious works were produced to add to the existing corpus of patristic writings. The best known authors of this period are Gregory the Great, Bede, Alcuin, Hrabanus Maurus, John the Scot, Walafrid Strabo and Peter Damian, but there were a host of others. By the time Peter Damian died in 1072 the religious literature of the west, which formed part of the tradition of the church, had grown to mammoth proportions. It fills 145 volumes of Migne's *Patrologia Latina*, which is printed in double columns with very small type, and this represents only a selection of the total corpus. A man seeking to discover the church's teaching about some point of doctrine in the works of the Fathers was, by the eleventh century, like someone looking for a specific book in a large library which has no catalogue.

Scholastic theology

A way out of this dilemma was found when the lost Latin translation of part of the logical works of Aristotle was discovered in the late tenth century, and the teaching of dialectic introduced in the syllabus of higher education. This was deductive logic, based on the use of the extended syllogism. By the twelfth century a training in dialectic had become the hallmark of most educated people in the west and this affected the study of theology in two ways.

First it stimulated original thought by leading men to examine traditional beliefs in the light of human reason. St Anselm, abbot of Bec and archbishop of Canterbury (†1109), formulated the ontological proof for the existence of God. Taking as his premise the proposition 'God is that than which nothing greater can be conceived' he developed his argument to prove the necessary existence of such a being. Unlike most other statements by medieval theologians, the ontological proof has retained a perennial interest for western thinkers, since even those for whom the subject matter is of no intrinsic interest are intrigued by the method of argument.

Anselm lived at a time when dialectic was a new and intoxicating discipline. Later medieval theologians were forced to recognize its limitations and to con-clude that, while it was possible to demonstrate that revealed truth was not incompatible with human reason, reason could only reach authoritative con-clusions about the material universe, whereas certainty about the eternal realities could be attained solely through divine revelation.

The second effect of the revival of logic on the study of theology was a practical one: it made systematic study possible. During the twelfth century the schools of Paris became pre-eminent as a centre of theological scholarship, and Peter Lombard (†1160), who taught in them for twenty years, wrote the *Four Books of Sentences* which, despite an initially hostile reception, came to be used as a fundamental text in all the theology schools of western Europe in the following centuries. It is a comprehensive and lucid survey of the Christian faith and uses the dialectical method in which all students had been trained. The author proposes a doctrinal thesis, cites authorities for and against it, and argues a conclusion.

This kind of study became known as scholastic theology because it originated in the twelfth-century schools. Some of those schools evolved into universities and the same method of study was used in their theology faculties throughout the Middle Ages. The scholastic theologians reduced to order the amorphous body of writings which made up the western tradition, and provided succinct accounts of the main Christian teachings, which could be used as a basis for further study. All areas of belief were dealt with in this way, and some received systematic treatment for the first time in the church's history. Thus whereas the early councils had examined the doctrines of the Trinity and the Incarnation, medieval theologians were the first to consider systematically the ways in which God is present in his church.

The seven sacraments

It had always been believed that the sacraments were important means of receiv-ing God's grace, but before the twelfth century there was no consensus about how many there were. Peter Lombard argued that Christ had instituted seven: bap-tism, confirmation, the eucharist, penance, marriage, ordination, and unction (the anointing of the sick). This view was in time accepted by everybody. The scholastic theologians were responsible for establishing a theology of the sacra-ments by considering the conditions which needed to be fulfilled in order to render them valid, that is efficacious as a means of grace. They concluded that these conditions were threefold: right matter must be used, for example in the eucharist no other materials could be substituted for bread and wine because the church had no power to change Christ's instructions; secondly, the right form should be used, for example a minister at a baptism could not substitute his own form of words for those given by Christ as recorded in the Gospels; thirdly an intention of doing what the church intended to do when conferring a sacrament was essential.

There was considerable controversy about whether a sinful minister could validly confer the sacraments, but consensus was finally achieved that the unworthiness of the minister did not impede the efficacy of the sacraments. This might be termed a victory for common sense, for, since only God could tell whether a minister was in a state of mortal sin, uncertainty on that issue would have placed the validity of all sacraments in doubt in the minds of the scrupulous. It was decided that if sacraments were performed using right matter and right form and with the right intention, they were efficacious *ex opere operato*, by virtue of their performance. This was an affirmation that the true minister of all sacraments is Christ and that the church's ministers are merely his representatives and powerless to hinder the grace which Christ offers to his people. Nevertheless, sacramental grace was not mechanical, and it was believed that if a Christian received any sacrament while in a state of mortal and unrepented sin, he was incapable of obtaining any spiritual benefit from it.

The eucharist

The scholastic theologians examined all the sacraments systematically, but paid special attention to two of them, the eucharist and penance. In the medieval west the eucharist was normally called the mass, and that term will henceforth be used. The earliest account of the institution of this sacrament, and of the significance which the first Christians attached to it, is that given by St Paul:

> The Lord Jesus, the same night in which he was betrayed, took bread; and when he had given thanks he brake it and said: 'Take, eat: this is my body which is given up for you: do this in remembrance of me. After the same manner he took the cup . . . saying, 'This cup is the new testament in my blood: this do ye, as oft as ye drink it, in remembrance of me'. For as often as ye eat this bread and drink this cup [St Paul comments] ye do shew the Lord's death till he come. Wherefore whosoever shall eat this bread and drink this cup of the Lord unworthily, shall be guilty of the body and blood of the Lord (I Cor., 11, 23–7).

The word 'remembrance' and the Latin word *memoria* used in this passage by the medieval church, are imperfect attempts to render the Greek work *anamnesis* used by St Paul, which has a different force, implying a re-calling, not simply a calling to mind. The Greek sense accords with the belief universally held in the medieval west, that Christ was truly present in the consecrated bread and wine. No attempt was made to explain this mystery until, in the eleventh century, it was seen to pose an intellectual problem: the consecrated bread and wine retained their normal characteristics when perceived by the senses, and it was therefore difficult to understand in what way they could be described as truly the body and blood of Christ. A decision was made about this by the Fourth Lateran Council of 1215, which defined the doctrine of transubstantiation. This definition was included in a general statement about belief:

> There is one universal church of the faithful, outside which nobody may in any way be saved, in which Jesus Christ is himself both priest and sacrifice. His body and blood are

contained in the sacrament of the altar under the appearances (*sub speciebus*) of bread and wine, which have been transubstantiated by divine power, the bread into the body, the wine into the blood, so that to complete the mystery of unity we receive from him [Christ] that which he received from us. And indeed nobody is able to celebrate this sacrament except a priest who has been validly ordained in accordance with the powers of the church which Jesus Christ granted to the apostles and their successors.

In this definition the eucharist is seen in the context of the incarnation: Christ who received from mankind a human body, gives his body and blood to men in holy communion. Through this sacrament he, the church's head, remains ever present among his faithful people. The terminology of the definition is Aristotelian, based on the distinction between the appearance of material objects and their essential qualities. Thus it is affirmed that while the eucharistic elements retain the appearance of bread and wine, their real qualities become those of Christ, present in them.

This definition also refers to Christ as the sacrifice of the church. St Paul said that the eucharist was intended to 'show forth the Lord's death', that is, to represent the sacrifice of Christ on Calvary at the crucifixion. For that reason it was customary throughout the Middle Ages to speak of the mass as a sacrifice. There was complete agreement about the purpose of the mass as a sacrifice: the offering to God of bread and wine, transubstantiated into the body and blood of Christ, was the supreme act of worship which the church could perform, and that sacrifice was also the highest form of intercession for the needs of all Christians, living and dead. But there was no consensus about the relation between the sacrifice offered by Christ on Calvary and the re-enactment of that sacrifice by the church in the eucharistic mystery. Thus whereas some theologians supposed that at each mass Christ offered himself for sacrifice again, St Thomas Aquinas held that there was only one sacrifice, that of Calvary, which was 'shown forth' in time at each mass for the particular needs of God's people.

The sacrament of penance

Scholastic theologians paid special attention to the sacrament of penance because of the pastoral needs of the church. It was a traditional part of Christian belief that all men suffered from original sin: this was characteristic of being human, inherited from the ancestors of the human race who had fallen from grace, and it prevented men from leading the life of perfection. In addition, each individual had the capacity to commit personal sin by deliberate acts of free will. Baptism alone could cleanse men from original sin, and it also conferred remission of all personal sin. The sacrament of penance was ordained to forgive sins committed after baptism. It was necessary only in the case of serious sins, and in the early church it involved confession of those sins to a bishop or his delegate and the performance of a harsh and lengthy penance. In the early centuries it could only be received once in a lifetime.

Medieval theologians made a distinction between two kinds of post-baptismal sin. Venial sins, which were trivial in character and not deliberate acts of will, were not the concern of the whole church, but could be privately confessed to God. Mortal sins, which were serious offences committed with full knowledge and with the intention of doing wrong, could only be forgiven in the sacrament of penance, which during the Middle Ages could be administered by any priest.

Three conditions were necessary for the forgiveness of mortal sins: the penitent must feel truly contrite; he must confess his sins to a priest; and he must perform the penance enjoined on him. It was, however, agreed that this sacrament might be received by any Christian as often as was necessary.

Since the third century penance had been regarded as an act of reparation to God for sin, that is, as evidence of the sinner's sincere desire to make amends, but it was the scholastic theologians who first worked out the implications of this belief. They pointed out that the penances which the church enjoined might not be adequate reparation in the sight of God for the sins which had been committed and that it therefore followed that any discrepancy would have to be made good in the next life. Furthermore, when dying men made their confessions they were unable to perform any penances for their sins, and in such cases the entire penance would have to be performed in the next life.

The doctrine of purgatory

These considerations led the church to re-examine its teaching about the afterlife. It was agreed that those who died in a state of unrepented mortal sin would go to hell, although it was forbidden to believe that any particular person had been damned, since only God knew whether a man had repented at the instant of death. It was also agreed that if a man died in a state of grace, and had performed full penance for all his sins, he would go straight to heaven. Souls who died in a state of grace, but who had not completed their penance, however, constituted a problem: they would not be damned, but they could not perform penance in heaven, which was a state of perfection.

It was this dilemma which led the church to formulate a fully developed doctrine of purgatory. This was, in effect, an ante-chamber to heaven, since all who went there would, when they had completed their purification, enter the presence of God. Although belief in an intermediate state after death was implicit in the Catholic tradition from an early time, it was, as J. Le Goff has recently shown, only fully schematized by western theologians in the twelfth and thirteenth centuries. Before that time some authorities seem to have considered that purgation involved a temporary experience of hell. The doctrine of purgatory was formally defined as an article of faith by the council of Florence in 1439.

Scholastic theologians could reach no common mind about the fate of non-Christians after death. The church taught that after his crucifixion Christ had descended to hell and released the souls of all righteous men who had been held captive there since the fall, but it ventured no opinion about the position of unbelievers since Christ's coming. Some theologians took the rigorist view that the unbaptized would be damned, but others inclined to accept St Augustine's doctrine of 'baptism by desire'. While conceding that baptism was the means of salvation, Augustine suggested that a desire to be baptized would be accorded equivalent reward by God. This doctrine was capable to extension to include those who would have wished to be baptized had they known about Christianity, and those who knew about it and rejected it, but would have wished to accept it had they understood it properly.

Children who died unbaptized before the age of reason were admitted by everybody to fall into a different category, since although they suffered from original sin by reason of being human, they were too young to have committed a mortal sin. The ingenious minds of scholastic theologians postulated the existence of a spiritual state called Limbo in which, according to St Thomas Aquinas, such souls existed in complete happiness although they were unable to enjoy the vision of God.

The doctrine of indulgences

The harsh penitential discipline of the medieval church proved self-defeating, because large numbers of people refused to make their confessions until they were dying and unable to perform penances. It was this which led the popes from the late eleventh century onwards to offer indulgences. In its earliest form a plenary indulgence enabled a man to substitute an act which he found congenial, like going on crusade, for all the penances imposed by the church for the sins he had previously confessed. At a later period it was extended to include those penances which he would otherwise have to perform in purgatory. The popes based their claim to grant such privileges on the power of the keys, granted by Christ to St Peter: 'whatsoever thou shalt loose on earth shall be loosed in heaven'.

Theology was accounted a science in the Middle Ages, and it had this in common with other sciences, that its practitioners were not content to know that things happen, but also wished to discover why they did. Scholastic theologians sought to explain how the system of indulgences worked and devised a kind of celestial accountancy known as the treasury of merits. This was made up of the merits of Christ, which were infinite, and of those saints who, during their lifetimes, had performed acts of penance far in excess of those required as reparation for their own sins, and the pope, as successor of St Peter, had the power to apply those merits to help other souls in need. This doctrine is framed in very legalistic terms, but it expresses a belief, deeply rooted in Catholic tradition, that no arbitrary limit can be drawn in the spiritual life between the living and the dead, but that all Christians throughout the ages are members of one church and have a collective responsibility to help each other to attain salvation.

Continuing speculation

Many of the views of the scholastic theologians, but by no means all of them, became part of the tradition of belief of the western church, but few of them were defined as articles of faith. The church used its powers of definition sparingly. At the end of the Middle Ages it would have been possible to list the articles of belief defined by General Councils, but these would not have formed a comprehensive statement of the Catholic faith, or even a statement of the minimum which Catholics were required to believe. Many doctrines had not been defined because they were not controversial: no Catholic had ever questioned, for example, that the Holy Spirit was conferred on the believer at confirmation by the laying-on of hands, and it had therefore never been necessary to define this as an article of faith. Yet it would have been heresy to deny it, or to deny the large body of other, uncontroversial beliefs which formed part of the church's tradition.

There were, however, various matters about which no consensus existed and about which it was legitimate to speculate. One of these was the doctrine of the atonement. It was believed that Christ's sacrifice on Calvary had reconciled man to God, but a variety of explanations existed about why it had done so. St Anselm in his *Cur Deus Homo*? (*Why did God become man?*) saw in Christ's death a sacrifice offered to God the Father in satisfaction for the offence caused to his justice by the sins of men. Only God could offer the unlimited sacrifice which divine justice required, and only by becoming man could God the Son represent men before God the Father in this sacrificial role. Peter Abelard advanced the quite different argument that Christ's sacrifice was effectual, not because it gave satisfaction to God's justice, but because it showed men the depth of God's love for them, and evoked in men a corresponding love. Medieval opinion found Anselm's theory more congenial, but it never received the official approval of the church, and the Catholic tradition has never endorsed any single explanation of this central mystery of the Christian faith.

Another doctrine which remained a subject of controversy throughout the Middle Ages was that of the immaculate conception of the Blessed Virgin Mary. Whereas some theologians, like Duns Scotus († 1308), argued that Mary had at her conception been freed from original sin in order to become the Mother of God, thereby anticipating the freedom which all Christians enjoy through baptism, this was strongly denied by St Thomas Aquinas and other Dominican theologians.

There were many areas of belief during the Middle Ages which remained open to speculation and that is perhaps the chief reason why the theology faculties of western Europe attracted, as G. Leff has pointed out, the intellectual heavyweights of the time. Medieval Catholicism, despite the systematization imposed upon it by the scholastic theologians, remained a living tradition, capable of developing fresh insights into the faith which it had received from the apostles.

The role of individual revelation

It is a universal Christian experience that God speaks to individual members of the church in the context of prayer. The majority of such communications are of a strictly personal kind and of no interest to the church at large, but some people in the Middle Ages claimed to have received revelations which were of general concern. Discernment was necessary when considering such cases, because the people who made such claims might prove to be fraudulent or deluded or might have misunderstood a genuine revelation.

The church nevertheless accepted that God did sometimes speak to men in this way, but it ruled that genuine revelations could not of their nature add to, or contradict, the revelation given by Christ, for St Paul had warned, 'But though . . . an angel from heaven preach any other gospel to you . . . let him be accursed' (Gal., 1,8). The church accepted that some of its members had genuine gifts of prophecy: that God revealed the future to them in general or specific terms. St Hildegarde was credited with such powers and was treated by her contemporaries, both lay and clerical, as a kind of oracle. The Cistercian abbot, Joachim of Flora (†1202), wrote mystical treatises about the future pattern of human history, based on a close study of the scriptures, and these were very influential because they were widely regarded as prophetic works.

Other people claimed revelations which had a more immediate application. St Catherine of Siena (†1380), for example, believed that she had a divine mandate to persuade Gregory XI to move the papal court back to Rome from Avignon. The pope accepted her claims as genuine and acted on her advice and she was subsequently canonized. A quite different experience was that of the English anchoress, Lady Julian of Norwich, who claimed that in 1373 Christ had appeared to her on sixteen occasions and spoken with her. She wrote an account of this, *The Revelations of Divine Love*, which the church accepted as a genuine record of her own experiences which might be read with profit by other Christians.

It is always difficult for any religious institution to balance the claims of personal revelation against those of the received tradition, but it is important to remember that the medieval church made that attempt and did not seek to stifle the prophetic voice of the community, which had occupied so important a place in the primitive church. Western religious experience was undoubtedly enriched as a result, for prophetic gifts were not the monopoly of trained theologians or of the clergy, but were shared also by lay people. A high proportion of those who possessed them were women, who had no voice in church councils or theology faculties, but were in this way able to contribute to the continued growth of a living tradition of faith.

5
Public Worship

One of the earliest descriptions of the Christian church states that its members 'continued steadfastly in the apostles' doctrine and fellowship, and in breaking of bread and in prayers' (Acts, 2,42). From the beginning faith and worship were inseparable and they cannot be understood in isolation from each other, for it was through worship that the Christian community experienced God and came to understand its faith more fully. 'The breaking of bread', a term used in the New Testament for the eucharist, and the recitation of communal prayers continued to be the chief forms of worship during the Middle Ages. Collectively these activities were known as the liturgy, a word meaning 'public duty', for worship was the chief duty of the church.

Church architecture

Churches were built and furnished to meet the needs of the liturgy which was performed in them. Those dating from the late Roman period were usually rectangular in shape and had a semi-circular apse containing the altar, at which mass was said. The choir was placed in the middle of such churches and was separated from the congregation by a low screen. These churches were designed for a liturgy in which the congregation took a full part, and it was normal practice in late antiquity for the celebrant to stand behind the altar and say mass facing the people.

By the ninth century a new style of church architecture became dominant in the west and remained so throughout the rest of the Middle Ages. The new churches were often cruciform in shape: the nave represented the foot of the cross, the two transepts the arms of the cross and the sanctuary its head. The altar was built against the east wall of the sanctuary* so that the priest said mass with his back to the congregation. The choir sat on either side of the sanctuary, which was separated from the main body of the church by a rood-screen of wood or stone, so called because it was normally surmounted by a rood, or cross. The congregation could see the liturgical action through the lattice-work in the upper half of the screen. Before the thirteenth century no seating was provided for the worshippers, but thereafter wooden benches began to be placed in the naves of some churches.

If enough money was available churches were decorated with works of religious symbolism: groups of sculpture adorned the exterior of the building; the

*It is customary to describe church interiors on the assumption that the main altar is always at the east end.

capitals of columns were carved with religious scenes; the walls were embellished with frescoes and the windows filled with stained glass. Only very rich churches possessed all these features, but the poorest contained some crude examples of religious art. When a worshipper passed through the doors of a church he entered a different world: an enclosed space, consecrated to God, in which everything he saw directed his attention to the mysteries of the faith.

Liturgical rites

Medieval churches were built on the assumption that the congregation would take little part in the services. This came about because all public worship was conducted in Latin, which was known only to the educated, except in Rome and some parts of central Italy, where it remained comprehensible to the whole population until at least the eleventh century. Latin had originally been used by the western church because it was the official language of the Roman empire, but it was retained in the post-Roman era in order to distinguish Catholics from the Germanic invaders who were Arian heretics and used a vernacular liturgy (see chapter 1). Although in the ninth century the papacy licensed a translation of the liturgy into Old Slavonic for use by missionaries in central Europe, this concession was permanently adopted only in a few dioceses on the Dalmatian coast, and the rest of Catholic Europe worshipped in Latin.

Before the eleventh century a variety of liturgical forms, or rites, existed in the west: the Roman rite, the Ambrosian rite of Milan, the Mozarabic rite of Spain, the Celtic rite and the Gallican rite of the Frankish kingdom. All churches used some variation of one of these rites. Charlemagne sought to standardize forms of worship in the Frankish empire by imposing the Roman rite there, but Gallican forms proved resistant to change and consequently a hybrid liturgy, the Romano-Gallican rite, grew up in northern Europe in the ninth and tenth centuries. This was introduced in Rome in the eleventh century by reforming popes from northern Europe and displaced the old Roman rite. From *c.*1050 the papacy strove to enforce the use of the Romano-Gallican liturgy throughout the western church and gradually succeeded, so that by 1500 it was used everywhere except in the province of Milan, where the Ambrosian rite was retained.

Before the invention of printing it was very difficult to standardize texts, and so considerable variation existed in the wording and rubrics of the Romano-Gallican liturgy used in local churches. Attempts were made to standardize local practice by encouraging the churches in a diocese or province to conform to the Use, or custom, of a cathedral. Thus many English churches in the later Middle Ages came to adopt the liturgical customs of Salisbury cathedral, known as the Use of Sarum, but complete uniformity was not achieved.

Mass vestments and liturgical vessels

The principal church service, and the only one which lay people regularly attended, was the mass. It might, without irreverence, be described as a sacred drama, for its purpose was 'to show forth the Lord's death'. The officiating clergy wore distinctive vestments, which had originally been the formal dress of the late Roman period, but which in the Middle Ages were reserved for liturgical use. There were five principal vestments: the alb, a full-length, white, linen garment, with long sleeves, held in at the waist by a girdle; the chasuble, an oval vestment, without sleeves, but with a hole in the centre for inserting the head, not unlike a Latin American *poncho* in design; the tunicle and dalmatic, each a slightly different form of an unbelted, short-sleeved tunic, reaching below the knees; and the cope, an ankle-length cloak, with an attached hood, secured on the chest by a metal clasp.Bishops and certain privileged abbots had the right to wear a mitre, a headdress made of fabric in the shape of an inverted shield, with two pendant lappets at the back.

From the twelfth century it became customary to vary the colour of vestments in accordance with the liturgical season or feast. White or gold vestments were universally worn on great feast days and black vestments on Good Friday and for funeral masses, but there was no fixed rule about the other colours. Red, green, blue, purple and sometimes yellow vestments were used in rich churches, but poor parishes often had only one coloured set of vestments to use when white was inappropriate.

A number of 'properties' were needed to stage the sacred drama of the mass. Before it began the altar was covered with a white linen cloth and the altar candles lit: these varied in number but were never less than two. On a small table beside the altar were placed a basin and towel, to enable the celebrant ritually to wash his hands; two small bottles containing wine and water; and a box filled with thin wafers of white, unleavened bread, known as hosts, from the Latin word, *hostia*, a victim, because, when consecrated, they would become the body of Christ crucified. A cup, or chalice, on which was placed a small plate, or paten, both if possible made of precious metal, were also placed on the side table and covered with an embroidered cloth. At solemn celebrations of mass additional 'properties' were needed: a processional cross, portable candlesticks, a holy water stoup, a box of incense and a thurible to burn it in.

The liturgical calendar

The text of the mass retained an unvarying form throughout the year, but allowed for considerable variation in detail. Those parts which never altered were known as the ordinary of the mass, and those which changed as the 'proper' of the mass, because they were liturgical forms proper for use on certain days.

The church observed a liturgical year which began on the fourth Sunday before Christmas Day. This marked the start of Advent, a season which lasted until Christmas Eve and was concerned with meditating on the Second Coming of Christ and the Last Judgement. This was followed by Christmas, the remembrance of Christ's first coming, which was kept for twelve days. The weeks after Christmas were 'ordinary' time in that they commemorated no special aspect of the church's teaching. This period varied in length in accordance with the date of Easter, which could fall on any day between 22 March and 25 April, because the First Council of Nicaea had ordered that it should be kept on the Sunday after the first full moon to occur on or after the spring equinox (21 March). Easter was preceded by the penitential season of Lent, which began on Ash Wednesday and lasted for forty days. The last week of Lent was known as Holy Week and commemorated the events leading up to Christ's death, culminating in the remembrance of the crucifixion on Good Friday. Christ's resurrection was celebrated on Easter Day, and Eastertide lasted for forty days, the time of Christ's presence on earth after rising from the dead. This season ended on Ascension

Day, commemorating Christ's return to heaven. Ten days later the feast of Pentecost was observed (which is better known in the English-speaking world as Whitsunday), celebrating the descent of the Holy Spirit on the apostles. This season lasted for eight days, and the rest of the year until the first Sunday in Advent was 'ordinary' time in which no special doctrine was commemorated.

The church also observed a festal cycle, which was based on the calendrical year. Feasts were kept each year on fixed dates, for example that of St Michael the archangel, or Michaelmas, always fell on 29 September. Elaborate rules were devised to determine which form of service should be used if there was a conflict between the seasonal calendar and the festal calendar. Broadly speaking the festal cycle took precedence on ordinary weekdays, but the seasonal cycle took precedence on Sundays, unless a very great feast fell on a Sunday. From the eighth century the whole church observed the same seasonal calendar, but there was always considerable local variation in the festal calendar. As the Middle Ages wore on and the number of saints commemorated grew larger, there were very few weekdays which were not saints' days. However, on weekdays when no saint was commemorated, the proper of the mass for the previous Sunday was used.

The solemn celebration of mass

The celebration of a solemn mass, with full ceremonial, involved quite a large cast. The celebrant was always a priest and so, usually, were his two assistants who took the parts of deacon and subdeacon. The servers who assisted with the ceremonial were often laymen, and, except in religious communities, choirs were usually made up of laymen. Except in convents, women did not serve as choristers and treble parts in all other choirs were sung by boys. There was a great development in liturgical music during the Middle Ages: the simple plainsong of the early centuries first became more ornamented, and then was replaced by polyphony from the early fourteenth century onwards. By 1500 this was fully developed in the work of composers like Josquin des Prés (†1521). The chant was at first unaccompanied, but organs began to be used in the central Middle Ages and were found in most large churches by the end of this period.

This is how the solemn mass of Easter Day would have been celebrated in a cathedral, or large monastic or parish church from the twelfth century onwards. The altar being prepared and the candles lit, the clergy entered in procession: first a server carrying the processional cross, flanked by two servers with lighted candles and followed by the thurifer, swinging a lighted censer; next came the other servers and the choir, all wearing albs; and finally the celebrant, wearing a gold cope over an alb, flanked by the deacon and subdeacon vested in albs and a gold tunicle and dalmatic. While the rest of the ministers took up their places in the sanctuary, the celebrant, accompanied by a server carrying a stoup, advanced into the nave and sprinkled the congregation with holy water, as the choir sang: 'I beheld water issuing out from the right side of the Temple, alleluia'. This ceremony was intended to remind the faithful that they had been cleansed from their sins in the waters of baptism.

The celebrant returned to the sanctuary, took off his cope and vested in a gold chasuble, as the choir sang the introit, the opening anthem for the feast: 'I have risen and I am still with you, alleluia'. While the celebrant, assisted by the deacon and subdeacon, censed the altar, the choir sang the ninefold *Kyrie*, 'Lord, have mercy upon us', the only part of the mass which was regularly said in Greek. This led straight into the hymn of praise, *Gloria in excelsis Deo*, 'Glory be to God on high'. The celebrant then chanted the collect, the prayer appointed for the day, and next the subdeacon chanted the first lesson, known as the Epistle, since it was normally taken from one of the letters found in the New Testament. After this the choir sang a collection of special anthems for the feast, while the deacon knelt to receive the celebrant's blessing, before carrying the Gospel book in procession to the north side of the sanctuary, facing the people. The Gospels were held open by a server, flanked by two servers holding lighted candles and a thurifer swinging a censer. Having censed the book, the deacon chanted the Gospel for the day. The choir then sang the Nicene Creed, followed by the offertory anthem proper to the feast, 'The earth trembled and was still when God arose to judgement, alleluia'. While this was being sung the celebrant, deacon and subdeacon prepared the elements for consecration, putting hosts on the paten and mixing wine and water in the chalice, both of which were placed on the centre of the altar. They then censed the altar once more and, as the anthem ended, the celebrant turned to the congregation and said: 'Pray, brethren, that my sacrifice and yours may be acceptable to God the almighty Father'.

This marked the beginning of the main part of the mass. The church on earth joined with the angels and saints in heaven in praising God as the choir sang the *Sanctus*, 'Holy, holy, holy, Lord God of hosts', and *Benedictus*, 'Blessed is he that cometh in the name of the Lord'. The celebrant then began to recite the canon of the mass, the prayer of consecration, which, except in very minor ways, never varied. The celebrant had his back to the people and normally said this prayer in a low voice, and so, in order to inform the congregation when the consecration had taken place, it became usual, from the eleventh century, for the priest to hold first the consecrated host and then the consecrated chalice above his head. Attention was drawn to this by the ringing of handbells, three times at each consecration. This practice was known as the Elevation of the Host and was the most impressive part of the eucharistic liturgy: the choir had fallen silent, the congregation knelt in silence, and the whole church waited on God until the chalice was elevated and the consecration complete. The celebrant continued the canon in silence, praying for the needs of the living and the dead, and concluded it by chanting aloud the Our Father. The choir then sang the *Agnus Dei*, 'O Lamb of God that takest away the sins of the world, have mercy upon us, grant us peace', while the celebrant and his assistants made their communion. Such members of the congregation as wished to receive holy communion entered the sanctuary at this point and knelt around the altar, and during the communion the choir sang the anthem proper to the feast, 'Christ our passover is sacrificed for us, alleluia'.

The celebrant then chanted a prayer of thanksgiving and gave the congregation his blessing. Finally, he read aloud the opening words of St John's Gospel, in which the mystery of the Incarnation is set forth. This being ended, the clergy, servers and choir formed up once more in procession and left the church singing a Latin hymn.

Sung mass and low mass

The majority of parish churches lacked the resources to celebrate solemn mass: they were served by only one priest, they had no choir, and they could not afford incense. On Sundays and holy days the priest, assisted by one or more servers, sang the parts of both choir and celebrant to simple chants, although he said the prayer of consecration silently. In the later Middle Ages the mendicant orders introduced the custom of saying mass instead of singing it. This was known as low mass in contrast to sung mass, or high mass. Low mass was characterized by a complete absence of ceremonial: frequently the priest read the entire service in a low and inaudible voice with his back to the congregation throughout. Such celebrations, sometimes described as 'the blessed mutter of the Latin mass', were not unpopular, because they had the supreme merit of brevity. Nevertheless, they did not become the universal alternative to solemn masses in the Middle Ages, for masses continued to be sung, particularly in country parishes, into the sixteenth century.

Medieval church services were not designed to edify the congregation: their sole purpose was to offer worship to God, and lay people were encouraged to be present at mass in order to associate themselves with that worship. Nevertheless, the presence of a congregation was not essential. From the ninth century, when most monks began to be priested, it became normal for each of them to say a private mass each day as well as assisting at the solemn community mass. At a private mass the priest was usually attended only by a server and no congregation was expected. This custom spread to the rest of the clergy. Whereas in the early Middle Ages parish priests had normally only said mass on Sundays and holy days, they later began to celebrate mass every day. Since on working days lay people were unable to attend, the priest was often assisted only by a server.

The Divine Office

Unlike the mass, the Divine Office, which formed the other main part of the church's public worship, was not intended for lay participation. It originated in the monasteries as a daily system of communal prayer and was adopted subsequently by all the religious orders. There were eight services in each daily cycle. Mattins, said in the middle of the night, consisted on ordinary days of three psalms and three readings taken from the Bible and other edifying books, and on Sundays and great feast days of nine psalms and nine readings. It was normally followed immediately by Lauds, at which four psalms and two canticles were recited, followed by prayers. Canticles form a regular part of the Office: they are biblical songs of praise, such as the *Magnificat*, the song of the Blessed Virgin Mary (Luke, 1, 46–54). The Office of Prime, consisting of three psalms followed by prayers, was said at dawn; those of Terce, Sext and None were recited at the third, sixth and ninth hours of the day and were each devoted to the reading of part of psalm 119 (Vulgate, 118), followed by prayers. Vespers, consisting of five psalms, the *Magnificat* and prayers, was said at sunset; and the eighth Office, Compline, was recited before the community retired to bed: it began with an examination of conscience which was followed by four psalms, a canticle and prayers.

The original purpose of the Divine Office was to ensure that a community recited the entire psalter each week and read most of the Bible each year; for the psalms were arranged on a weekly cycle, and the readings on a yearly cycle, starting on the first Sunday in Advent. The Divine Office, like the mass, had 'propers' which varied from week to week: these consisted of antiphons (verses recited before and after each psalm), responsories (short litanies said after each reading), special hymns and special prayers. The system failed in its purpose because the festal cycle took precedence over the seasonal cycle on weekdays, as explained above. Each feast day had its own Office, consisting of a special set of psalms, readings and prayers, antiphons, responsories and hymns. As the number of feast days increased so the seasonal Office was rarely said except on Sundays. Thus throughout much of the year the Divine Office lacked overall cohesion, and the Office for each day became a self-contained unit, commemorating a particular feast, but having no connection with the Office of the next day.

In the eleventh century the Little Office of Our Lady was composed: this was an exact replica of the eightfold Divine Office, but it was much shorter and its forms never varied. In most religious houses the Little Office was a voluntary devotion and was said privately by some of the brethren, but the Cistercians and Carmelites sang it communally each day in addition to the Divine Office.

Unlike the mass, the Office had no dramatic potential. Choir-monks wore surplices, calf-length linen tunics, with wide sleeves, over their habits during the Office, and the altar candles were usually lit, but the services did not lend themselves to elaborate ceremonial. They did, however, offer scope for elaborate musical settings. Originally the Office had been said, and St Benedict's Rule allows about four hours a day for that purpose, but by the ninth century the Office was normally sung and, as chants grew more elaborate, so it came to occupy longer periods of the monastic day. As Noreen Hunt has shown, at Cluny in the late eleventh century almost eight hours a day were spent in singing the Divine Office on every day of the year.

The Divine Office was not suited for public recital in all churches. The canons in most cathedrals, or their deputies, the vicars-choral, sang the day Offices, but the night Offices were sung only in cathedrals administered by a religious community. The secular clergy were supposed to recite the Divine Office each day, but when they observed this rule they normally did so in private and made no attempt to read the Office in church. Lay people were not discouraged from attending Offices in places where they were publicly sung, but unless they understood Latin there was little inducement for them to do so.

Liturgical books

In the early Middle Ages the texts of the mass and the Divine Office were contained in a variety of books. The ordinary of the mass, together with the prayers for use throughout the year were contained in the sacramentary, but the readings were contained in the epistolary and the evangeliary, while the proper anthems were found in the antiphonary and the gradual and ceremonial directions in the *ordo*. Missals, containing all the necessary texts and rubrics for the celebration of mass throughout the year, began to be produced from the ninth century, although they did not become universal until the later Middle Ages. A similar problem existed at first in regard to the Divine Office: the psalms were in a psalter, the antiphons in an antiphonary, the hymns in a hymnary, and the readings in a lectionary. From the eleventh century all these texts began to be assembled in a single volume, the breviary.

Although simpler to handle than the multiplicity of volumes which they replaced, the missal and breviary could only be used by clergy with a technical training, since the directions they contained presupposed a sound liturgical knowledge. Thomas Cranmer, trained in the medieval method of saying mass and reading the Office, surely spoke from the heart when he said in the preface to the 1549 Prayer Book:

> Moreover the nombre and hardnes of the rules . . . and the manifolde chaunginges of the service, was the cause, that to turn the boke onlye, was so hard and intricate a matter, that many times there was more busines to find out what should be read, than to read it when it was founde out.

The use of interdict

In conclusion it should be noted that the church claimed the right to suspend public worship. Such a sanction was known as an interdict. Any bishop might impose this on a parish or town in his diocese, but the pope alone had the right to apply it to a wider area. During an interdict the sacraments might be administered privately to individuals, for example children might be baptized, lay people married and the last rites administered to the dying, but mass might not be celebrated publicly nor might the Divine Office be said in choir. Churches remained closed unless they had been specifically exempted from the interdict by the pope, as was the case with the chapels of some religious orders. Interdict was usually employed as an ecclesiastical weapon during the course of a quarrel between the church and lay authority.

6
Knowledge of the Bible

The text of the Bible

The New Testament read by the medieval church contained the same canonical books as those found in any modern edition, but the medieval Old Testament contained a number of additional books not found in modern Protestant editions (see Appendix I for details). The Old Testament used in the Middle Ages was based on the Septuagint canon, the Greek translation of the scriptures made for the Jews of Alexandria. This contained books which have not been preserved in Hebrew, but which are known only in Greek. St Jerome distinguished between those books which existed in both Hebrew and Greek, which he deemed canonical, and those which were known in Greek only, which he called ecclesiastical, because they were read by Christians but not accepted as divinely inspired by Jews. The Protestant reformers observed St Jerome's distinction, but the medieval church did not. It accorded canonical status to the entire Septuagint canon, because this version had been cited by some New Testament authors, which seemed to validate it, and also because it had been accepted as authoritative by the early church.

The Vulgate of St Jerome

The earliest Latin translations of the Bible date from the third century and are known collectively as the *Vetus Latina*, or Old Latin version. In 382 pope Damasus I commissioned St Jerome to make a new translation of the whole Bible from the Greek and Hebrew originals. This work, completed in 404, was known as the Vulgate, or the Bible in the common speech. Although it was intended for use as a standard version throughout the western church, this proved an impossible goal in an age before the invention of printing. The *Vetus Latina* continued to be read alongside the Vulgate for centuries, and readings from the older version were often incorporated in new transcriptions of the Vulgate text.

Exemplars of the Vulgate were sent from Rome to Northumbria in the seventh century and copies derived from them were used by Charlemagne's religious adviser, the English scholar Alcuin (†804), as the basis for his revision of the text of the Bible. Alcuin's edition became widely diffused in northern Europe and a version of it was adopted as authoritative in the theology schools of Paris during the twelfth century. Because Paris became pre-eminent as a centre of theological study, the Alcuin Vulgate came to be accepted by the whole western church in the later Middle Ages, although texts were never completely standardized and some families of manuscripts continued to contain a high proportion of readings derived from the *Vetus Latina*.

Vernacular translations

The Vulgate had been intended for popular use, since Latin was the language of all educated people in the west in St Jerome's day, and was spoken by most people in towns, where Christianity was strongest, but it soon became obsolete in many parts of Europe. The Germanic invasions of the fifth century led gradually to the evolution of a different society: the Roman system of secular education collapsed, urban life decayed, and new vernacular languages began to evolve within the former imperial frontiers. The church did not immediately respond to this new situation by translating the Bible into the common speech. Part of the reason for this was that the church identified Germanic languages with heresy, for many of the invaders were Arians (see chapter 1) and used a Gothic translation of the Bible made in the fourth century. Catholics therefore distanced themselves from the invaders by continuing to read the scriptures in Latin, and, of course, for a long time after the invasions began, many Catholics were able to understand Latin. It was not until *c*.600 that in most of northern Europe Latin had become a monopoly of the clergy; while in parts of Italy, including Rome, the vernacular remained close to Latin until at least the eleventh century, so that when the Vulgate was read in church the laity could grasp its general sense quite clearly, although no doubt it sounded archaic.

But in northern Europe after *c*.600 the Vulgate was no longer understood by lay people, and so churchmen encouraged the making of vernacular poems based on Biblical themes in order to make people familiar with the scriptures. The Anglo-Saxon clergy took a lead in this: the earliest known author of this kind is the Northumbrian poet Caedmon, who in the seventh century composed works on the creation of the world, the Exodus and the life of Christ, under the patronage of the abbess of Whitby. This genre of writing spread to the continent, perhaps through the influence of English missionaries: in *c*.830–40 the Gospel narrative was retold in epic form in a vernacular poem composed in Saxony, called the *Heliand*, the *Saviour*. Such poems were designed for public recital, and were an excellent way of instructing new converts in Biblical knowledge.

A tradition of making vernacular paraphrases of parts of the Bible persisted throughout the Middle Ages. Some were composed in verse, others in prose, but most were designed to be read aloud to a wide audience. Such works naturally concentrated on the narrative parts of the Bible, but they did serve to familiarize lay people with the scriptural account of man's salvation from the creation of the world to the Last Judgement.

Concurrently with these developments, literal vernacular translations were being made of parts of the Bible. This was done for the benefit of clergy in the church schools who were learning to read Latin. Such translations often took the form of interlinear glosses, like the word-for-word rendering into Anglo-Saxon of the Latin text of the Lindisfarne Gospels, written between the lines of the manuscript in the tenth century. G. Shepherd has argued convincingly that the translation of St John's Gospel, on which Bede was said to have been engaged at the time of his death, was a work of this kind, intended as a teaching aid for his pupils in the school of Jarrow, not for pastoral use.

These literal translations prepared the way for the making of literary translations: before 1000 the Gospels had been translated into West Saxon, and during the twelfth century the four Books of Kings (see Appendix I) were translated into Old French. By 1200 it would appear that vernacular translations existed of the entire Bible, although no complete translation had been made into any single language.

The church did not object in principle to vernacular translations, nor did it attempt to prevent lay people from owning or reading such translations before 1200. A change in attitude is perceptible after that time, because in the late twelfth century dissident groups, notably the Waldensians and Cathars (see chapter 18), made vernacular translations of the entire New Testament and parts of the Old and encouraged their followers to understand them in an unorthodox sense. In areas where such movements were strong, the church authorities not merely condemned the heretical interpretation of scripture, but also banned the reading of vernacular Bibles by lay people. The synod of Toulouse in 1229 took the extreme step of forbidding lay people to own copies of the Bible in any language, even Latin.

Enactments of this kind were sufficiently widespread to create a belief, summed up in a decree of the emperor Charles IV in 1369, that: 'It is not permitted in canon law for lay people of either sex to read the holy scriptures in any vernacular translation'. In fact this was a misapprehension: no law of that kind had been promulgated for the universal church. Indeed, the only papal ruling on the subject was that given in 1199 by Innocent III about Bible-reading heretics at Metz, a ruling incorporated in the *Decretals* published by Gregory IX in 1234 and therefore part of the canon law of the church. Innocent condemned the separatist tendencies of the heretics of Metz and the erroneous way in which they interpreted the Bible, but he did not condemn the study of vernacular translations of the Bible by lay people if carried out in an orthodox way, but observed that:

> The desire to understand holy scripture and the attempt to encourage others to live in accordance with its teachings is unexceptionable and indeed praiseworthy.

The distinction which Innocent here makes between the right and wrong uses of the Bible by lay people was observed by the church as a whole. For despite the prohibitions of vernacular Bibles enacted by local councils in areas affected by heresy, the production of vernacular translations for use by Catholic laymen proceeded without hindrance. A complete text of the Bible in the *langue d'oeil*, the speech of northern France, was compiled in the later thirteenth century, and in the fourteenth century vernacular Bibles circulated freely in Italy, Aragon, Castile, Germany and Burgundy.

By that time heresy had declined throughout much of western Europe and churchmen no longer regarded Bible reading with suspicion as a possible symptom of heterodoxy. England, however, was an exception to this general rule. The first complete translation of the Bible into English was that made by John Wycliffe (†1384) and his followers, the Lollards, who were condemned as heretics. For that reason the council of Oxford in 1407 forbade the use of vernacular scriptures made during or since Wycliffe's time, unless a bishop's license was first obtained, and it also forbade the making of new, unlicensed translations. The bishops did not object to the Lollard Bible in itself, for they sometimes granted licenses to lay people to read it, but they disapproved of its use by the Lollards as a source of unorthodox teaching.

The situation in fifteenth-century England was exceptional. There is no evidence that episcopal permission was required by laymen who wished to read the Bible in the vernacular in any other part of the western church. Indeed, when the theology faculty of the university of Cologne was asked by conservative German churchmen in 1398 whether lay people might read the scriptures in the vernacular, it ruled that this was legitimate. By the fifteenth century there were devout lay people all over western Europe, except in England, who owned and read vernacular Bibles. Whereas before 1350 the majority of such Bibles had been in the possession of kings and great noblemen, after that time their ownership was spread over a wider social spectrum, including prosperous burgesses. This reflects the cheaper costs of book production in the later Middle Ages.

The cost of producing Bibles

Complete texts of the Bible were in relatively short supply throughout much of the Middle Ages because of the unusually high costs of book production. Whereas in the ancient world Egyptian papyrus was used for preparing cheap copies of texts, while a relatively high degree of literacy enabled *scriptoria* to produce multiple copies of a work by the process of simultaneous dictation to a group of scribes, thereby reducing the costs of transcription, neither of these conditions obtained in the early Middle Ages.

Because literacy declined there was no longer a demand for cheap books. Early medieval books were luxury goods and were extremely expensive to produce. Very little papyrus was imported in the early Middle Ages and until *c.*1300 books were written on parchment, that is, animal hides, usually sheepskin. Each folio had to be specially prepared so that the surface was smooth, it had to be cut to size and it had to be lined to ensure even spacing. Multiple copies were no longer needed: each text was written out separately and the number of man-hours involved in copying an entire Bible was immense. Most early medieval Bibles were therefore *de luxe* copies, they were often illuminated with miniatures and were richly bound, some having covers made from ivory or encrusted with cabuchon jewels.

Only cathedrals and great monasteries could afford Bibles of that kind, and the only individuals who were rich enough to own them were some bishops or kings and great noblemen, who displayed them as prestige objects in their private chapels. Some parts of the Bible were distributed more widely: copies of the Gospels and the psalter were quite common, but separate manuscripts of other parts of the scriptures, such as the Epistles or the Pentateuch, were also produced. But most churches and small monasteries had no copy of even part of the Bible, and had to rely on lectionaries, books containing the lessons read during public worship.

The growth of theology schools at Paris and elsewhere from the twelfth century onwards led to a demand for multiple texts of the Bible for use by students. The ancient practice of mass production by simultaneous dictation to a group of scribes was therefore re-introduced, and costs were also reduced by omitting luxury features like illuminated capitals, and by writing in double columns and adopting standard abbreviations, which meant that less parchment was needed.

In this way portable, one-volume texts of the Bible were produced, but they remained expensive, for they contained about 450 folios each.

In the late thirteenth century paper began to be used in book production and as this became more generally available the overhead costs were substantially reduced. The introduction of printing in the fifteenth century did not immediately reduce costs, for early printed books were expensive and cheaper books were not produced until the early modern period. Nevertheless, Bibles written on paper were cheaper than earlier Bibles had been, and more clergy and literate laymen began to have copies of their own. Even so, many parish churches, specially those in rural areas, still relied solely on lectionaries as a source of Bible readings at the end of the Middle Ages.

Bible reading in the Middle Ages

Although all the clergy were supposed to understand Latin, few of them had access to a complete text of the Vulgate. The secular clergy knew those parts of the Bible which were read at mass. In the Romano-Gallican rite used in most western churches after the eleventh century (see chapter 5) two lessons were appointed for most masses, one from the Gospels, the other from the Epistles, although occasionally a reading from some other part of the Bible might be substituted for this. On weekday masses of the season no special lessons were appointed and the Sunday lessons were read again, except during Lent when each of the forty days had its own readings. Special lessons were, it is true, appointed for each feast day, but this produced less variety than might be supposed, since many feasts shared the same readings. Thus the first reading on the feast of a martyr was usually the same passage of the Book of Wisdom: 'The souls of the righteous are in the hand of God'. Mass readings were usually brief, except during Holy Week, when the four Gospel narratives of Christ's Passion were read in their entirety on consecutive days, while twelve Old Testament prophecies foretelling Christ's life were read at the vigil preceding the first mass of Easter. Thus a priest whose knowledge of the Bible depended solely on the readings appointed for mass would know the Gospels well and the Epistles reasonably well, but would have little acquaintance with the rest of the Bible.

Members of religious communities, who said the Divine Office each day, and secular clergy, who read the office in their breviaries, would know those parts of the Bible appointed to be read each day at Mattins. Originally the three readings on ordinary days and the nine readings on great feasts had all been taken from the Bible, but during the Middle Ages passages from other religious works came to be substituted for some of them. Thus all the readings for weekdays during Lent came to be taken from Biblical commentaries, and not from the Bible itself, while on saints' days, which came to occupy an increasingly important place in the late medieval calendar (see chapter 5), the third reading was always taken from the life of the saint. Furthermore, the Bible readings appointed for saints' days were self-contained and bore no relation to the readings appointed for the season. Thus a monk or priest who said the Divine Office regularly would come to know the entire psalter by heart and would read a random selection of passages from the Old and New Testaments in the course of a year, but would not have any systematic knowledge of the Bible.

Biblical scholarship

Nevertheless, throughout the Middle Ages there was always a small group of scholars who knew the whole of the Bible very well. In the early centuries they were mostly monks, living in communities which had good libraries and working in isolation from each other. Men like Bede, who wrote extensive Biblical commentaries, and Alcuin, who sought to revise the text of the Vulgate, worked in that tradition. The growth of centres of higher education in the twelfth century made systematic Biblical scholarship a possibility. The majority of students did not, of course, read theology: this study was confined to a relatively small group of men who had completed their preliminary training in the liberal arts.

The medieval theology schools have left their mark on modern editions of the Bible. Since that time the books of the Old and New Testaments have always been arranged in the same order and the chapter divisions which were introduced then are still universally observed (verse divisions only date from the sixteenth century). Biblical concordances were also first produced in the thirteenth-century schools as aids to study.

Medieval theologians attempted to revise the text of the Vulgate and eliminate the errors of earlier copyists. With the help of Jewish scholars they revised the Vulgate Old Testament in the light of Hebrew texts used by the Jewish communities of western Europe. The Vulgate text was not superseded, but lists of *correctoria*, or alternative readings, were compiled by this method for use in the theology schools.

Comparatively little work was done on the text of the New Testament. Greek texts were not available in most of western Europe, but had to be procured from the Byzantine empire or Sicily, and few western scholars were able to read them. During the fifteenth century the study of Greek became part of the educational syllabus favoured by the Renaissance humanists, who also developed sound techniques for the editing of classical texts. This kind of training could be applied to Biblical studies, and it enabled Erasmus to produce a critical edition of the New Testament in 1516 together with a new translation into classical Latin.

The concern to establish an accurate text of the Bible had been present in the west throughout the Middle Ages, but it was not until the very end of the period that the necessary linguistic and technical skills were developed to make such an undertaking possible. Cardinal Ximenes, archbishop of Toledo and Inquisitor-General of the Spanish kingdoms, financed and commissioned the publication of the Complutensian Polyglot, or Bible in many languages, edited at the university of Alcalà (Latin, *Complutum*). This work occupied six volumes and was completed in 1517. The Vulgate text of the Old Testament was printed between the Hebrew text and the Greek text of the Septuagint, while the Vulgate New Testament was printed in parallel with the original Greek, and the Syriac paraphrase was appended at the foot of each page.

Biblical commentaries

The medieval church inherited a large corpus of Biblical commentary from the church of late antiquity. It also inherited from the early church a belief that there were four senses in which the scriptures could be understood. First there was the literal sense: this included both the grammatical study of the sacred text and a consideration of its meaning as a statement of fact (this was sometimes called the historical sense). Secondly there was the moral sense: any passage in the Bible, in addition to its literal meaning, might have some more general application which could edify the reader. For example, the story of Daniel in the lions' den, taken in a moral sense, showed that God defended those who obeyed his law even when this involved breaking the law of the land. Thirdly there was the allegorical sense: this interpreted passages in the scriptures as symbols of the life of Christ on earth and of the work of his church. Christ himself had interpreted the Old Testament in this way when he had likened his death and resurrection to the fate of the prophet Jonah, swallowed by a whale and then restored to the world of men (Matt., 12, 39–41), while St Paul had interpreted Abraham's domestic life as an allegory of the Jewish and Christian dispensations (Gal., 4, 22–31). Fourthly there was the anagogical, or mystical, sense: this interpreted the scriptures as symbols of ultimate realities, and assumed that a careful study of the Bible would increase man's knowledge of God who was, in a final sense, its author. Thus the author of the Epistle to the Hebrews interprets the rituals and sacrifices of the Mosaic law as symbols of the nature of God who, in Christ, offered himself as a sacrifice for the sins of the world.

Although examples of all four senses can be found in the New Testament, Clement of Alexandria (†215) was the first Christian writer to tabulate them, but thereafter they became an accepted part of Christian commentary. The literal and moral senses might be applied to any part of scripture, but the allegorical and mystical senses were at first normally applied only to the Old Testament. In time, however, they came to be applied to the New Testament as well. For example, commentators remarked that when Peter and John came to the empty tomb on the first Easter morning, John saw the grave clothes lying on the ground but did not enter the tomb, whereas Peter went in and examined them. They interpreted this as an allegory: the graveclothes represented the prophecies contained in the Old Testament about the resurrection of the dead; John represented the Jewish synagogue, which knew the prophecies but did not examine their meaning; and Peter represented the Christian church which examined the meaning of the prophecies and believed what they proclaimed.

Of course, not all parts of the Bible were patient of exposition in all four senses. It would, for example, be very difficult to interpret the opening verses of St John's Gospel, which describe the relation of the Divine Word to the Creator, in anything but a mystical sense; it would be almost as difficult to interpret parts of the Book of Proverbs in anything but a moral sense. Nevertheless, a high proportion of scripture did prove susceptible of multi-level interpretation and the volume of Biblical commentaries grew throughout the early Middle Ages.

When the systematic study of theology was developed in the twelfth century an urgent need was felt for a standard, authoritative commentary. This was met by the brothers Anselm and Ralph of Laon, the authors of the *Glossa Ordinaria*, a brief commentary on the entire Bible, which incorporates the consensus of interpretation found among the church Fathers. Part of this work was once wrongly attributed to the Carolingian scholar, Walafrid Strabo, but Beryl Smalley has elucidated its true authorship. The *Glossa* was adopted by Peter Lombard, the chief founder of the theology schools of Paris, as a standard text, and it was frequently incorporated in manuscripts of the Vulgate as an interlinear and marginal gloss. It thus became the starting point for the study of Biblical exegesis in the theology faculties of western Europe during the later Middle Ages.

New and detailed commentaries continued to be written throughout the medieval centuries. But although some scholars, like the Franciscan, Nicholas of Lyra (†1340), concentrated on the literal sense of scripture, most commentators continued to consider all four senses.

Why the quadripartite interpretation was valued

Although the literal and moral levels of interpretation are straightforward enough, the allegorical and anagogical interpretations advanced by medieval scholars often strike a modern reader as far-fetched and irrelevant. It is certainly true that some commentators were carried away by an excess of ingenuity. Thus Alcuin, writing of the verse in the *Song of Songs*, 'Thy lips, O my spouse, drop as the honeycomb', interprets the honeycomb as the literal sense of the holy scriptures and the bride's lips as the doctors of the church who show the many spiritual senses concealed within the sacred writings. Yet it would be wrong to dismiss the fourfold interpretation as theological fantasy, for the medieval church valued it because it helped to solve certain problems which beset all Christians who accept the Bible as a divinely inspired work and use it for devotional purposes. Those difficulties fall into three main groups.

First, from at least the time of Marcion (†c.160), Christians have been troubled by the seeming disjunction between the anthropomorphic portrayal of God in the historical books of the Old Testament and the transcendent God of love and mercy to whom Christ bore witness. The medieval church accepted that Christ's revelation of God was true, and was the measure by which all other accounts of God in the Bible had to be assessed. Thus if Old Testament writers described God as acting in ways contrary to his nature as revealed by Christ, such passages could not be true on the literal level but had to be understood in an allegorical or mystical sense.

Secondly, there were parts of the Bible which, if understood only in a literal sense, had no relevance to the religious needs of most Christians. Notable examples of this in the Old Testament were those parts of the Pentateuch concerned with Jewish law and ritual, and the Song of Songs which was a celebration of sexual passion. But there were also passages of a similar kind in the New Testament, for instance parts of St Paul's letters in which he addressed himself to the problems of first-century Christians, which had no application on a literal level to the circumstances of Christians in later ages. All these passages became relevant if read in an allegorical or mystical sense. The commentators did not deny that the passages had a literal sense, but supposed that it was of no religious value or interest to their readers. Thus while pointing out that the Song of Songs was part of a genre of poetry known as epithalamia, the commentators discussed it as an allegory of the love which exists between Christ and his church, which is likened by St Paul to the physical love between husband and wife (Eph., 5, 25–32). The Mosaic rituals were seen as prefiguring the sacrifice of Christ; while Paul's discussion of the significance of circumcision, or of abstaining from meat sacrificed to idols, was glossed in a spiritual sense and thus made relevant to the life of medieval Christians.

Finally, there were parts of the Bible which could not be understood in a literal sense. Origen (†c.254) had pointed this out forcefully, and his work was read in the west throughout the Middle Ages in the Latin translation of Rufinus:

> Who is so ignorant as to suppose that God, as if he had been a husbandman, planted trees in Paradise, in Eden towards the east, and a tree of life in it, that is a visible and palpable tree of wood, so that anyone eating of it with bodily teeth should obtain life and, eating again of another tree should come to the knowledge of good and evil?

These and other similar statements, Origen argued, and educated opinion in the Middle Ages believed, must be understood in a spiritual sense, since the God revealed by Christ could not have acted in so arbitrary a way as a literal understanding of Genesis would lead one to suppose.

The fourfold interpretation of scripture, which was employed during the first 1500 years of the Christian era, yielded impressive results. The entire Bible, when read in this perspective, became a profoundly Christian book: Jesus son of Mary stood at the centre of human history; the Old Testament was a detailed and many-layered prophecy of the Incarnation; and both Testaments revealed, in part, the nature and mind of God the Father. A minute and cohesive symbolism was identified throughout the sacred writings, so that it could be argued, for example, that the Magi had known that they should watch for the star of Bethlehem, foretelling Christ's birth, because of the prophecy of Balaam to king Balak of Moab at the time of the Exodus, that 'there shall come a star out of Jacob' (Num., 24, 17).

The influence of the fourfold interpretation

Although a detailed knowledge of the huge body of Biblical commentary was confined to a small group of specialist scholars, the fourfold interpretation of scripture affected the way in which all Christians understood the Bible during the Middle Ages. First it shaped the liturgy, which was almost entirely made up of passages drawn from the Bible. These were chosen because they were considered relevant to a particular theme, but their relevance was determined by the fourfold interpretation. This can be seen, for example, in the choice of propers for the midnight mass of Christmas. The literal meaning of the feast is set out in the Gospel appointed for the day, St Luke's account of Christ's birth and of the annunciation to the shepherds. The moral meaning of the feast is explained in the Epistle, in which St Paul tells Titus that the Incarnation should enable all men to live righteously. But the proper anthems are drawn from three psalms, which in an allegorical sense were understood as prophecies of Christ's birth. Psalm 2, 'Why do the heathen so furiously rage together?' prophesies the powerlessness of God's enemies to prevent the establishment of his kingdom upon earth; psalm 96, 'Let the heavens rejoice and let the earth be glad before the Lord, for he is come', prophesies the events of the first Christmas night, when angels and men united to praise the birth of God's son; and psalm 110, 'The Lord said unto my Lord, sit thou on my right hand', prophesies that God will give his son lordship over the whole world and will establish his priesthood for ever. Thus the Old and New Testaments were called to bear witness in the liturgy to the birth of Jesus, son of God and son of Mary.

The fourfold interpretation of scripture also influenced religious iconography. A great deal has been written about this and one example must suffice here. E. Mâle has drawn attention to the juxtaposition in the stained glass of Bourges cathedral of the crucifixion and four Old Testament scenes: the death of Abel, the Brazen Serpent, the waters of Meribah and the grapes of Eshcol. Each of these incidents was thought to be an allegory of Christ's death. Abel, whose sacrifice was acceptable to God, was murdered by his brother, just as Christ, whose sacrifice was acceptable to God the Father, was put to death by his own people. Christ himself compared his own forthcoming death on the cross to the erection of the Brazen Serpent by Moses, which gave healing to all those suffering from scorpion bites who looked towards it. Just as water gushed from the rock of Meribah when Moses struck it, and refreshed the Israelites in time of drought, even so water gushed from the side of Christ when the centurion pierced it with a lance, and brought spiritual refreshment to men. The grapes of Eshcol, brought from the promised land by an Israelite raiding party, were evidence to the people in the desert of the good things that awaited them there, just as Christ, the True Vine, was evidence of the blessings which awaited all men in the heavenly kingdom.

Although only the learned clergy could understand all the allusions contained in such recondite symbolism, this way of interpreting scripture did in some measure influence everybody. Even simple people could recognize references to Christ as the Lamb of God, and know that the image of a winged lion holding an open book was a representation of the evangelist St Mark.

The Bible occupied a very important place in the life of the medieval church. It was distinguished from all other kinds of Christian writing because it was believed to be divinely inspired. No other written source, however ancient it was, or however respected its author may have been, carried that guarantee. Other works were received only in so far as they were consonant with the mind of the church, whereas the Bible expressed the mind of God and the church could not be selective in its approach to it, accepting some parts and rejecting others. The entire work had to be accepted, and the church's role was simply to interpret the revelation which it contained.

7
Methods of Instruction

Techniques of evangelization

Preaching occupied a central place in the conversion of pagan peoples: they could not be expected to accept the Christian faith unless it was explained to them. There was a good deal of variation in preaching method among medieval missionaries. Thus Bede tells how St Aidan, first bishop of Lindisfarne, when seeking to convert the Northumbrians

> ... always travelled on foot ... and whenever he met anyone, whether high or low, he stopped and spoke to them. If they were heathen he urged them to be baptized; and if they were Christians he strengthened their faith. . . .

A very different approach was adopted by the priest Thangbrand, sent by king Harald Tryggvason of Norway to preach the faith in pagan Iceland in c.1000. The *Saga of Burnt Njal* relates how

> Thangbrand toured the country evangelizing and ... [at] Stafafell the farmer ... Thorkel opposed the new faith strongly and challenged Thangbrand to a duel. Thangbrand defended himself with a crucifix instead of with a shield, but even so he managed to defeat Thorkel and kill him.

Once Christianity had been established in a new area and the first generation of converts instructed in the faith, it became self-perpetuating. Parents would teach their children the prayers which they had learnt, tell them the stories which they had heard about the creation of the world and the life of Christ, and explain the significance of the main church festivals. There was a danger that if no other kind of instruction was available, only a vestigial understanding of the faith would be preserved after a few generations. Nevertheless, in much of the west during the early Middle Ages the faith was very largely transmitted in that way because there was a lack of properly trained clergy to give formal instruction.

The training of priests

Arguably the greatest defect in the organization of the medieval church was the lack of any provision for training the secular clergy. Although a few seminaries were endowed by private patrons in the fifteenth century, they were exceptional and could only offer places to a few students. Before then the only institutions which offered a professional training to ordinands were the choir-schools attached to some cathedrals, for example that of St John Lateran in Rome. Such schools were not found in most dioceses; those which did exist could only take a small number of pupils and, because the boys who attended them became highly qualified, they did not normally undertake ordinary parish work but became canons of cathedrals or church administrators.

Before 1100 most ordinands were trained by their parish priests, who taught them how to read the Latin service books, how to celebrate the sacraments and conduct public worship, and how to exercise the cure of souls. Until priestly celibacy was enforced in the twelfth century ordinands were often the sons of priests and learned their fathers' skills just as all other village boys did in that very conservative society. The weakness of such a system was that defects in priestly training could not easily be remedied: this was particularly true of the low standard of Latinity which obtained among the secular clergy. It is clear from the complaints made time and again by church synods that many priests had only a formal knowledge of Latin. They could read the Latin liturgy, but they could not understand what they read. In the early Middle Ages there were few other opportunities for an ordinand to learn Latin: he might seek entrance as an extern pupil of a monastery school, or attend one of the small cathedral schools to be found in a few north European cities, but most candidates could not afford to do either of these things.

In the later Middle Ages general education was much more widely available. Elementary schools were founded in most towns of moderate size in which boys could learn how to read and write Latin and acquire the rudiments of numeracy, while from the thirteenth century universities existed in most parts of the west. As a result of this the general level of clerical learning improved, although in some rural areas ordinands continued to be trained solely by their parish priests and in consequence remained very poorly educated. The element of apprenticeship continued to be present in the training even of those ordinands who had attended school or university, for they had received no instruction about priestly duties and had to receive that from ordained priests.

When their training was complete ordinands were presented to the bishop, who charged his archdeacon or one of his chaplains to examine them. The throughness of such scrutinies varied a good deal and many officials were satisfied if the candidate possessed minimum qualifications: a knowledge of how to read Latin, celebrate the sacraments and operate the church calendar. No doubt it would have been impossible to obtain a sufficient number of priests if higher qualifications had been demanded. On receiving a satisfactory report the bishop ordained the candidates on one of the twelve Ember Days set aside for ordinations each year.

After 1200 the whole church benefited from the improvement in standards of clerical learning because of the work of the mendicant Orders. The Dominicans were from their inception a learned Order and the Franciscans became so within a generation of their founder's death. The level of education which was provided by these Orders for their members was so high that friars were exempted from reading a first degree in Arts when they wished to attend a university. The preliminary training which the mendicants provided in their houses of study was designed for the needs of priests. The mendicant Orders were committed to pastoral work, and after 1300 all bishops were required to license a certain number of friars to serve parishes in their dioceses.

Thus the standard of education among the secular clergy varied a great deal throughout the Middle Ages. All of them had received a practical training in how to administer the sacraments and conduct public worship, but their knowledge of the Latin language and of church doctrine was very unequal and a significant proportion of priests was ill-educated and ignorant, although this was undoubtedly a more general problem before 1100 than later.

Preaching

Although it was through preaching that the first generation of converts learned about their faith, the sermon did not form a normal part of public worship in the early Middle Ages. The bishop alone had the right to preach: he could delegate that right to subordinates, but it was not automatically delegated to all parish priests in the early Middle Ages. A bishop was expected to preach in his cathedral on Sundays and great feast days and the council of Mainz in 813 enacted that if he were absent or ill on those days he should license a deputy to preach on his behalf.

The preaching tradition remained alive in some monasteries. Collections of homilies were preserved in some libraries and read by some monks, who thus learned how sermons should be constructed, for preaching is a specialized skill which combines rhetorical and didactic abilities. In some communities it became the custom to preach in the vernacular at the chief mass on Sundays and holy days at which some lay people would usually be present. But the parish clergy did not normally preach at all, or know how to do so.

Bishops began to think it desirable that priests should preach regularly. The synod of Limoges in 1032 enacted that 'all priests in charge of parishes ought to edify the people by preaching on all Sundays and feast days', but it noted that trained preachers were few and exhorted bishops to encourage any clerk or monk who had the ability to preach to undertake that ministry. As a way of overcoming this difficulty, bishops suggested that priests who did not know how to preach should read to their congregations some of the great sermons delivered in the past by men like pope Gregory I, but this solution was quite impractical. Such texts could only be used in translation and it was beyond the capacity of most parish priests, even if they were given copies of the Latin originals, to make good, idiomatic renderings of them.

A more sensible expedient was devised in the Old English church. Aelfric, a Benedictine monk at Cerne Abbas, composed a set of vernacular homilies, based on the writings of the Church Fathers and suitable for use on Sundays during Lent and feast days, and presented a copy of this work to the archbishop of Canterbury in 995. The homilies were intended for the use of parish clergy and they circulated quite widely in the pre-Conquest church. Nevertheless, the expense of copying a text of this kind precluded its being used in all churches: it would only have been available in those which had rich patrons.

Despite such experiments, preaching remained comparatively rare before 1095 when Urban II launched the first crusade. This movement owed its success to preaching which the pope and his bishops organized. Throughout the twelfth century the papacy continued to coordinate preaching for particular purposes, such as the launching of new crusades, the introduction of new reforms and the combating of heresy. For heretical leaders attracted large followings through their preaching, particularly in those areas where there was no tradition of regular preaching among the Catholic clergy. Many of the new Catholic preachers were members of religious Orders, like the Cistercian abbot, St Bernard of Clairvaux (†1153).

Yet until the mendicant Orders were founded in the early thirteenth century preaching, though more common than it had been 200 years earlier, was still infrequent. The mendicants considered preaching an important part of public ministry. The Franciscans were at first concerned to stimulate in their hearers a desire to repent and to practise the Christian life more fully, but the Dominicans sought to instruct people in the Catholic faith in order to counteract heresy, for they believed that heresy spread because many Catholics were too ill-instructed to recognize it as false teaching.

The two great mendicant Orders, together with the lesser Orders of friars, made a great impact on the religious life of the west. They spread very rapidly and by 1300 most towns of any size had at least one convent of friars, and the brethren also toured the neighbouring countryside, preaching in village churches. Although after 1350 the friars lost much of their fervour, they continued to preach regularly in the parishes which they ran. Moreover, in the fifteenth century there was a revival of preaching zeal among the Observant members of both main Orders. The Dominican, Vincent Ferrer (†1419), drew large crowds when he toured Spain, France and the Empire preaching the need for penitence, while the Franciscan, Bernardino of Siena (†1444), was so popular a preacher that Pius II likened him to a new St Paul.

Thus by the fifteenth century the sermon had come to occupy a central place in much of the western church. Many of the secular clergy, certainly those who were well educated, preached regularly on Sundays and holy days, as did those members of religious Orders who exercised cure of souls. Although there were some rural parishes where the clergy never preached, nobody who lived in a town would have found any difficulty in hearing a weekly sermon. Gifted preachers, not unnaturally, considered that listening to sermons was an essential part of the Christian life. St Bernardino of Siena went so far as to say that if a man had only time to hear a sermon or attend mass he should 'let the mass go, rather than the sermon'. The church did not endorse that view: it was left to the choice of the individual layman whether he attended a preaching service and, if a sermon were preached at the only mass of the day, some laymen at least felt free to leave the church during that time and return when it was over.

Catechizing

The church did not make attendance at sermons obligatory because it did not envisage that they would be the sole, or even the chief means of instructing lay people. Except in the missionfield the function of the sermon is not to teach the ignorant the rudiments of Christianity, but to build up the faith of those who have already been instructed.

In the early church, when adult conversions were common, anybody who wished to be baptized had first to undergo a lengthy period of instruction known as *catechesis*. During the Middle Ages, when infant baptism was universal, this instruction or catechism was supposed to be given by parish priests to the children in their charge. Although elaborate catechisms were drawn up for instructing novices in monastic schools, no written catechisms for lay people were produced in the early Middle Ages. Provincial synods legislated regularly about the form which catechizing should take: each priest should ensure that his parishioners were taught simple prayers, the principal articles of the faith, the significance of the sacraments, the meaning of the church's year, and the way to lead the Christian life. It depended entirely on the parish priest how far these injunctions were fulfilled. Some priests seem to have ignored them completely, while others were too ill-educated to give more than a superficial account of the faith, but there were always some priests who gave clear and detailed instruction. There is little evidence before the thirteenth century about the circumstances in which such teaching was given: the priest presumably gathered the children of the parish together to be catechized, perhaps on great feast days.

The situation is clearer after 1215 when the Fourth Lateran Council enacted that all men above the age of fifteen and women aged twelve and over should go to confession and receive holy communion once a year at Easter. This made first communicants an identifiable group and priests had thereafter to prepare girls under twelve and boys under fifteen to receive the sacraments. Instruction might be spread over a number of years, but it had to be completed before those ages. In order to help poorly educated priests, manuals of instruction were drawn up by learned clergy. Such works were not available in every parish, but they did circulate quite widely and the level of instruction among lay people was markedly improved in the later Middle Ages.

Religious art

The opinion that religious art was an important means of instructing illiterate lay people about their faith needs to be treated with some caution. Such art was not didactic in intention, but was intended to glorify God. This had practical consequences, for much of the detail of the stained glass in Gothic cathedrals, for example, erected for the consideration of God the All-seeing, could not be seen from ground-level without the help of magnifying lenses of a type which did not exist in the Middle Ages. Moreover, Romanesque and Gothic art uses a symbolism which is only fully comprehensible to those who have been trained in scholastic theology and in the quadripartite interpretation of scripture. Although almost the entire system of Christian belief was visually expressed in the glass, sculpture and painting of a great cathedral like Chartres, an illiterate layman would not have found that visiting such a church helped him to understand his faith any better. Isolated images might have spoken to him, but he would have lacked the technical training to appreciate the assumptions which underlay the iconographic scheme.

Parish churches contained fewer works of art and those, paradoxically, were more useful as a means of instruction. They were a familiar part of the parishioners' environment and priests could therefore refer to them when instructing children or when seeking to illustrate some point in a sermon. Sometimes a visual symbol could be used to explain a very complex idea to simple people: the Tree of Jesse, found in many late medieval churches, is an example of this. Jesse, the father of David, is shown asleep at the foot of the painting, while a tree grows from his side. In its branches his descendants are shown, each holding a scroll which identifies him, and at the top of the tree stands the Virgin with the child Christ in her arms. This simple image explained why the stories in the Old Testament were of relevance to Christians at all: they represented the human inheritance which Christ had received from his mother and from her ancestors.

The religious art of the Romanesque and Gothic ages was concerned with expressing supernatural concepts in visual terms: the Virgin and Child, for example, were portrayed not simply as a mother and a baby, but as the Mother of God holding on her knee the Second Person of the Trinity. People who learned to conceptualize their faith by looking at such images could not think of God and the saints in human terms: the nature of the art forced them to recognize that religion was concerned with a different mode of being.

The Florentine Renaissance of the late fourteenth century introduced a new convention of religious painting to the west, one which represented the divine in terms of perfected humanity. This kind of art spread to much of Europe during the fifteenth century. Like Gothic art it employed an elaborate symbolism drawn from a learned tradition, but it also spoke directly to those who were ignorant of that tradition. Nativity scenes in this genre ceased to be abstract statements about the nature of the Incarnation and portrayed instead the love of a mother for her new-born child. In Filippo Lippi's Nativity, for example, the child lies in a cradle, while a very realistic ox and ass look on and the Virgin kneels before him, marvelling at the new life to which she has given birth. In such works, basic human emotions are placed in a universal context to which everybody can respond.

In one way Renaissance painting was more useful as a means of instruction than Romanesque and Gothic art had been, since there was less that needed to be explained before the work could be understood by the simple. Yet in another sense this art was more difficult to use: the sense of the Other, so powerful in medieval art, had been lost. Angels had ceased to be supernatural beings and had become young men with wings, just as Mary had ceased to be the Mother of God and had become simply the mother of an ordinary baby.

There was one central way in which all religious art was limited as a means of instruction: it is not possible to convey the meaning 'like' in visual terms, yet 'like' is a crucial word in theological definition. The church was conscious that faith was concerned with a state of being which human language is inadequate to express. Thus although churchmen might speak of the fires of hell or the torments of purgatory, these were only figurative terms used to describe spiritual states. But a painting could not express that nuance: people who were ignorant of the learned tradition conceived the afterlife in the visual terms through which they had learned about it: hell and purgatory were places of material torment, angels had wings, devils had pitchforks. Similarly it proved impossible to express in art the great gulf which in orthodox belief separated the Blessed Virgin from God: he was the infinite creator, while she was a finite creature. Yet as she appeared in art, crowned queen of heaven and holding the Christ-child in her arms, she looked like one of the great queen-regents of medieval Europe who held power on behalf of minor heirs, as Blanche of Castile did for St Louis of France. Mary in popular belief thus became credited with a degree of authority which in orthodox theology she did not possess.

After the invention of printing woodcuts became an important means of instructing the illiterate. Illuminated manuscripts could not serve the same purpose in the Middle Ages, for they were *de luxe* objects which only the very rich could afford, and although they could be used by chaplains of great households as teaching aids, they could not be used more generally. Possible exceptions are the *Biblia Pauperum*, or poor men's Bibles, found in a number of early fourteenth-century manuscripts which are thought to be based on older prototypes. They consist of thirty-four or more miniatures, depicting the principal scenes from the lives of Jesus and Mary. Each miniature is flanked by two others illustrating Old Testament prototypes and is surrounded by four medallions containing relevant prophetic texts. Although it is uncertain whether these works were designed as memory aids for preachers, or as visual aids for use by preachers talking to small groups, they represent a genuine attempt to convey the richness of the learned tradition to lay people lacking the skills needed to read and understand Biblical commentaries based on the fourfold interpretation.

Liturgical ceremonies

The liturgy should have been the principal, regular means of instruction, but the language in which it was performed made it incomprehensible to most people. Nevertheless, there were certain occasions in the church's year when the dramatic qualities of the liturgical action conveyed the meaning of a particular feast very clearly. Examples of this were the blessing and distribution of candles at the beginning of mass on 2 February, Candlemas Day, which were then lit and carried in procession to symbolize that Christ was the light of the world; the imposition of ashes on the foreheads of the congregation at the beginning of the mass on Ash Wednesday with the words, 'Remember, O man, that thou art dust and unto dust thou shalt return'; the blessing of palm branches at mass on Palm Sunday, which were carried through the parish in procession to commemorate Christ's triumphal entry into Jerusalem; and the custom on Good Friday whereby the entire congregation genuflected three times before a large crucifix and each kissed the feet of the figure of Christ.

The most impressive ceremonies of the year were those of Easter Eve when, late at night, a fire was kindled outside the church from which the paschal candle was lit. This was a large candle, designed to burn through the forty days of Eastertide, and symbolized the risen Christ, the light of the world. Inside the church the congregation stood in total darkness, holding candles, which were lit from the paschal candle when it was carried in procession. The light spread from one candle to another, until the whole church was ablaze with candlelight as the deacon began to sing the *Exsultet*, the proclamation of the church's joy at the resurrection of Christ.

New ceremonies evolved during the Middle Ages. The crib, a familiar part of the Christmas liturgy in many modern churches, is said to have become popular after St Francis of Assisi had celebrated the midnight mass in a stable at Greccio in 1223. While not imitating the saint's realism, other priests began to use models of the stable at Bethlehem, containing figures of the Christ-child, Joseph and Mary, the ox and the ass, and to bless them at the midnight mass. This devotion proved immensely popular, and acted as a focus for lay piety: in some parishes cribs reached huge sizes as the community added new figures year by year to the central tableau.

In the fifteenth century Stations of the Cross were introduced in some western towns, a devotion which originated in Jerusalem. The Stations were stopping places on Christ's journey from the judgement hall of Pilate to Calvary. At each Station a plaque was erected showing the incident which was being commemorated, for example, Christ's speaking to the women of Jerusalem, and prayers were appointed to be read at each Station. Initially the number of Stations varied considerably, but the present set of fourteen was first introduced at Louvain in 1505 and spread from there to the rest of the church. This devotion might be performed by individuals or in groups and enabled men to re-enact and meditate upon the events leading up to Christ's death.

Religious drama

Liturgical ceremonies were performed in all churches, but religious drama only in some of them. The earliest known examples of such plays were brief dramas enacted by the clergy during the liturgy on certain feasts, for instance, a dialogue between the angel at the sepulchre and the three Marys coming to anoint the body of Jesus on the first Easter morning. These plays date from the late tenth century, but later versions were more elaborate and became dissociated from the liturgy. They began to be performed by laymen under ecclesiastical direction. Some of the actors were professionals, but more commonly they were amateurs. In the later Middle Ages these plays were usually performed in the open air. They covered a wide range of religious themes and in some places the tradition developed of performing mystery cycles which surveyed the whole sacred drama from the creation of the world to the Last Judgement.

In the later Middle Ages such plays were commonly performed at Corpus Christi, the Thursday after Trinity Sunday, which always fell in late Spring when the weather was fine. The performance of one of the great mystery cycles afforded an opportunity of seeing the entire framework of human history set forth in a single day, and there was no other way of experiencing this survey of the faith so rapidly and vividly. The actors, who were often drawn from a wide sector of the community, must have been led to reflect on the significance at least of their own part of the cycle and so to come to understand it better. People came from a wide region to watch such plays but as they were performed only in some large towns their influence as a medium of instruction was limited.

By the end of the Middle Ages the church had made serious attempts to produce a well instructed laity. A high proportion of parish priests catechized the children in their charge and preached regularly on Sundays and holy days; in addition, Observant members of the mendicant Orders carried out preaching missions in many parts of the west. Religious art and liturgical ceremonial helped to increase men's understanding of the faith they professed and in some places religious drama deepened their awareness of it even more. Nevertheless, at the end of the period there were some remote, rural areas which had been little affected by these developments, which had been concentrated chiefly in the towns and their immediate hinterlands.

8
The Quest for Perfection

The medieval church recognized two ways of leading the Christian life, the active and the contemplative. The active life was spent in the world and was the vocation of most people, whereas few were called to the contemplative life which involved withdrawal from the world in order to cultivate the interior life of prayer. Both vocations had the same objective: the attempt to live conformably to God's will in this world and to enjoy the vision of God in the next. Contemplatives lived under a rule, designed to aid them in their search for perfection (see chapter 3), but lay people who led the active life, though not required to observe a rule, were offered various kinds of spiritual counselling about the best ways of consecrating their lives to God's service.

The vocation of kings and knights

In the early Middle Ages the class which appeared to need most spiritual direction was that of the warriors, for their violent life-style was almost totally at variance with Christian teaching. Kings stood at the apex of that class and the church recognized that they had a special religious vocation. At their coronation they were anointed with holy oil, a ritual derived from the Old Testament, which by the tenth century was used in all the monarchies of western Europe. Anointing gave the king a sacred character: thirteenth-century canon lawyers argued that it conferred on him the status of deacon or subdeacon, and the kings of France and England claimed that they could heal scrofula by the laying-on of hands, a practice known as 'touching for the king's evil'. But the church recognized that the king's exercise of secular powers, in the government and defence of his realm, was also a religious function which his consecration empowered him to perform.

The church also attempted to give knights a sense of Christian vocation. This was a gradual process: from c.950 it became customary to bless the sword of a new knight in a religious ceremony, although the investiture took place in a secular context. This was a symbol that the power of the sword was God-given and should be used in God's service. In the late tenth century the church began to foster the growth of voluntary associations of knights who undertook to uphold the Peace or the Truce of God. Members of Peace leagues swore not to harm non-combatants, while members of Truce leagues promised to refrain from fighting on holy days and during penitential seasons: both movements were designed to limit the evils of private warfare. During the eleventh century the church encouraged knights to fight the infidel rather than fellow-Christians, a policy which reached its climax in Urban II's appeal to the knighthood of the west to support the first crusade.

In these ways knights were schooled to use their expertise as warriors in the defence of the weak and oppressed and to protect the church of God against the infidel. These ideals found institutional expression in the Military Orders (see chapter 3), but also influenced the ways in which knights regarded their social role. During the thirteenth century the ritual for making a knight became completely liturgical, and the prayers which were used emphasized his religious vocation.

The spiritual training of other laymen

At first the church did not consider it necessary to offer any special training to lay people who were not warriors because it was thought that they would find no special problem in adopting Christian standards of behaviour. There were, however, some devout lay people who desired spiritual direction and in the late eleventh century they began to form themselves into communities of beghards (for men) and beguines (for women). Members of such groups placed themselves under the direction of a religious superior, and lived a common life, but they took no vows and were free to leave and to marry at any time. The communities were self-supporting: some members did charitable work, but others went out each day to undertake paid employment. In the fourteenth century beguines and beghards were suspected of heresy, unjustly it would seem, and many of their houses were suppressed, but the Council of Constance (1414–18) gave its approval to those which remained, and they continued to be centres of Catholic lay piety throughout the fifteenth century.

Communities of this kind could only minister to the needs of single people, or of widows and widowers. St Francis of Assisi was the first churchman to consider the spiritual direction of the far larger class of married people. In 1214 he wrote an open letter to 'all the faithful in Christ', setting out the principles of the life of perfection which he was seeking to implement in his Order and inviting all men and women to 'receive these words of our Lord Jesus Christ and cheerfully put them into practice and observe them perfectly'. He does not seem to have wanted to form an élite group of laymen, for he believed that the principles which he enjoined were those of the Gospels and thus within the capacity of all men to follow. Yet even in his lifetime those lay people who wished to associate themselves with the work of the saint were formed into a Third Order by a tidy-minded church. The members of this Order were lay people, engaged in ordinary work, who bound themselves to observe a rule of life entailing a regular programme of religious observances. They met together regularly and appointed officers to preside over their affairs and scrutinize the admission of new members. Later in the thirteenth century the Dominicans and Carmelites founded similar Third Orders.

From the start the members of Third Orders enjoyed certain clerical privileges, notably exemption from military service, although, as they were not ordained, they could waive that right if they chose. As time passed the Third Orders became increasingly clerical in character, and this would seem to have happened because the members wished it, not because of any pressure from the hierarchy. By 1300 some members of Third Orders had begun to take the three monastic vows and to live in single-sex communities, while continuing to work in lay occupations. By 1400 some Third Order communities had accepted total enclosure and, except for differences in their rule, were virtually indistinguishable from the professed members of the First and Second Orders. Yet there also continued to be married men and women in the Third Orders who lived in the world but followed a common rule of life.

The most influential attempt in the later Middle Ages to enable lay people to cultivate the life of holiness was the movement known as the *devotio moderna*, or 'new spirituality'. Its founder, Gerard Groote of Deventer (†1385), formed single-sex communities of lay people and clergy who followed a common rule of life, but took no vows and were free to leave when they wished. Their object was to study the faith and to meditate on it in order to live the Christian life fully. These communities were known as Brethren of the Common Life. Later monastic communities were founded by some Brethren, which adopted the rule of the Austin Canons: thirty-seven houses of men and eight of women were established, and they supported themselves chiefly by copying manuscripts and took a major part in running schools.

The Brethren of the Common Life spread through much of northern Europe and had a profound effect on the life of the late medieval church. Through their teachings and their writings, of which the best known example is probably Thomas à Kempis' *Imitation of Christ*, they influenced a wide circle of lay opinion. The kind of spirituality which they advocated, although it derived from the monastic tradition, could be implemented by married, lay people following secular careers. The movement influenced the spiritual development of early modern Europe, for abbot Cisneros of Monserrat was deeply indebted to the *devotio moderna* and wrote Spiritual Exercises which helped to form the thought of St Ignatius Loyola, the founder of the Jesuit Order.

Why the contemplative ideal was considered superior

These various forms of spiritual direction were intended to enable lay people to consecrate their daily activities to God's service. Yet they never succeeded in eradicating the belief that the contemplative life was a higher vocation than the active life. Part of the reason for his was the explanation which medieval commentators gave to a passage in St Luke's Gospel, which relates that when Jesus visited the sisters, Mary and Martha of Bethany, Martha was concerned to produce a large meal, while Mary sat and listened to what he had to say and he commended her:

> Martha, thou art careful and troubled about many things: but one thing is needful: and Mary hath chosen that good part which shall not be taken away from her (Luke, 10, 41–2).

The commentators saw in Mary the symbol of the contemplatives who devoted their lives to prayer, while those who lived the active life were like Martha, 'troubled about many things' and unwilling to listen to God's voice.

The interpretation of one brief passage of scripture would not in itself have determined the values of an entire society; but this interpretation was known to learned churchmen who wrote the lives of the saints and they were concerned to show that all saints, irrespective of the circumstances of their lives, had wished to be like Mary of Bethany and to choose 'that good part', contemplation. The saints occupied a very important place in medieval western thought, because they were the most universally admired members of society. Not only had they attained salvation, which everybody wanted to do, they had also become members of the court of heaven to whom God delegated power in this world.

The cult of the saints

The saints were the holy ones, the souls of men and women who had attained perfection and entered the presence of God. The church taught that they prayed for their fellow Christians on earth and that it was lawful to ask for their prayers, a practice known as the invocation of the saints. They had no power in their own right, but it was believed that God sometimes granted them the power to work miracles in this world, just as he sometimes granted it to living men. God also, it was thought, sometimes used the saints as his messengers to men and on such occasions they were sometimes allowed to manifest themselves in human form, although they did not any longer have physical bodies. The number of the saints was known to God alone, and from the mid-ninth century the church kept the feast of All Saints on 1 November to commemorate the company of heaven most of whose names it did not know.

Some saints were known by name, and these fell into three main groups. First there were the saints of the New Testament, among whom was Mary, the mother of Jesus. She was regarded as the greatest of all saints because her willingness to do God's will had made the Incarnation possible. The reverence in which she was held in the western church steadily increased throughout the Middle Ages and St Thomas Aquinas (†1274) considered that she was worthy of *hyperdulia*, a degree of veneration greater than that accorded to any other creature, because she alone was privileged to be the Mother of God. The distinction between Mary and God was nevertheless held to be absolute. Although in liturgical poetry she was called Queen of Heaven, it was a sin to offer worship to Mary (or for that matter to any other saint) for that belonged to God alone.

The saints of post-apostolic times were divided into two main groups: the martyrs who had died for the faith and the confessors, who had died from natural causes, but who during their lives had borne witness to God through their sanctity. The martyrs were a clearly defined group, but it was more difficult to determine who had the right to be accounted confessors.

In the early Middle Ages people were canonized, or placed in the official list of saints, by popular acclamation. Such cults needed the approval of the local bishop but of no higher authority. From the late tenth century the papacy began to intervene in the process and in the pontificate of Alexander III (1159–81) canonization was reserved to the holy see. The procedures to be followed were set out in the revised code of canon law of 1234: the church required evidence that the candidate had lived a holy life and that miracles had been performed through his intercession since his death. If the examining judges were satisfied, the pope canonized the new saint and licensed his cult. The papacy sometimes ordered older cults, for which there was no good historical evidence, to be suppressed, but such investigations were haphazard and many saints continued to be venerated for whom there was little sound evidence. It also proved impossible to eliminate completely the spontaneous growth of local cults even after the process of canonization had been centralized (see chapter 13).

The cult of some saints was licensed for the entire church, while that of others was licensed only in certain dioceses. In the area where the cult was permitted the saint's feast day was solemnly observed each year and proper forms of the mass and the Divine Office were composed in his honour. Any Catholic might privately invoke the prayers of a canonized saint, and reverence might be paid to his images and relics (see chapter 13). Churches were dedicated to saints and placed under their protection, and children were given saints' names at their baptism and thus placed under their patronage.

The lives of the saints

The cult of the saints was attractive partly because they had all once been ordinary men and women. Moreover, they were drawn from all ranks of society for, unlike the medieval west, where much of the time there was little social mobility, heaven was completely classless. All Catholics had an equal chance of being canonized simply by living holy lives.

There was thus a great demand for information about the saints and this generated a huge literature. From the thirteenth century onwards the lives of new saints were based on the evidence submitted at their canonization processes and are thus well documented, but earlier lives are very uneven in quality. Some were written by contemporaries and are accurate and well informed, while others were only written centuries after the saint's death and are entirely fictional. Saints' lives were widely known. Brief versions of them were read among the lessons of mattins on the saints' feasts and in this way the clergy became familiar with them. Lay people heard the stories in sermons, or were told them when they went on pilgrimage to shrines; and the themes were frequently illustrated in stained glass or wall-paintings. The stories were very popular and as lay literacy increased people wished to read them for themselves. One of the first works to be printed in England by Caxton was a translation of *The Golden Legend* of James of Voragine (†1298), a collection of saints' lives arranged in order of the church's year.

Part of the attraction of these writings was that they contained good stories, as the following examples will show. St Eustace was said to have been one of the emperor Trajan's generals. One day while hunting near Tivoli he met a stag carrying a crucifix between its antlers, and was so moved by this sight that he and his entire family were baptized. After a life distinguished by generosity to the poor, he and his kin were roasted to death inside a bronze bull because he refused to sacrifice to the emperor at a victory parade. St Eustace was a saint whose feast was kept by the universal church, but equally vivid stories were told about local saints, like St Kenelm, a child martyr venerated at Halesowen in Worcestershire. He was said to have become king of Mercia at the age of seven and to have been murdered on the orders of his ambitious elder sister, who coveted the throne, while he was hunting in the forest of Clent. Although his murder was successfully concealed from his subjects, the truth was made known to the pope, for, while he was celebrating solemn mass in St Peter's a dove deposited a scroll on the high altar, containing this cryptic message:

In Clent in Cowbage, Kenelm, king born,
Lieth under a thorn,
His head off shorn.

People did not read or listen to the lives of the saints solely as escapist literature, but as evidence of how the successful members of their society had made good. This is the kind of interest which is closely linked to imitation. Martyrs like St Eustace and St Kenelm did not provide useful paradigms for people living in a Christian society in which it was rare to be required to die for the faith. People sought personal guidance in the lives of confessors, but the authors of those lives tended to stress the world-renouncing virtues of their subjects, because they believed that the contemplative life was a higher vocation than the active life.

The theme of renunciation

Monastic saints naturally conformed to this pattern for by reason of their profession they had renounced the world. Some monks, it is true, became very involved in the life of the world they had left, but if such men were canonized their biographers were at pains to emphasize their desire for renunciation. St Hugh of Cluny (†1109), for sixty years one of the greatest political figures in Europe, is praised in his life for his extreme mortification and secret fasting. Similarly, saintly bishops, who were called to the active, not the contemplative life, were praised for their contemplative virtues. Thus St Antoninus, archbishop of Florence (1446–59), was admired for despising the wealth to which his office entitled him: he employed only six servants in his huge palace, kept no horses, but walked everywhere, and gave all his surplus revenues to the poor.

Canonized laymen were also often shown as contemplatives in disguise and this to some extent offset the encouragement which the church tried to give to royal and knightly vocations. Thus of the four kings canonized after 1100, when the process came to be largely controlled by the pope, two were represented as men with monastic proclivities, for both the emperor Henry II (†1024, canonized 1146) and Edward the Confessor of England (†1066, canonized 1161) were said not to have consummated their marriages. Yet continence, which is a virtue in monks, is a vice in kings, for deliberate failure to beget an heir leads to the evils of a disputed succession.

Canonized knights were also often shown as wishing to renounce the world. One of the most famous of them was St William of Orange (†812), a kinsman of Charlemagne's who had recaptured Barcelona from the Moors, but who ended his life as a Benedictine monk at Gellone which he had founded. A parallel case was that of St Gerald of Aurillac (†909), who when a young man wanted to become a monk, but was persuaded by his bishop to remain in the world because society had need of just rulers. Gerald therefore agreed to become count of Aurillac, but he received the monastic tonsure secretly, never married and gave much of his wealth to found a monastery. He was a model secular ruler, but tried always to observe the monastic rule in as far as it was compatible with his other duties.

Canonized laywomen were described in much the same terms. St Elizabeth, queen of Portugal (†1336), renounced her greatness when widowed to become a Franciscan tertiary and devote her life to the poor. Similarly, St Frances of Rome (†1440) wished to become a nun but was forced to marry by her father. Having brought up a large family and been a devoted wife and mother, she was widowed and able to join the religious order which she had earlier founded for the relief of the poor.

The saints themselves do not seem to have taken so negative a view of the active life as their biographers pictured them as doing, but were prepared to consecrate the life that they were leading to the service of God rather than desiring all the time to escape from it. In the case of Louis IX, king of France (1226–70), we possess a life written after his canonization in 1297 by his companion, John of Joinville. This is a biography rather than a hagiography and does not emphasize the world-renouncing aspects of Louis' character, but shows him as taking a positive pleasure in the government of his kingdom, the defence of Christendom and the conduct of his family life. Equally, on a domestic level, St Frances of Rome understood the need to consecrate everyday tasks to God and once said:

> It is most laudable in a married woman to be devout, but she must never forget that she must be a housewife, and sometimes she must leave God at the altar to find him in her housekeeping.

The writers of hagiography did not share this view. That is evident from the fictional lives of confessors which they composed, one of the best known of which is that of St Alexius. He was said to have been the son of a Roman senator who was forced to marry against his will. He fled from home on his wedding-night and went to live as a recluse in the desert near Edessa. Years later he returned to Rome, took service in his father's house where, of course, nobody recognized him, and after performing menial tasks in an exemplary way, died in a cupboard under the stairs which had been assigned as his living quarters, holding in his hand the text of his autobiography.

The most striking evidence of the low regard in which hagiographers held the active life is shown by accounts of the life of the Virgin. The Gospels relate that Mary was married to Joseph, a carpenter, and that she brought up four other boys and at least two girls as well as Jesus. Medieval commentators were unanimous in supposing that Mary's marriage to Joseph was never consummated and that the 'Lord's brethren', the *christadelphoi*, were either adopted children, or the children of Joseph by a previous marriage. Nevertheless, this did not in itself affect the domestic circumstances of Mary's life: she and Joseph had a great deal in common with most lay people. But little attention was paid by hagiographers to these aspects of Mary's life, and St Joseph received almost no attention, for his feast was not observed in the western church during the Middle Ages. Attention was focused rather on the way in which Mary differed from other wives and mothers through her virginity, and virginity was an attribute of the contemplative vocation, not of the active life.

The power of the contemplative ideal

The power of the contemplative ideal may be seen also in the speculative and imaginative writing of the medieval west. Adso of Montier-en-Der (†992), whose treatise on Antichrist had a profound influence on medieval concepts of the future pattern of world history, invented the figure of the Emperor of the Last Days. This ruler, of Frankish race, would reconstitute the whole of the ancient Roman empire and would then go on pilgrimage to Jerusalem and lay down his crown and sceptre at the Mount of Olives, thus leaving the way open for Antichrist to seize power. The Emperor's abdication was not interpreted by the author or his readers as a dereliction of duty, but as a supreme act of piety. Similarly the hero of Ramon Lull's (†1316) novel, *Blanquerna*, having given up the life of a knight to become a monk, is called from the cloister to be a bishop and is finally elected pope; yet, having reformed the church, he abdicates in order to follow the highest vocation of all, that of a hermit.

Men who conformed to this ideal really existed. It is true that Celestine V, the hermit who in 1294 briefly became pope and then abdicated to resume the eremitical life, was a victim of political circumstances and therefore a controversial figure, even though he was later canonized, but no ambiguity attached to the career of St Peter Damian. He was a member of an Order of hermits, who was called from his community in 1057 by pope Stephen IX and consecrated cardinal-bishop of Ostia. Peter never wanted this preferment and pope Alexander II (1062–73) allowed him to return to Fonte Avellana and live in his hermitage provided that he was willing to undertake the duties of a cardinal when necessary. Peter could have been criticized for neglecting his diocese and taking only a minimal part in the affairs of the sacred college, but instead his contemporaries viewed with awe and admiration the spectacle of the senior cardinal living withdrawn from the world and only occasionally and reluctantly leaving his cell to carry out some mission on the pope's behalf.

Most medieval people, while revering the contemplative saints, did not seek to emulate them, but led lives which were guided by self-interest, or, in many cases, by the fight for survival. Yet the contemplative ideal was accepted by them and would sometimes surface unexpectedly, causing men and women to leave the security of their homes and kin-groups in order to set out on long and dangerous pilgrimages, or to abandon successful careers in order to enter the cloister or live as recluses.

Such choices were respected. Society saw nothing eccentric in the spectacle of men and women who renounced power, wealth, prestige and even human affection in order to live as pilgrims, monks, or solitaries. For there was an awareness in medieval society that all human achievements were transitory and that the only permanent satisfaction available to man was that which awaited him in heaven.

Part II

The Practice of the Christian Life

9

The Christian World Picture

The Middle Ages are sometimes called the Christian centuries. This phrase does not mean that the entire population of western Europe at that time was fervently Catholic, for that was far from being the case. The medieval west was Christian in the sense that everybody shared a common understanding of the world in which they lived based on Christian premises. Only the very learned had full and detailed knowledge of the whole world picture, but everybody understood some part of it.

Nine choirs of angels

Certainly everybody knew that there was one God in three Persons, Father, Son and Holy Spirit, who was the sole creative principle. The first act of God of which men had any knowledge was the creation of the angels. These were incorporeal, immortal beings, with far greater intellectual capacities than man. There were nine choirs of angels, who were ranked as follows in descending order of importance: seraphim, cherubim, thrones, dominations, virtues, powers, principalities, archangels and angels. This surprisingly coherent account of the invisible world was constructed from the evidence of scattered Biblical references by the anonymous author of *The Celestial Hierarchy*, probably written in Syria in *c*.500, whose aim was to interpret Christianity in terms of the neoplatonic thought dominant among educated people in late antiquity. This work owed its subsequent importance to a wrong attribution, for it was ascribed to Dionysius the Areopagite, one of St Paul's Athenian converts (Acts, 17, 34), and was thus thought to represent apostolic teaching. It was translated into Latin by John the Scot (†*c*.877) and accepted as authoritative by the western church throughout the rest of the Middle Ages. *The Celestial Hierarchy* was influential not only as a guide to angelology but also as a guide to social structure. For the hierarchical organization which it showed as existing in the perfect society of heaven was regarded by most Christian thinkers throughout the Middle Ages as a model which should be imitated on earth, both in church and state.

All angels had been created perfect, but some of them had fallen from grace. By pondering various Biblical allusions to this event the church Fathers worked out a coherent account of what had happened. Lucifer, the greatest of the angels, had wished to make himself equal to God (Isa., 14, 12–15), and had led some of the angels in a revolt. He had been opposed by the rest of the angelic host, commanded by the archangel Michael, and together with his followers had been cast out of heaven (Rev., 12, 7–9). Lucifer, the lightbearer, became Satan, the adversary, his attendant angels became demons and their abode was hell. This story will be familiar to some readers because it is the theme of the opening books of Milton's *Paradise Lost*.

The spiritual creation influenced the life of men on earth. The angels, like the saints, were regularly invoked, because it was believed that they could help men by their prayers. Sometimes, it was thought, they were used as divine messengers and were allowed to manifest themselves to men. The devil and his angels were also credited with considerable powers in this world, for it was here that they continued their warfare against God, trying to enlist men on their side. Demons could show themselves to men in a variety of forms, some of them deceptively attractive.

It used commonly to be said by writers who were unsympathetic to scholastic theology that medieval theologians debated how many angels could stand on the point of a pin. Nobody has ever found the text of such a disputation and this is not surprising because any educated churchman would have known that it was a nonsensical topic. Its modern equivalent would be a discussion between physicists about how many neutrons there are in a hundredweight. Spiritual beings were by definition incorporeal and could not occupy space: this was not a matter of opinion but of category. The same was true of the 'places' they inhabited: heaven and hell had no physical location, but were states of being; heaven was where God was, hell where God was not. Popular understanding of the spiritual creation was rather different, since it was derived from verbal or visual images. Heaven was thought of in terms of the symbolism used in the book of Revelation and hell was pictured as a place of material torment. Most people undoubtedly believed that heaven and hell were located somewhere: outside the visible creation, perhaps, but not outside space and time. The concept of a spiritual state was as difficult for most medieval people to understand as that of a fourth dimension is for most of us. But the learned and the simple were agreed that a spiritual creation did exist and that the physical universe was a battleground in the war between the forces of good and evil.

The Ptolemaic universe

It was agreed by everyone that the visible universe had been created by God *ex nihilo*. The accounts of the creation contained in the first two chapters of Genesis were believed to be divinely inspired, but few educated people supposed that they were to be understood in a strictly literal sense: the seven days of creation, for example, could not be those of a normal week, since during the first three neither the sun nor the moon existed to determine their duration. Genesis was important not because it gave a factual account of how the world came into being, but because it revealed that the cosmos had been created by God, which man could not have deduced through natural reason alone. Moreover, when interpreted in a spiritual sense, Genesis also explained the relationship which existed between God and the natural order and man's place in the universe.

The Christian revelation says nothing about the physical structure of the universe, and medieval thinkers accepted the scientific explanations which they had inherited from the ancient world. The most important astronomical work was that of Claudius Ptolemy (*fl*. 140 AD) which encapsulated centuries of observations made in the observatory of Alexandria. This treatise, normally known by

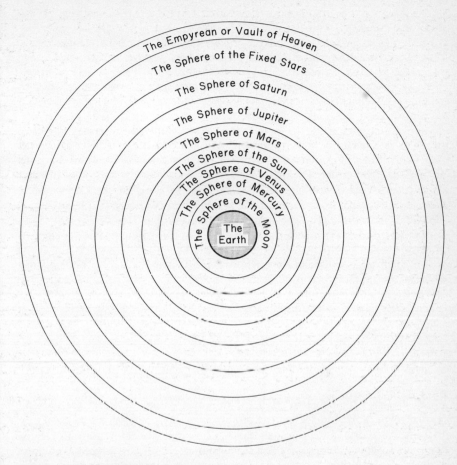

Figure 1 The medieval universe

its Arabic title, *The Almagest*, or The Great Work, was not translated into Latin until the twelfth century, but even during the early Middle Ages the Ptolemaic model of the universe had been known in the west through the work of late Latin encyclopaedists. *The Almagest* supplied the detailed evidence on which that model was based.

The Ptolemaic system assumed that the earth was a static sphere at the centre of the universe round which all the heavenly bodies moved. Greek science distinguished between the moving stars, which continually changed their positions in the heavens, and the fixed stars, which remained in a constant relationship to each other. The moving stars were the sun, the moon and the five planets visible to the naked eye, Mercury, Venus, Mars, Jupiter and Saturn. The relative distances of the different bodies from the earth was computed by observing how long it took each of them to make a complete circuit of the heavens. The moon was clearly the nearest, for it circled the heavens in a month. The sun took a year to complete the circuit and was therefore further away; but the two inner planets, Mercury and Venus, were a problem, since they escorted the sun on its annual journey, but sometimes preceded it and at other times followed it. Thus Venus is sometimes the morning star and sometimes the evening star. It was accepted as an unproven hypothesis that both had orbits between the moon and the sun and that Mercury's was nearer to the moon, while that of Venus lay between Mercury and the sun. The outer planets were straightforward: Mars takes two years to complete the heavenly circuit, Jupiter almost twelve and Saturn nearly thirty, so their order was not in doubt.

Beyond Saturn were the fixed stars. Ancient astronomers believed that they were all equidistant from the earth, although they differed in size and were classified in five orders of magnitude. Scientific thought was particularly interested in the stars of the ecliptic, the belt of fixed stars through which the path of the sun ran. This was the circle of the zodiac and was divided into twelve sections, each named after a dominant constellation. It was observed that the sun did not return precisely to the same point in the circle of fixed stars at each spring equinox, which marked the start of a new year. When observations were first made in Alexandria in the third century BC the sun began the year in the sign of Aries, but by about the beginning of the Christian era it had moved into the sign of Pisces. This phenomenon is known as the precession of the equinoxes, and it was explained by the hypothesis that the fixed stars moved round the earth, just as the planets did, but that their movement was almost imperceptible because they were so remote. It was estimated that they made a complete circuit of the heavens every 36,000 years. This period was known as a Great Year, and it was surmised that at the end of that time the sun would return to exactly the same point in the ecliptic at the spring equinox as it had occupied at the beginning of the cycle. Beyond the fixed stars, immeasurably remote, was the empyrean, the vault of the heavens.

The earliest Greek scientists had supposed that the heavenly bodies all moved in perfect circles and although detailed observation showed that this was not so, the concept of perfect circular motion was preserved by postulating a series of epicycles, or extra circles, each conceived as being centred on the circular orbit of a star. In this way the irregularities of astral movement could be explained in terms of perfect circular motion. Greek scientists spoke of the orbits as spheres and distinguished nine of them: those of the moon, Mercury, Venus, the sun, Mars, Jupiter, Saturn, the Fixed Stars and the Empyrean, all of which moved on a common axis, passing through the earth. The ancient astronomers, it would seem, did not attribute a physical reality to the spheres and epicycles or to the axis of the heavens, but considered them as mathematical abstractions which accurately described the observable movements of the stars. Medieval thinkers probably shared that view, using the term sphere much as modern scientists would use the term orbit. However, some educated people may have considered that a celestial mechanism was needed to hold the heavens in place (for this was a pre-Newtonian universe in which the laws of gravity were unknown), but that if such a structure existed it was made of some ethereal substance and was not visible to man. Various speculations were possible on that score. Hrabanus Maurus (†856), for example, seems to have thought that the sphere of the Empyrean was made of some kind of crystal and that it contained freezer compartments on the outside in which God had placed 'the waters above the firmament' mentioned in Genesis, 1,7.

Medieval scientists could make no significant advance in the study of astronomy. *The Almagest* accounted for all the movements of the heavens visible to the naked eye and the telescopic lens was not invented until the seventeenth century. Theoretical speculation was, of course, always possible and in 1440 Nicholas of Cusa did suggest that the earth itself might be in motion although this would not be perceptible to men living on it. Had this opinion been accepted it would have revolutionized astronomical study. The Ptolemaic view of the universe, however, was never challenged during the Middle Ages.

People who accepted that model of the cosmos saw in the heavens evidence not merely of God's creative power but also of his perfection, for the stars never changed and they were thought to move in their courses in perfect circular motion. It was sometimes suggested that the distances between the spheres had significance as musical intervals and that the universe was like a great musical score whose harmonies its creator could read. Astronomy was an important study in Christian terms, because it enabled men to contemplate the visible perfection of the creation: no other science afforded that opportunity because no other part of the material creation was perfect.

The world beneath the moon

The Middle Ages inherited from antiquity a belief that the entire universe was composed of four elements, earth, water, fire and air. Yet it was evident that whereas, during centuries of observation, the heavenly bodies never changed, the world beneath the moon was subject to constant fluctuation. Transitory bodies like comets and shooting stars appeared in the sky of the sub-lunar sphere, while the earth was subject to seasonal change and to the recurrent cycle of life, decay and death. The earth was a place of mutability, where the elements existed only in combination and kept changing their pattern, whereas in the heavens they existed in pure and unchanging forms.

Yet the earth and the heavens formed part of an organic whole and it was this fact which made it possible for the stars to affect life on earth. The belief that they did so rested on scientific observation: the moon clearly regulates the tides, and the sun determines the seasons, so that, given a geocentric model of the universe, it was rational to suppose that all the stars influenced the earth in some way and that further study would elucidate how this system operated. The belief that certain stars have an affinity with certain stones, plants or living creatures is now considered an astrological superstition, because the Ptolemaic model of the universe is no longer accepted, but the Middle Ages regarded that belief as a scientific fact. The church did not dispute that astral influence existed, but merely condemned astral determinism, the belief that the fate of individuals was 'written in the stars' (see chapter 17).

It is often wrongly assumed that people in the Middle Ages believed that the earth was flat. No doubt many simple people did, including the three Mesopotamian monks who set out to look for the horizon and whose Latin life was widely read in the medieval west, but no educated person doubted that the earth was a sphere. Its circumference had been accurately computed by Eratosthenes (†196 BC) at 24,662 miles, but this figure was not very widely known in the Middle Ages, although some scholars, like Hermann of Reichenau in the eleventh century, knew an approximation of it.

Medieval scholars were naturally aware that their knowledge of the earth was confined to a part of the northern hemisphere. They did not doubt that it would be possible to explore the whole of that hemisphere given the right opportunities, but uncertainty existed about the accessibility of the southern hemisphere. Classical geographers had inferred, quite correctly, that the world must have five climatic zones: that the arctic and northern temperate zones must be balanced by antarctic and southern temperate zones in the other hemisphere; and that the two temperate zones must be separated by a torrid zone centred on the equator. But they also erroneously supposed that the torrid zone was too hot to support human life, and this led some Fathers of the church, from the time of St Clement of Rome (c.100), to question whether the antipodes could be peopled, since that would have necessitated a separate creation, a view which did not appear to be sanctioned by scripture.Bede, however, was willing to concede that separately created animals might exist in the antipodes. This opinion came to lose its force as western travellers, like Marco Polo, journeyed near to the equator, until in the fifteenth century the Portuguese explorers proved that the belief was groundless.

The medieval west also inherited from the ancient world a tradition of natural science. This was descriptive and consisted in compiling lists of animals, vegetables and minerals and recording their properties. Medieval bestiaries, herbals and lapidaries were based partly on observation and partly on classical sources and contained a strange mixture of accurate information and myth. Many of the mistaken ideas which people in the Middle Ages held about the nature of the world around them resulted from their having too great a respect for ancient authorities. This was largely a consequence of the break in tradition which occurred in the early medieval west, since it meant that when Graeco-Roman learning was recovered in the twelfth century western scholars were awed by the sheer volume of knowledge which ancient writers had possessed. This led Bernard Sylvester of Chartres to say, 'We are dwarves standing on the shoulders of giants'. Consequently very few medieval scholars were prepared to contradict classical writers and so some endearing mythical fauna found its way into the bestiaries, like the amphisboena, a snake recorded by Lucan in his *Pharsalia*, which has a head at either end of its body and is thus able to clasp its two heads together and form itself into a circle, and to move by bowling itself along like a hoop.

The entire natural world was seen as an expression of the mind of the creator who had called it into being, and men, enlightened by the Christian revelation, were able to understand its symbolism. The natural world was like the Bible, in that both were expressions of the creative Word of God, and both could therefore be interpreted in the same fourfold way. Thus animals and plants and stones were, on a literal level, themselves; but it was also possible to discern a moral in the behaviour of some animals, or in the properties of some plants or stones; just as it was possible to find allegories of the life of Christ and mystical intimations of the nature of God in the world about one through the devout study of the natural sciences.

The mirror of history

Just as the natural world was viewed as an expression of the mind of God, so the whole of time was seen as an unfolding experience of the will of God. Medieval theologians spoke of the *speculum historiale*, the mirror of history, meaning by this that all historical study enabled men to learn more about God.

Although educated opinion in the Middle Ages did not suppose that each of the six days of creation was twenty-four hours long, no real concept of geological time existed then. There was no need to postulate it, for during the Middle Ages and for centuries afterwards scholars considered that each species of plant and animal life, including man, was a distinct creation. The church's tradition about this was essentially Platonist: every species was the realization of a thought in the mind of God. Yet without the need for evolution, there was no need for vast geological time spans in which life could develop.

Moreover, the Middle Ages had no concept of pre-history. Scholars then believed that the first people on earth had been perfect specimens of *homo sapiens* and had enjoyed greater intellectual and physical capacities than any of their descendants. Ever since that time man's physical powers had degenerated and his life-span had declined from a millennium to less than a century, while the greatest modern intellect could not rival that of the ancestors of the human race because sin had impaired man's capacity to think clearly. There was no need to postulate millions of years in which man could gradually evolve, for man had been created perfect. Nor was man's early history at all obscure, since the Old Testament provided a clear account of precisely what had happened since the creation, and this was a framework into which other sources of historical information could be fitted.

It is true that few medieval scholars shared the confidence of archbishop Ussher of Armagh (†1656) that all the years mentioned in the Bible were of standard length, so that it was possible to compute the creation of the world as 4004 BC; nor did they all consider that every event recorded in the Old Testament should be understood in a literal sense. Nevertheless, few of those who ventured an opinion about the date of the creation of man were willing to place it much earlier than *c*.5000 BC and they all agreed that the general outline of human history contained in the Old Testament was literally true.

The historical perspective of the Middle Ages was very different from that which is prevalent now. We see history as a linear progression of events stretching back from the present day to some indeterminate point in the past at which it merges with palaeontology and geology; but medieval people saw history as a cosmic drama which began with the fall of Lucifer and reached its climax with the Incarnation of Christ. Everything which happened before Christ's coming was in some sense a preparation for it. The narrative of human history recorded in the Old Testament was interpreted in that way (see chapter 6) and medieval scholars incorporated all other historical information available to them within the scriptural framework. The writings of Greek and Roman historians and the traditions of the Celtic, Germanic and Scandinavian peoples were all synchronized with Jewish history. This became so much a habit of mind that when Geoffrey of Monmouth wrote his legendary *History of the Kings of Britain* in *c*.1136, he placed the troubled reign of king Lear at the time when 'Isaiah was making his prophecies'.

Medieval theologians, following the lead of the church Fathers, found evidence of prophets outside Israel who had foretold the coming of Christ, like Virgil, who in his Fourth Eclogue had predicted the imminent birth of a saviour. The church came to accept that, although the Jews had been specially prepared for Christ's coming because he was to be born among them, the Holy Spirit had also prepared all mankind for the reception of his teaching. Consequently all earlier human history was seen as a preparation for the coming of Christ.

History since the Incarnation had centred round the triumph of Christ in his church. This was a further episode in the struggle between the forces of good and evil which had been raging since the fall of Lucifer, for, even in the Christian era, evil remained powerful, working through human sin and self-interest in an attempt to frustrate the purpose of God. Initially the primitive church had faced the overt hostility of the Roman empire, but although the emperor Constantine had granted the church peace and protection, the spiritual war was by no means over. The church had continually to face assaults from tyrannical rulers and also from heretics and schismatics working within Christendom, as well as the hostility of unbelievers who attacked Christians and hindered the spread of the faith.

The medieval view of history was unusual in that it included also an account of the history of the future: this was known from the teachings of Christ and from the Revelation of St John the Divine which ended the New Testament canon. At some unknown time in the future a number of portents would occur heralding the coming of Antichrist. He would be the antithesis of Christ, a mortal man, subservient to the devil, claiming to be Christ returned to earth again and demanding to be paid divine honours. Many Christians, it was supposed, would accept his claim and apostatize, while those who refused to worship Antichrist would be persecuted. His dominion would be ended by the return of Christ to earth in majesty. He would slay Antichrist and summon the living and the dead to Judgement. Then the present universe would be dissolved and God would create a new heaven and a new earth.

The instrument of ten strings

The Christian world picture was nothing if not comprehensive: it began with the creation of the angels and it ended with the creation of a new heaven and earth. All human history was related to the cosmic contest between good and evil which reached its climax in the Incarnation. Moreover, all human knowledge was integrated into this religious pattern, because everything which existed was an expression of the divine mind and was therefore a means whereby man might learn more about his creator. This was even true of the interior workings of the rational mind, since these were all divine gifts, and by contemplating his own methods of knowing man could learn more about God.

All study of the phenomenal world therefore increased man's knowledge of God.

Vincent of Beauvais († 1264), the author of a huge encyclopaedia, encompassing all branches of human learning, arranged in 9,885 chapters, called this work the *Speculum Maius*, or Great Mirror, because he believed, as did all his contemporaries, that the universe mirrored its creator.

Man occupied a central place in the divine order, for, being composed of a physical body and an immortal soul, he alone shared simultaneously in the life of both the spiritual and material creations. Man was not the greatest work of God: he was inferior in intelligence to the angels, and was arguably morally inferior to the animal creation, which had never sinned. Yet God had given man a dignity greater than that of any other creature by himself becoming man. St Paul had taught that the entire Christian revelation was not simply concerned with the salvation of man, but formed part of the cosmic struggle between good and evil (Eph., 3, 10). Medieval theologians expressed this mystery of man's role in the spiritual drama in terms of a poetic image, the instrument of ten strings. This was drawn from a phrase in the Psalms, 'Praise him on an instrument of ten strings' (Ps., 33, 2; Vulgate, 32, 2), which was interpreted as a prophecy of how, when the spiritual war was ended and harmony restored to the universe, God would be praised not merely by the nine choirs of angels, but also by man.

The whole of this world picture was understood fully only by the learned, but it influenced the way in which the universe and man's place in it was comprehended at all levels since, if any reflective person asked a question about any field of human knowledge, the answer he received would come from this total world-view. Although, as will be seen in Part III, the western world during the Middle Ages was not hermetically sealed from contact with other cultures, a full understanding of those non-Christian traditions was rare. It was, of course, possible for people living in western Christendom to question the received tradition, but to do this on a broad scale required an independence of mind and an intellectual capacity which are rarely found in any age. Most people accepted the prevalent world-picture in broad outline, even if they were ignorant of much of the detail, or sceptical about certain points in the tradition. Consequently, since that world-picture was a Catholic Christian one, it is possible to speak of almost all people in the west during the Middle Ages as being Christian: intellectually they thought of the world in mainly orthodox Christian terms because no alternative system was available to them. This is, of course, a very different matter from fervent commitment to a religious faith, or even moderate practice of it.

10
The Legacy of Paganism

The church views paganism as a modern aberration

Although on a rational level people in the medieval west accepted the Christian account of the nature of the universe and of man's place in it, older concepts, derived from the pagan religions of the west, lingered in their consciousness and helped to shape their attitudes in ways which were not Christian at all.

The church did not see in paganism an attempt by primitive peoples to express their religious impulses in unorthodox ways, but considered that all forms of paganism were idolatrous and false. This was a consequence less of intolerance than of the universally held, foreshortened, historical perspective of the medieval west, which envisaged that the entire world had been re-peopled by the descendants of Noah at some unspecified but recent date, probably during the third millennium BC. This had important consequences for the understanding of other religions. It was clear from the Biblical account that Noah and his sons had worshipped the one true God and it therefore followed that pagan cults could only have arisen because Noah's descendants had wilfully adopted polytheism. Such a retrograde step must have been diabolically inspired. Indeed, the sources which medieval scholars viewed as authoritative led them to the opposite conclusion from that favoured by modern historians of religion: that is, they supposed that monotheism had once been the universal religion and that polytheism had succeeded it in comparatively recent times. The church explained the origin of pagan gods in two ways: either they were demons who had manifested themselves to men in attractive forms and deluded them into regarding them as gods, or they were men who had been falsely deified after death.

The gods of Olympus

The gods of Olympus, who under a variety of names made up the official pantheon of the Roman empire at the time of its conversion to Christianity, were not at that time a serious threat to the church. Educated pagans were, for the most part, theists who did not believe in the literal existence of those gods, while simple people, who perhaps did believe in them, were more concerned with the worship of local and household divinities. The church condemned the Olympians as demons and suppressed their public cult, but found it impossible to erase an awareness of them from the Christian mind.

For the pagan gods figured prominently in classical Latin literature, particularly in the poets. These works were read by educated people throughout the

Middle Ages: not merely were they enjoyed as literature, they were also considered a necessary part of a good education because they were examples of golden-age Latin style. The church made some attempt to demythologize these works by treating them as Christian allegories: this was done even with so unpromising a text as Ovid's *Ars Amatoria*, whose explicit sexual references were interpreted, like those of the Song of Songs, as an allegory of God's love for the soul, or for the church. Yet although such exegesis may have been found helpful in the secluded atmosphere of monastery schools, it met with little response among the secular students of the twelfth-century cathedral schools and their university successors, who preferred the literal meaning.

Successive generations of churchmen viewed the pagan poets as dangerous. St Odo of Cluny (†942) was warned in a dream about the perils of reading Virgil, whose works he saw as a beautiful ship which, when he boarded it, was full of serpents. 'He understood by the serpents', his biographer relates,' the teaching of the poets'. Almost 400 years later the same anxiety about the danger inherent in reading the pagan poets were expressed by Nicholas of Nonancourt, chancellor of the university of Paris.

Churchmen did not, of course, fear a revival of the cult of the Olympian gods, yet the dangers of which they spoke were real enough, because the religious values of pagan poets were not merely different from, but were often diametrically opposed to, those of the Christian faith. They lacked, for the most part, any sense that it was meritorious to renounce the good things of this world, which the medieval church regarded as the highest form of spirituality. Moreover, some of the gods and goddesses extolled by those poets represented principles which in Christian terms were sinful. This was particularly true of Bacchus/Dionysus, god not only of wine but also of human nature unrestrained by reason, and of Venus, goddess of love in all its forms. Churchmen were afraid lest those who read and admired the pagan poets should come to share their religious values and to regard some sinful human reactions as praiseworthy and justified because they were attributes of the Olympian gods.

Some readers certainly responded to classical poetry in that way in their own writings and used pagan religious imagery to express their feelings. The anonymous twelfth-century writer known as the Archpoet says in his autobiography, for example:

Quicquid Venus imperat
Labor est suavis,
Que nunquam in cordibus
Habitat ignavis.

('Whatever Venus commands is a labour of delight, for she never dwells in the hearts of those who lack spirit'.) The frank paganism of the Archpoet distressed at least one modern critic, F.J.E. Raby, who said of him: 'The very shamelessness of this 'confession' is without parallel', and it is therefore not surprising that this and other works of this genre troubled medieval churchmen.

Despite all the misgivings with which they were viewed, classical poets were too firmly ensconced in the learned tradition of the west and in its educational syllabus to be displaced. During the Italian Renaissance of the fifteenth century the corpus of classical literature available to western readers was enlarged and it was studied once more in a humanist way which had been absent from higher education since the twelfth century. Yet the problems which this created for the church were not new: they had in some measure been present throughout the Middle Ages. Scholars who read and admired classical literature were believing Catholics, but their thought was in part shaped by pre-Christian values expressed in pagan religious symbolism.This seldom led to unorthodox belief, but it did produce an ambiguous response to the practice of the Christian life sometimes, because the distinction between pagan and Christian definitions of virtue became blurred.

The northern gods become heroes

The paganism of northern Europe, unlike that of imperial Rome, was a living faith when Christianity became established there. The church had no consistent policy about categorizing the gods of the Celts, the Germans and, later, the Scandinavians, but it tended to euhemerize them, that is, to treat them as men and women who had really lived and had been accorded divine honours after death. In the church's view diabolical malice was the cause of such idolatry, but the gods were not themselves demons, but exceptionally gifted human beings whom the devil had deluded men into treating as gods. This approach was probably dictated by political caution. All the northern kings in pagan times claimed descent from the gods and exercised authority in virtue of this, so the church's mission would not have been aided by a doctrinaire assertion that the royal ancestors were demons whom all Christians should abhor.

The church's attitude made it possible for Christian kings to continue to claim descent from pagan gods, but those gods had to be fitted into the historical framework of the Old Testament. This was achieved with varying degrees of ingenuity. The *Anglo-Saxon Chronicle* traced the pedigree of Alfred the Great's father, king Ethelwulf, to the god Woden, but then traced Woden's descent from Sceaf, an otherwise unknown son of Noah, born in the Ark. When dealing with the pagan Norse gods, Snorri Sturluson, a Christian Icelander writing in the early thirteenth century, suggested that Thor was a grandson of king Priam of Troy, thus linking the old gods to classical history, which was itself tied in to Old Testament chronology in the Christian historiographical tradition.

One consequence of this approach was that churchmen were prepared to write down the pagan religious traditions of the peoples of northern Europe, since these could be read as straight history. The pagan mythology of Ireland and Scandinavia was recorded in great detail, and that of the rest of northern Europe in more fragmentary form, by churchmen who thought in this way. It did not prove possible to reduce the gods to human stature in these legends, even though they were written and edited by Christian clergy. Thus Odin, who sat in Valhalla of the 640 gates presiding over the assembly of the gods and of the souls of warriors slain in battle, and who had hung for nine nights and days on the world tree,

> struck with a spear
> and given to Odin,
> myself given to myself

as the *Havamal* states, was clearly more than an early Norse king. Long after they had ceased to be objects of religious worship the pagan gods of the north retained a vital place in the Christian imagination of those regions even though they did not fit into any of the categories of Christian cosmology.

The growing population of hell

Although the church sought to avoid any kind of syncretism by excluding all pagan deities from heaven, it was less discriminating about the population of hell. All religions have supernatural figures who are hostile to man: Hecate and the Eumenides are examples of this in Graeco-Roman religion, the Giants and the Norns in Norse religion; while there were also hosts of lesser spirits of a malignant or mischievous kind found in all the pagan traditions of the west. The church regarded all these creatures as demons. This was the obvious course to take: pagan converts believed in the objective existence of these malignant forces, the church believed in the existence of demonic powers and it simply reclassified the malignant, pagan beings as demons.

Its wisdom in doing so is open to question. In the Christian tradition the demons were all fallen angels, spiritual beings more intelligent than man. Goblins, trolls and ogres did not belong in that company. Except for the fact that they were both opposed to good and hostile to man, there was nothing in common between a fallen angel, which was an incorporeal intelligence, and a troll which lived in the hills and which would turn to stone if exposed to the common light of day. Yet it is clear from the way in which devils are represented in medieval art that the pagan view of evil spirits won out over the more rarefied beliefs of the church Fathers. The imagination of the west continued to be haunted by symbols of evil far older than those of the Christian tradition and even learned churchmen conceded that hell was peopled with a motley assembly of malignant spirits with varying degrees of power and intelligence. This deviation from the tradition of the primitive church had a long-term effect on western thought, for it was accepted without question by both Catholics and Protestants in the early modern period.

The Christianizing of pagan rituals

Paganism did not disappear suddenly when a ruler established Christianity as the religion of his people. Although it was possible to perform mass baptisms, there were seldom enough priests to instruct new converts in the practice of the faith, and a network of local churches was established only very slowly. Consequently in many parts of Europe paganism was practised alongside a nominal form of Christianity for centuries.

The church sought to make the transition from paganism easier by adopting a policy of compromise about matters which did not involve questions of principle. In the late Roman period the church calendar was arranged so that some important feasts should be kept on the same date as pagan festivals: thus from the fourth century Christ's birth was observed on 25 December, the feast of Sol Invictus, and the Nativity of St John the Baptist on 24 June, the summer solstice in the Julian calendar.

Pope Gregory I suggested that the pagan temples of Anglo-Saxon England should be reconsecrated as churches and that the festivals at which the pagan Saxons had been accustomed to sacrifice oxen in honour of their gods should be replaced by new Christian festivals at which oxen should be killed to provide a banquet for the worshippers. He added:

> If the people are allowed some worldly pleasures in this way, they will more readily come to desire the joys of the spirit.

As a result of this policy, which was implemented throughout the west, many pagan customs became replaced by Christian ones and many pagan sites became Catholic shrines. This attitude was very long-lived: as late as 998 when the church of S. Bartolomeo was built in the ruins of the temple of Aesculepius on the Tiber Island in Rome, the sacred well of the temple was incorporated in the chancel of the new church, where it remains to this day as a liturgical curiosity, a Christian holy well, performing no function, and awkwardly sited in the middle of the chancel steps. When nineteenth-century anthropologists first discovered the degree of continuity between Catholicism and paganism in the early Middle Ages they were deeply scandalized by what they regarded as evidence of religious syncretism. In fact no sacrifice of principle was involved, for the church sought merely to accommodate neutral features of the old religions so that new converts would not experience too violent a cultural break.

Paganism becomes folklore

By the eleventh century overt paganism had disappeared throughout the west except in newly converted areas like Scandinavia and Hungary. Yet a range of practices remained which, though no longer part of a living tradition of paganism, had not been assimilated to the new religion either. These had turned into folk magic, the vestiges of an old religion practised by people who on most conscious levels were Christian.

Some of these customs had become so divorced from their religious context that the church was prepared to tolerate them as secular traditions. For example, the maypole was a descendant of pagan representations of the sacred world tree which held up the heavens. Symbols of this kind had once had considerable religious power: Charlemagne in 772 destroyed the Irminsul, the sacred tree near the chief Saxon temple at Marseburg, because he considered it a focus of pagan worship, but throughout much of northern Europe in the following centuries Christians continued to erect and decorate maypoles, having forgotten their religious significance. The church authorities viewed this custom benignly. The church of St Andrew Undershaft in medieval London, for example, was so called because it was dwarfed by the giant maypole erected outside it each year, round which its parishioners danced after hearing mass on the feast of Sts Philip and James. There were many other customs of a similar kind: beltane fires, lit in many parts of Europe on Midsummer's Eve, round which young people danced and over which they jumped, were no longer thought of as part of sun-worship, but as a preliminary to the festivities of St John the Baptist's day; the kissing bough, hung in houses at Christmas, was no longer considered part of a fertility ritual, but another symbol of the general goodwill which prevailed at the season of Christ's birth.

In many parts of the west throughout the Middle Ages groups of mummers enacted plays in springtime about the ritual killing and bringing back to life of a symbolic figure, usually wearing a costume of leaves or of some other vegetation. Such dramas have plausibly been interpreted as survivals of pagan rituals relating to the dying and rising god on whose actual or ceremonial death the fertility of the crops was once held to depend. Similarly at harvest time it was the custom in many places to deck with flowers the last sheaf scythed in a village and to ritually wring its neck, a practice with animistic overtones, since it presupposed the existence of a corn-spirit. The church was prepared to tolerate such customs, which had lost their religious meaning and become occasions for secular festivals or, at most, good luck ceremonies. Certainly nobody regarded them as substitutes for Christian rites.

The persistence of pagan beliefs

Where it was possible to do so the church substituted Christian for pagan rituals. Sometimes this was a relatively simple matter, which involved the replacement of a pagan by a Christian invocation, for example in a blessing spell. It was not possible to adapt cursing spells in the same way, for although the church did have cursing rituals, of which the Commination Service in the Book of Common Prayer is the only modern example licensed for public use, they might not be pronounced in private by individuals, but could only be used publicly in a liturgical context. Private cursing formed part of the practice of *maleficium*, the use of religious formularies to harm others, which had been condemned even in pagan times and was similarly outlawed by the church (see chapter 17).

But there were certain beneficent pagan rituals which were believed to be powerful yet which it was impossible to recast in Christian form. In parts of Germany, for example, the following rain-making ritual was used in the early eleventh century in times of drought. The women of a village took all the unmarried girls and appointed one of them leader. She was led out of the village, stripped naked, and made to dig up a henbane plant with the little finger of her right hand. The plant was tied with a string to the little toe of her right foot and the other girls, holding small branches, took her to a stream and, dipping their branches in it, sprinkled her with water. The leader was then made to walk backwards to the village, still naked, and this ceremony was believed to ensure rain. There was no way in which such a ritual could be Christianized: the church considered it sinful, because pagan, and prescribed a penance for the adult women who organized it. This is merely one of many pagan customs listed in the nineteenth book of the *Decretum*, written by Burchard of Worms in c.1008–12, which was used as a major source by J. Grimm in his pioneer study of German folklore.

Clear evidence of how difficult it could be to eradicate pagan beliefs is found in parts of southern France where, as late as 1300, tumuli, containing burial-chambers of a pagan Celtic type, were built just outside villages. The bodies of the dead were buried in the local churchyards in consecrated ground, but the burial chambers in the tumuli were used for depositing grave-goods. Earth from the village was placed in them, together with dead animals and broken pottery, and some chambers had apertures at surface level through which libations could be poured. Clearly the belief was widespread that the spirits of the dead remained earthbound, at least for a time, and needed ministrations. This was contrary to the teachings of the church and the persistence of such a belief is remarkable in a part of France where Christianity had been established since the second century. Since the church refused to compromise its teachings by allowing grave-goods to be buried with the dead, these spirit-chambers were erected by lay people to deal with the problem.

There is no evidence to suggest that the people who built these chambers, or the German women who practised rain-making rituals, were crypto-pagans, just as there is no warrant for thinking that the women in Protestant households of Devon in the early years of this century who made the sign of the cross with a spoon when mixing a junket were crypto-Catholics. In both cases the conscious acceptance of a new religious tradition had not been able to eradicate centuries' old beliefs.

The imaginative legacy of paganism

Moreover, a thousand years proved too short a time in which to Christianize the imagination of Europe. Indeed, by euhemerizing many of the ancient gods the church helped to perpetuate a pagan, imaginative tradition, for although mythology was treated as history, the mythological figures continued to move in a supernatural context which was pre-Christian. On an intellectual level there was no room for such a context in the Christian thought-world. Yet pagan supernatural beliefs had a very secure place in the imagination of most medieval Christians and this influenced their creative writing. This can be seen in the Arthurian legends, which took the form in which we know them during the period 1160–1230, and became known as the Matter of Britain. As the early French writers on these themes admitted, they had learned the stories from Breton minstrels and many of those stories ultimately derive from pagan, Celtic folklore.

The heroes and heroines of the Matter of Britain are depicted as twelfth- and thirteenth-century Catholics, but the world in which their adventures occur is peopled with figures from a far older tradition. King Bagdemagus of Gore, whose realm few may leave, and which may be approached only across a bridge of knife-blades, has many of the attributes of a pagan king of the dead; Sir Lancelot, though a mortal man, is surnamed *du lac* because he has been reared by a fairy princess, the Lady of the Lake; King Arthur has human parents, yet one of his sisters is a supernatural being, Morgan *la fée*; the wizard Merlin ends his life imprisoned in a tower of air by the enchantress Vivian, but does not die. Even the Holy Grail, which the authors of the romances strove assiduously to make a Christian vessel (though not necessarily the chalice of the Last Supper), devoting an entire book of the Prose Vulgate Cycle to that purpose, retained Celtic associations quite foreign to the Christian tradition. It is in the keeping not, as a relic would normally be, of the church authorities, but of a laymen, the rich Fisher King, who is wounded 'between the thighs' and, in some versions of the story, presides over a waste land. In all versions the king will only be healed if the questing knight asks the right question, and in some versions this will also cause water to flow again in the waste land. The Grail itself has thaumaturgic properties: great light shines from it and it can feed an entire company with the earthly food each of them most desires. Although each of these features is patient of an explanation in terms of Christian allegory, many of them are so primitive and pagan that it is difficult to conceive of any Christian poet inventing them, and clearly they are a re-working of older material which has not been completely freed of its pagan connotations.

The stories in the Matter of Britain were not unique: much of the imaginative writing of the Middle Ages shares this quality of combining descriptions of contemporary life with supernatural marvels which do not form part of the Christian world picture. This was precisely the mental world which the audience of these stories inhabited, for although their society conformed to Christian standards and their intellectual formation was consciously Christian, their imagination drew much of its symbolism from non-Christian sources.

The supernatural world of the medieval imagination might be described as a third spiritual dimension. It had nothing to do with the conflict between the armies of heaven and hell which was the setting for the Christian revelation of the supernatural order. The writers of romances were aware of this problem. The authors of the Prose Vulgate Cycle created Galahad, the perfect Christian knight, in order to impose orthodox values on the supernatural world of the Matter of Britain, but this attempt to Christianize the imagination of Europe was not entirely successful, because, of necessity, Galahad, being both perfect and human, remains a cardboard figure.

The persistence of a pagan imaginative world encouraged western people to think in non-Christian ways. For example, in the twelfth century it was widely believed in both Cornwall and Brittany that king Arthur was not dead, but would return to rule over the Celtic people, and at the end of the century a groom of the bishop of Catania claimed to have seen him sleeping, surrounded by his court, in a cave on the side of Mount Etna. In Christian terms such a belief was untenable: God might, as a special grace, prolong the lives of saints in that way as he had done to the Seven Sleepers of Ephesus, but Arthur was not a saint: he had been dead for centuries and in terms of Christian orthodoxy he could not return to reign. Arthur's immortality was possible only in terms of pagan Celtic belief, yet men who were entirely Catholic on any conscious level found no difficulty in imaginatively supposing that Christian rules about death and resurrection might not operate for some people.

Another example of the same phenomenon was the persistence of the belief in the existence of benign, though unpredictable, supernatural beings, the creatures of faëry whom Shakespeare portrays in *A Midsummer Night's Dream*. In Christian terms such beings, who were obviously not angels, must be demons, but such a view was considered irrelevant by most people who tended to behave as though such creatures existed and should be treated with cautious respect, and be propitiated with gifts, usually of food, as a sign of goodwill.

This three-layered view of the supernatural, consisting of the good and evil forces of Christian orthodoxy, together with a third, neutral force which did not conform to Christian categories, persisted throughout the Middle Ages and into modern times in much of the west. It did not represent a survival of conscious pagan belief, although its roots were undoubtedly pagan, nor did it denote any conscious rejection of the church. All-embracing though its world-picture was, the church could not accommodate alternative views of the supernatural order, yet these were so deeply ingrained in the thought of western Christians that they proved impossible to eradicate. The third supernatural area was a country of the mind in which the people of the west could move freely. Consequently even their religious attitudes were not immune from unorthodox reactions which drew their power from the pagan imaginative tradition.

11
Knowledge of the Faith

Because many clergy in the Middle Ages had little formal training (see chapter 7), they were unable to give much religious instruction to the laity in their care. Baptism, it is true, conferred full church membership, but people needed to know something about their faith in order to attempt to lead the Christian life. Medieval theologians debated what was the minimum which any adult Christian of sound mind needed to know, and St Thomas Aquinas concluded that no formal instruction was necessary, although it was highly desirable, and that it was possible to understand the fundamental points of Christian doctrine simply by attending the services of the church on Sundays and holy days.

Before the eleventh century a high proportion of lay people must have learned about their faith in that way and even in 1500 some people living in rural areas had received no formal instruction because their clergy were too ignorant to provide it. It would be wrong to assume that such people knew next to nothing about the faith, for the medieval church had a liturgy which was visually instructive, while the church's lavish use of representational art helped to make good its lack of verbal teaching.

What was known by the uninstructed

Belief in one God, the creator, would seem to have been universal throughout the Christian west in the Middle Ages. Any deviation from this, for example, the various shades of dualism professed by the Cathars (see chapter 18 below), was viewed as quite exceptional by the church authorities. Everybody knew the Our Father: no formal instruction was needed to transmit this prayer once it had been taught to converts, for mothers would quite naturally teach it to their children. God the Father was represented quite freely in western art, always in human form and usually as an old man. Consequently most people found no difficulty in conceptualizing God the creator.

The faith of the medieval west was profoundly Christocentric and its chief symbol was the crucifix. The way in which Christ was portrayed varied: until 900 he was always shown reigning from the cross, crowned and wearing the high priestly vestments, whereas after that time he was shown as the suffering Lord. However poor a church might be, and however little decoration it contained, it would possess one or more crucifixes, and in all churches these were in central positions, above the rood-screen or the altar, where the eye of the worshipper was drawn to them. Although in richer churches and cathedrals other scenes from the life of Christ would be portrayed in frescoes, sculptures and stained glass, the central act of Christ's life in the minds of western people was undoubtedly the crucifixion.

In the church's liturgy the crucifixion was inseparably linked with the resurrection. On Good Friday churches were stripped of their ornaments, the stone altar stood bare, statues were veiled and the clergy wore black vestments as they did for a funeral mass. At the centre of the Good Friday liturgy was the veneration of the cross, when, led by the clergy, the entire congregation came to kneel three times before the crucifix and to kiss the feet of the crucified Lord. On Easter Day the church was decked with flowers, the Paschal candle burned in the sanctuary, the clergy vested in white or cloth-of-gold, and the dominant word in the liturgy was *alleluia*. In the pre-industrial society of the medieval west, where the entire population was conscious of the seasons of the agricultural cycle on which their livelihoods and, indeed, their survival depended, no explanation was needed to elucidate these ceremonies. Easter was the spring festival and nature itself reinforced the church's message, proclaiming the death of winter and the rising to life again of all the natural world. The resurrection was not a difficult concept for an agrarian society to accept.

Although the death and resurrection of Christ were at the heart of popular understanding of the faith, the theological significance of these events was less clearly perceived. Most people could not have explained the connection between Christ's death on Calvary and its re-enactment in the mass. Yet they did believe that Christ was truly present in the mass under the appearances of bread and wine and that they could contemplate that divine presence during the Elevation of the Host. They believed, moreover, that the mass was a sacrifice, the only sacrifice which a Christian could make, the offering of Christ to his Father for the needs of the living and the dead. The universality of this belief in the spiritual power of the mass is self-evident: people in the Middle Ages were willing to spend considerable sums of money in payment for masses and to support large numbers of priests whose sole function was to say mass for their benefactors.

Christ's presence in the mass was experienced in a transcendental way: he descended from heaven to be present with his people. Medieval men had no difficulty in believing that Christ was God, because that was how they experienced him. For that reason they had a problem in understanding why the Incarnation was relevant. Christ was represented as a man in religious art, and the liturgy commemorated events in his earthly life, such as his birth, death and resurrection, but what spoke most vividly to medieval Christians about Christ's humanity was the cult of Mary his mother.

This had reached western Europe from the eastern churches in the early Middle Ages and had spread rapidly. By the twelfth century representations of the Virgin Mother had become almost as common as those of the crucified Lord: almost no church was without at least one statue of the Virgin and in the later Middle Ages most churches had a Lady chapel, or at least a Lady altar, dedicated to the Virgin. The degree of veneration in which Mary was held in the western church in the later Middle Ages was necessary to prevent men's concept of Christ from becoming completely spiritualized. Motherhood was confined to this world: the angels in heaven had no mothers, but God the Son had a mother, and that was possible solely because he had become man.

Christians worship the Holy Trinity, Father, Son and Holy Spirit, but this doctrine has seldom had a very strong hold on the popular mind. Medieval people were aware of the teaching because the formula 'In the name of the Father and of the Son and of the Holy Spirit' was used so frequently in the liturgy. Most people probably knew the phrase and used it as a prayer when they crossed themselves, while most women knew the phrase as part of the formula to be used in emergency baptisms (see chapter 12). Yet there is little evidence that the Holy Spirit held a significant place in the religious thought of most people. Part of the reason for this was that in western iconography the Third Person of the Trinity was represented in various ways, sometimes as a young man, sometimes as a dove and, in depictions of Pentecost, as tongues of fire. The lack of a constant iconographic image made it difficult for most people to conceptualize the Spirit.

Although the church said little in its official teaching about the devil and his angels, they occupied almost as important a place as the hosts of heaven in popular belief. This can be seen from the services which lay people required from the priesthood: rites of blessing, invariably accompanied by rites of exorcism, abound in medieval service books. People wanted their houses blessed, their fields blessed, their food blessed, their weapons blessed. The assumption behind all those rites was that the devil was very powerful and that his influence must be excluded by the stronger rituals of the Christian faith.

Such a view was not necessarily theologically unsound: Christ himself had referred to Satan as 'the prince of this world' (John, 12, 31). Nevertheless, the great force which belief in the devil exercised over the minds of medieval people is almost certainly connected with the problem which the nature of evil posed for them. A wider gulf existed throughout much of the Middle Ages between Christian moral standards and the ethics of society than does in our own culture (see chapter 14), and lay people could not help but be aware of this. Few people in any age are willing, or indeed able, to accept full responsibility for the evil in their own characters: nowadays there is a tendency to claim diminished responsibility because of social circumstances, whereas in the Middle Ages part of the blame was placed on diabolical temptation. Belief in the power of the devil was reinforced by empirical observation. Men lived in a hostile environment, in which their well-being and day-to-day survival was at risk from the elements, or from epidemic disease, or cattle murrain, which they had no way of checking. This was seen as evidence of the power of the 'prince of this world' and of his minions, from whom men sought protection in the prayers and holy water of the church.

Everybody believed that man had an immortal soul. There was nothing specifically Christian about this doctrine, which had been held by all the pagan religions of the west and was a basic assumption of all Europeans. Christian teaching about the fate of the soul after death made an impression on the west, although it took some centuries to do so, and although older, pagan notions sometimes coexisted with it. People learned of heaven and hell chiefly from the paintings found in many churches, showing the ladder of life or the Last Judgement. They undoubtedly thought of hell as a place of material torment and heaven as a garden of virtuous delights, and preaching did not succeed materially in modifying this picture. The subtle apophatic method of defining heaven by negatives, and the abstract concept of hell as a spiritual state of being, formulated by the scholastic theologians, did not commend themselves to popular preachers, who used verbal imagery which confirmed their hearers' belief in hell fire and the music and feasting of paradise.

Although they may not all have been familiar with the doctrine of purgatory, which only began to be visually represented in the later Middle Ages, people must throughout the medieval centuries have accepted the existence of a third spiritual state, which some souls entered after death, in which they needed prayers in order to be admitted to heaven.

Most people seem to have accepted that it was necessary to make reparation to God for serious and wilful sins either in this life or in the next. This belief, not dissimilar from the church's doctrine of penance (see chapter 4), was conceived in far simpler terms, derived from the secular world. Throughout much of the Middle Ages western society, like that of ancient Israel, took the principle 'an eye for an eye and a tooth for a tooth' as axiomatic in human relationships. An offence demanded legal compensation. Most people seem therefore to have thought it reasonable to expect that God too would demand compensation for offences committed against him. They went to great lengths to perform harsh penances in expiation for their sins, and everybody seems to have thought that they would need to perform further penances in purgatory after death. This showed a proper mixture of humility and caution. In theological terms penance was only effective because of the redeeming death of Christ, and even the poorly instructed instinctively understood this. They wished to associate Christ with them in their penance, by imploring the aid of his sacrificial death for themselves and for others by offering masses for the repose of their souls.

Lay instruction before 1100

In the early Middle Ages when no proper parish system existed there must have been many people who had received no formal instruction, but there would also have been some people who had a more detailed knowledge of the faith. From the ninth century provincial synods urged clergy to arrange for the laity to be formally instructed. They were exhorted to teach them the Apostles' creed and to expound its meaning. This was the shortest profession of faith and had, since the fourth century, formed part of the baptismal liturgy:

> I believe in God, the Father almighty, maker of heaven and earth, and in Jesus Christ his only son, our Lord, who was conceived by the Holy Spirit, born of the Virgin Mary, suffered under Pontius Pilate, was crucified, dead and buried. He descended into hell. And the third day he rose again from the dead, he ascended into heaven and sitteth at the right hand of God the Father almighty, from thence he shall come to judge the living and the dead. I believe in the Holy Spirit, the holy catholic church, the communion of saints, the forgiveness of sins, the resurrection of the body and the life everlasting. Amen.

Clergy were also told to instruct their flocks in the significance of the chief feasts and fasts of the church's year and to train them in the practice of the Christian life by expounding the virtues and vices.

Had such programmes of instruction been implemented lay people would have obtained a reasonable, if somewhat simple, knowledge of the faith. From the regularity with which complaints were made about the neglect of these rulings, it is clear that they were frequently disregarded, although some priests may have tried to comply with them. It seems clear, for example, that a genuine attempt was made in the late Old English church to supply the parish clergy with manuals of instruction in the vernacular.

The nobility do not seem to have been any better instructed than the poor, for although they employed private chaplains, few of these were at all well-educated, but most were simply mass priests. Devout members of the high nobility did sometimes engage learned chaplains and study theology with them. This was true of women as well as of men: Adela of Blois, the mother of king Stephen of England, for example, knew a good deal about Christian doctrine.

The 'miles literatus'

In the early Middle Ages there were always a few laymen who had an unexpectedly good technical knowledge of theology. An example of this kind is the anonymous south Italian knight who wrote the *Gesta Francorum*, an eyewitness account of the first crusade. He says of the Turks,

> They have a saying that they are of common stock with the Franks, and that no men, except the Franks and themselves, are naturally born to be knights. This is true . . . that if only they had stood firm in the faith of Christ and holy Christendom and had been willing to accept One God in Three Persons, and had believed rightly and faithfully that the Son of God was born of a virgin mother, that he suffered, and rose from the dead and ascended in the sight of his disciples into heaven, and sent them in full measure the comfort of the Holy Spirit, and that he reigns in heaven and earth, you could not find stronger or braver or more skilful soldiers . . .

An earlier generation of scholars was so surprised to find this understanding of Christian doctrine shown by a knight, that they posited the existence of a clerical co-author who had written this and other theological passages in the work. Rosalind Hill has argued, surely correctly, that the book is the work of a single hand, that the author must have been a *miles literatus* to be able to write Latin, and that this is almost certain proof that he had been trained for the church and subsequently recalled to the world. His is not an isolated case, for Baldwin I, king of Jerusalem, had a similar career structure. There were always a few lay people who shared a knowledge of theology with the learned clergy.

The effect of preaching

From the twelfth century onwards there was a marked increase in preaching to the laity, and this trend was accelerated by the work of the friars in the thirteenth century (see chapter 7). Nevertheless, throughout the Middle Ages a substantial number of priests with cure of souls never preached at all and were not trained to do so. The clergy who did preach regularly attached enormous importance to the sermon in the formation of the Christian life. James of Vitry, when he became bishop of Acre in the Crusader States in 1216, was scandalized to find that the chaplains of the Italian merchant communities there never preached. When they refused to allow him to preach in their churches, which were exempt from his jurisdiction, he used to stand in the streets outside and preach to anybody who would listen.

The content of sermons differed a great deal. The early Dominicans tried to use the sermon as a vehicle for doctrinal teaching, for St Dominic was convinced that heresy had spread so fast in southern France because so few people knew anything about orthodoxy. The Dominicans may have achieved part of their aim, by explaining what was wrong about heretical teaching and by showing that the church had a coherent system of belief, but it may be doubted whether the sermon is a suitable medium for doctrinal instruction, since it is impossible for the preacher to discover whether his congregation has understood what he has said to them. Sermons can certainly be used to refresh people's minds about teachings which they already know, but their most common use is for moral or spiritual exhortation. The great majority of sermons preached to lay people in the Middle Ages were of that kind and by the fifteenth century even the Dominicans had come to accept that approach. Notable preachers from that Order, like St Vincent Ferrer (†1419), exhorted their hearers to penance and amendment of life and did not try to instruct them in the subtleties of doctrine.

For all its limitations the sermon, when it became at all general, increased lay people's understanding of the Christian tradition. Preachers often held the attention of their audiences by telling them stories, or *exempla,* chosen to illustrate some point in their discourse. Some of these were chosen from everyday life and are of great value to the social historian, but more frequently *exempla* were taken from the lives of the saints, the Gospels and the historical books of the Old Testament. These subjects were often represented in religious art and therefore became fixed in the minds of lay people from two sources. People certainly knew far more about the life of Christ in the late Middle Ages than they had previously done, particularly through the evangelical preaching of the Franciscans, but they also knew a certain amount about the Old Testament as well. Thus Chaucer makes the pardoner preface his tale with a reference to king Lemuel. This is a recondite allusion, for Lemuel is mentioned only once in the Bible as the source for the last chapter of the book of Proverbs. The pardoner's audience did not identify Lemuel, but supposed him to be talking of Samuel, for the pardoner impatiently remarked, 'Not Samuel, but Lemuel say I'. A similar audience 300 years earlier, which had heard no sermons, would not have heard of either Samuel or Lemuel.

Catechisms

Once annual confession and communion had been made obligatory for lay people in 1215 attempts were made to provide guidance for parish priests in the instruction of their flocks. Simple catechetical manuals were produced, giving details of the rudiments of Christian doctrine and practice which everybody should know. These circulated quite widely even before the invention of printing, although their influence should not be exaggerated, for many priests would not have owned such a manual and would have given very limited instruction or no instruction at all.

One of the most popular catechisms of the later Middle Ages was the *A,B,C des simples gens* written by John Gerson (†1429), chancellor of the university of Paris. A printed edition was published at Paris in 1495. This work shows what a well instructed layman might have known about his faith at the end of the Middle Ages. The catechism opens in a way well suited to the instruction of young children to whom, perhaps, it was chiefly directed, with a list of the five senses (sight, hearing, touch, taste, smell), but the amount of doctrinal instruction it gives is not great. The candidate was expected to know two prayers in the vernacular, the Our Father and the Hail Mary. The latter was a combination of the greetings given to Mary by the archangel Gabriel and St Elizabeth (Luke, 1,

28, 42), and was the standard form of invocation of the Virgin used in the western church in the later Middle Ages. The form then in use was briefer than that of the modern prayer:

> Hail Mary, full of grace, the Lord is with thee, blessed art thou among women, and blessed is the fruit of they womb, Jesus.

Gerson then gives a French translation of the Apostles' Creed and lists the seven sacraments. Details are provided only about two of them: the seven grades of holy orders are listed, as are the six branches of penance: contrition, confession and satisfaction, the three parts of sacramental confession; and fasting, almsgiving and prayer, the three chief kinds of penance. This had a direct pastoral application, since the catechism was used to prepare children for their first confession. The catechism ends with a long section on the afterlife. The seven gifts of glory are listed, that is, the blessings enjoyed by the saints in heaven. Three are for the soul: the direct vision of God, the love of God and an assurance of remaining in heaven forever; four are for the resurrected body: clarity, subtlety, agility and impassibility. This section seems over-ambitious, for although most people could probably understand the three gifts of the soul, concepts like agility relating to the resurrected body presupposed an intellectual training which they had not received. The catechism ends by listing the chief joys of paradise and the chief pains of hell.

But the greater part of the work is taken up with ethics and spirituality. Gerson lists the seven deadly sins, the seven contrary virtues, the ten commandments, the three theological virtues, the four cardinal virtues, the seven gifts of the Holy Spirit, the eight beatitudes, the seven spiritual works of mercy, the seven corporal works of mercy and the four evangelical counsels of perfection. There is thus a great imbalance between the doctrinal and moral content of the catechism. A far greater degree of sophistication is demanded of the candidate in grappling with Christian spirituality and ethics than with Christian belief.

Gerson gives no guidance about how these matters are to be explained: his catechism forms a framework within which priests may work, and whenever possible subjects are grouped together in sevens, a convenient mnemonic device. In the hands of a well educated and sensitive priest Gerson's text could have been used as the starting point for a quite wide-ranging consideration of the faith, but there must also have been well intentioned but stupid clergy who thought that they had fulfilled their duty if they made their charges learn this or some other catechism by heart without commentary.

If properly used Gerson's catechism no doubt achieved its object by giving lay people an understanding of the rudiments of their faith: the central doctrines are contained in the Apostles' creed and the exposition of the seven sacraments. The function of the institutional church could be explained by expounding the seven grades of holy orders, and the prayers which every Christian needed to know, the Our Father and the Hail Mary, could be examined clause by clause. Yet although this catechism shows that by the later Middle Ages the church was seriously attempting to train all its members in the practice of the Christian life, it suggests that it was content to provide them with an adequate but very simple understanding of the Christian faith. The same is true of works written for the advanced spiritual guidance of lay people by members of groups like the Brethren of the Common Life. The emphasis in such books is almost exclusively on devotional practice and little is said about intellectual faith. The authors seek to teach their readers how to pray, how to create a devout relationship between themselves and Christ, and how to lead holy lives, but they have little to say about doctrine.

This reticence is comprehensible. Medieval theology had been formulated in terms of scholastic logic. It had developed its own highly technical vocabulary and was the most taxing and rigorous intellectual discipline then known. To ask theologians to explain central Christian doctrines like the Trinity, the Atonement, baptismal regeneration and eucharistic sacrifice in terms which illiterate lay people could understand was like asking scientists now to explain quantum physics in terms comprehensible to people who have no concept of number. The gulf between the highly articulate and intellectual faith of trained theologians and the simple beliefs of the mass of the laity in the later Middle Ages was almost unbridgeable.

Theologically literate laymen

Yet by the fifteenth century a knowledge of Latin was no longer confined to the clergy. Since the twelfth century there had been some men, notably civil lawyers and doctors of medicine, who were not in holy orders, but who were university-trained and thus able to read theological works if they wished to do so. The number of men who were similarly circumstanced increased from the late fourteenth century as the Italian Renaissance, starting from Florence, came to affect most parts of western Europe. The renaissance humanists were not primarily interested in theology, which formed no part of their educational curriculum, but they had an excellent command of classical languages and the devout among them did not have to rely on vernacular treatises, mainly devotional in content, for their knowledge of the Catholic faith. Like the learned clergy they could read the Bible, the church service books, the Latin and sometimes the Greek Fathers, as well as works of scholastic theology.

There thus arose at the end of the Middle Ages a class of laymen who had a full knowledge of theology, and it is significant that when Luther's writings first reached England traditional teaching was defended by two laymen: Henry VIII, whose *Assertio Septem Sacramentorum* won him the title of Defender of the Faith from pope Leo X, and Thomas More, Speaker of the House of Commons, who in 1523 published the *Responsio ad convitia Martini Lutheri*.

12
Religious Observance I: The Sacraments

Baptism

Since the entire population of the medieval west was Christian, infant baptism was universal except in the mission-field. In most areas parish priests were given the right to baptize, although in some Italian cities until the central Middle Ages baptisms had normally to be performed in the baptistery attached to the main church. The holy oils used in baptism (together with those used in extreme unction) were blessed by the bishop each year on Maundy Thursday and distributed to his clergy, while priests blessed the waters of their fonts each Easter eve, but baptisms were not confined to Eastertide but were performed throughout the year.

Baptism was the sacrament of salvation. It freed a child from original sin and it was believed that if a baptized baby died it would go straight to heaven because it had committed no actual sin, whereas if it died unbaptized it would go to Limbo (see chapter 4). Since the infant mortality rate was extremely high, parents were anxious that their children should be baptized as soon as possible. The baptismal liturgy had been designed for adult converts and was long and elaborate. When used for infants, responses were made on the child's behalf by its godparents, of whom there were at least two, one of either sex. It was their duty to ensure that the child was instructed in the faith, but they also assumed secular obligations. Medieval godparents took their social duties seriously and treated godchildren as members of their own kin-group. For that reason baptism was an important social as well as religious occasion and it was the time at which a child was given his name.

The liturgy began with exorcisms and the godparents were then required to make a brief profession of faith on the child's behalf. The central part of the rite consisted of pouring water three times on the child's head with the words 'Baptizo te in nomine Patris et Filii et Spiritus Sancti' ('I baptize thee in the name of the Father and of the Son and of the Holy Spirit'). At that point the child was named, and in conclusion he was anointed with holy oil and marked with the sign of the cross.

If a child was in danger of death a shortened form of service might be used. This consisted in sprinkling water on him three times, using the baptismal formula cited above. Baptism in this form might be administered by anybody, even by a non-Christian, provided that they intended to do what the church intended to do when it baptized. This canon law ruling made it possible for a Christian woman living in a frontier region to arrange for the baptism of a sickly child if she were attended only by a Muslim midwife.

A large number of children must have been baptized by lay people, and chiefly by women, since men were not present during labour. All midwives and married women must have been instructed in how to baptize in an emergency. The sacrament might not be conferred twice, but if a sickly child lived it could be taken to church and anointed with oil and signed with the cross by a priest, although that was not essential. Because the sacrament could be conferred so easily, very few children can have died unbaptized in the Middle Ages.

Churching of women

The Purification of the Virgin (Luke, 2, 22) is the oldest of the Marian feasts observed by the church. Mary went to the Temple to be ritually cleansed after childbirth as Jewish law required, but the church understood the significance of her action differently, because clearly no ritual impurity could have attached to the birth of God's Son. From the sixth century Christian women were exhorted to imitate Mary by going to church to give thanks for the gift of a child, and in England this ceremony was known as churching. The priest met the woman at the door of the church, recited a few prayers of thanksgiving, sprinkled her with holy water and led her in to mass. Churching was not obligatory, but social pressures ensured that the custom was widely observed in the later Middle Ages.

Confirmation

Confirmation had originally been conferred immediately after baptism as part of a single rite of initiation, but during the Middle Ages the two sacraments became separated. Confirmation was very important because it conferred the seven gifts of the Holy Spirit (Acts, 8, 14–17), but since it could only be administered by a bishop it was often neglected. Medieval bishops had considerable secular duties, which left them with less time for religious functions, and poor communications made it impossible for them to visit all parts of their dioceses regularly. Consequently confirmations were performed erratically. The ceremony was brief: the bishop stretched his hand over the candidate's head and prayed that he receive the gifts of the Spirit, made the sign of the cross on his forehead with holy oil and read a few concluding prayers. There are accounts of bishops who confirmed children from horseback while riding through villages on their way to somewhere else.

It was not thought desirable to defer confirmation until adolescence. On the contrary, it was considered ideal to confer it as soon after baptism as possible. Some royal children were confirmed when only a few days old and it was normal to present for confirmation all the children of a parish who had been born since the bishop's last visit, irrespective of their age. Yet most people were never confirmed, and baptism alone was held to confer full membership of the church.

Marriage

Although the early church made rules about the marriages of its members, forbidding polygamy and divorce for example, the marriage ceremony remained entirely secular then. The earliest account of a church wedding in the west dates from the ninth century and such weddings did not become common until the

eleventh century when marriage law began to come exclusively under the jurisdiction of the church courts.

Theologians taught that marriage was the oldest of the sacraments, having
been instituted by God when he created man, and sanctioned for use by Christians through the presence of Jesus at the marriage of Cana. It was not an
ecclesiastical sacrament and the church had no part in conferring it: the ministers
were the bride and groom, the form of the sacrament were the vows which they
exchanged, and the sacrament operated through their sexual love, which became
a vehicle of God's grace.

The church did not devise a special rite of marriage: the marriage service used
in the Roman church, and subsequently adopted by most of the churches of the
west, was merely an adaptation of the ancient Roman civil rite of marriage. The
ceremony took place in the churchyard, or in bad weather in the church porch,
throughout the Middle Ages, a sign that it was not in origin a church service at all,
and the role of the officiating priest was simply that of chief witness. The medieval marriage service did not differ very much from that used in most churches
now. The couple first exchanged vows. In the Sarum Use, followed in much of
England, the groom said:

> I N. take thee N. to be my wedded wife, to have and to hold from this day forward, for
> better for worse, for richer for poorer, in sickness and in health, till death us depart, if
> holy church it will ordain, and thereto I plight thee my troth.

After the bride had plighted her troth in similar words (with no mention of
obeying her husband, which was a Protestant innovation), the groom placed gold,
silver and a ring on a plate, the priest blessed the ring and the groom said:

> With this ring I thee wed, and this gold and silver I thee give; and with my body I thee
> worship and with all my worldly chattels I thee endow, in the name of the Father, and
> of the Son and of the Holy Spirit. Amen.

The priest then blessed the couple and, if a nuptial mass was to follow, led them
into the church. A marriage accompanied by a mass was described as being
solemnized.

It was not essential to be married in church unless, as was the case in some
countries during the later Middle Ages, this was required by civil law. In much of
Italy throughout the medieval centuries marriages were contracted at a civil
ceremony in the presence of a notary. These were like modern Register Office
weddings, except that they had to conform to the requirements of canon law.

In an attempt to prevent clandestine marriages the Fourth Lateran Council of
1215 ordered that marriage banns should be called in the churches of the bride
and groom prior to a wedding. This provision lost much of its force, because
theologians decided that if two people, who were free to do so, took marriage vows
privately and then slept together they were validly married. Such a marriage
could be regularized by being publicly blessed by a priest, but it could not be
annulled. Parents objected strongly to this ruling which enabled their children to
make unsuitable marriages without their consent and allowed men to seduce girls
by offering them private marriages which they could subsequently deny had
taken place. The church did not change its position and on the whole continued to
regard marriage as a natural sacrament which need not take place in church, while
lay people, for social and legal reasons, encouraged church weddings.

Attendance at mass

Lay people were required to attend mass on Sundays and holy days for Christ himself had instituted the eucharist, whereas all other church services were of human devising and attendance at them was optional. The number of holy days kept increasing and at the end of the Middle Ages about fifty were observed in some parts of Europe. In the early Middle Ages people who lived in former Roman cities, which were well provided with churches, and noblemen who had domestic chaplains, could attend mass regularly, whereas in many rural areas there were no churches and mass was only said occasionally by a visiting priest from a local minster or monastery. People living in such places may have made an effort to walk to the nearest church to hear mass on great feasts, but they were unable to do this every week.

By the eleventh century rural parishes had been established throughout much of the west, while many towns had a superfluity of churches. In Henry II's reign (1154–89), for example, there were thirteen large conventual churches and 136 lesser churches in London and its suburbs. People were supposed to attend mass in their parish churches: in the country they had no alternative, but town-dwellers often attended the chapels of religious orders. Complaints were made about this from the twelfth century, but it was not until 1517 that Leo X declared that people might fulfil their obligation by hearing mass in any church they liked.

Since Sundays and holy days were public holidays everywhere, people after *c.*1100 had little excuse for not going to mass regularly unless they lived on remote farms. The mendicant Orders certainly tried to promote church attendance as part of their evangelization of the laity during the thirteenth century. They met with only a limited success among young men: complaints were regularly made in the later Middle Ages that apprentices played football while they should have been at mass, while menservants lounged and gossiped outside churches but seldom attended them. The friars did succeed in producing an extremely devout group of lay people who not only heard mass every Sunday but every weekday as well. Indeed, the most zealous among them sometimes heard four consecutive masses daily. Such commitment was exceptional, but a quite high proportion of laymen in the later Middle Ages did consider that they should put in an appearance at mass on most Sundays.

There was little inducement for them to attend the whole service unless they could read Latin. Rather more townsmen were able to read the vernacular in the later Middle Ages, but there were no vernacular translations of the missal because it was considered irreverent to translate the sacred text. There were some vernacular devotional works, but they were more like the mass books written now for the use of small children, which explain what the priest is doing, but do not give a text of the service. Thus the *Lay Folks Mass Book*, popular for centuries, first in a Norman French version and then in Middle English, paraphrased parts of the mass, like the *Gloria*, but provided a set of meditations to be read during the prayer of consecration:

> All my life and all my living
> Wholly have I of thy giving.
> Thou bought me dear with thy blood
> And died for me upon the rood . . .

Most lay people could not read and they had little to do in church. On certain feasts the congregation took an active part in the liturgy: walking in procession with lighted tapers at Candlemas and with palm branches on Palm Sunday, being signed with ashes on Ash Wednesday and venerating the cross on Good Friday, but this degree of participation was unusual. The early missionaries in northern Europe had taught their converts to join in the *Sanctus* and the *Agnus Dei*, but this practice was abandoned in the tenth century and thereafter western congregations made no responses during mass.

Throughout much of the Middle Ages lay communion was infrequent, but until the thirteenth century *pain bénit* was quite commonly distributed at the end of mass, a practice which persisted into this century in parts of France. This was an ancient custom, representing the sharing out of bread which had been offered for the celebration of mass but which had not been used at the consecration. Such bread was sprinkled with holy water and distributed to the non-communicant laity, who valued it because it gave them some share in the liturgy.

Sunday masses were usually sung, as canon law required, but if there was no sermon and nobody communicated mass only lasted about half-an-hour. Nevertheless, laymen became bored and wanted to know how much of the mass they needed to attend. Most theologians broadly accepted the opinion of Amalarius of Metz (†851) that a layman need only be present from the offertory to the final blessing, since it was during that part of the mass that Christ's sacrifice was pleaded. People therefore tended to come into mass at different points during the service, and the clergy also complained that they walked about the church and chattted to each other. Free movement was possible because most medieval churches had no seating for the congregation.

The one part of the mass in which lay people wished to share was the Elevation of the Host (see chapter 5). The congregation knelt in complete silence when handbells were rung and the celebrant held first the consecrated Host and then the consecrated chalice above his head. Christ had, in the opinion of the people, once again fulfilled the promise made at his Ascension, 'Lo, I am with you alway, even unto the end of the world' (Matt, 28, 20): they could look on their Saviour and plead his sacrifice for their needs.

The Elevation of the Host united the sophisticated and the simple in a common act of worship. St Thomas Aquinas, the *doctor angelicus*, wrote of it:

> Iesu, quem velatum nunc aspicio,
> Oro, fiat illud quod tam sitio;
> Ut, te revelata cernens facie,
> Visu sim beatus tuae gloriae.

(O Christ whom now beneath a veil we see/May what we thirst for soon our portion be/To gaze on thee unveiled and see thy face/The vision of thy glory and thy grace.)

The laity felt parallel sentiments. Matthew Paris relates how Henry III of England and Louis IX of France once discussed the relative merits of going to mass and hearing a sermon. In Matthew's view Henry III won the argument by saying that it was better to go to mass because it was always preferable to see a friend than to hear him well spoken of.

Many laymen undoubtedly felt that they had fulfilled their obligation by being present at the Elevation and left mass immediately afterwards; but a curious superstition developed among the devout urban laity in the later Middle Ages, who on Sundays ran from one church to another, trying to be present at as many Elevations as possible.

Confession and holy communion

Christians have always emphasized the importance of receiving holy communion only when in a state of grace. St Paul warned the Corinthians:

> Let a man examine himself, and so let him eat of that bread and drink of that cup. For he that eateth and drinketh unworthily, eateth and drinketh damnation to himself, not discerning the Lord's body. (I Cor., 11, 28–9)

Venial sins did not debar a man from holy communion, but mortal sins did and they could only be absolved in the sacrament of penance (see chapter 4).

Until the late sixth century the penitential system was very harsh: the sacrament could be administered only once in a lifetime, confession was public, the penance was long and severe and the penitent was, in addition, bound to refrain from fighting and to observe strict chastity for life. Those who had committed mortal sins tended to defer confession until they were dying and no longer able to perform penance, but meanwhile they did not communicate when they attended mass.

The number of those in that position steadily increased in the early Middle Ages, because there was a wide divergence between the way in which people in fact lived in the barbarian kingdoms of the west and the way in which the church taught that they should live. Society was violent, its sexual standards were different from those of the church and pagan religious practices were common, and all these things were mortal sins in the view of the church. Consequently few lay people made their communion at all.

In order to help laymen to escape from this *impasse* a new form of penance was introduced in France in the late sixth century by Celtic monks. It spread first to England, and then, by the ninth century, to the whole western church. This was auricular confession, in which the penitent confessed his sins privately to a priest, and it was an adaptation of the monastic practice of spiritual counselling, whereby a monk confessed venial sins to his director and sought advice about how to combat them. Auricular confession was intended to deal only with mortal sins, but unlike the older form of penance it could be repeated as often as necessary and the penitent was not bound to abstain from sex and fighting for life. At first absolution was only granted after the penance had been completed, but from the eleventh century the penitent was absolved immediately after his confession.

The penances enjoined by the new system remained extremely harsh. Earl Swegn Godwinson, the brother-in-law of Edward the Confessor, had to walk barefoot from Bruges to Jerusalem in 1052 as penance for treacherously murdering a kinsman, and although young and healthy he died at Constantinople on the return journey, worn out by its rigours. Less serious sins attracted less severe penances, but none of them were lenient, prolonged fasts on bread and water being common. Manuals were drawn up to guide priests in administering the sacrament, and Regino of Prüm, in the manual which he drew up in 906 for the archdiocese of Trier, directed priests to exhort their parishioners to make their confessions if necessary each Ash Wednesday.

Some laymen heeded these injunctions. From the early eleventh century there is evidence that some kings and queens had begun to appoint confessors, which implies that they used the sacrament regularly. Notorious offenders against public morality were sometimes forced to do penance, either because of the strength of social disapproval, or because they had been excommunicated by their bishop. Excommunication debarred a man from being present at church services, but it also sometimes had political consequences, for example, the vassals of an excommunicate ruler might renounce their allegiance to him. In such a case he had to seek reconciliation with the church in the sacrament of penance.

In some cases it was possible for rich men to circumvent the harshness of penance by practising commutation. This provision had been introduced to help sick penitents, but was open to abuse when more widely applied. Thus fifty psalms might be recited in lieu of a day's fasting, but a layman, who did not know the psalms, might substitute almsgiving. Not all penances could be commuted in this way, while payment in lieu of penance was not a practical alternative for most people. Clearly there was a large group of men who were deterred from making their confession by the harshness of the penitential system. This is evident from the enthusiasm with which the crusade indulgence of 1095 was greeted, for this allowed men to substitute fighting the infidel and making the pilgrimage to Jerusalem for all other kinds of canonical penance.

Crusaders made their confession when they took the cross, and they also went to confession on the eve of major battles during the campaign. This became a normal feature of war against the infidel and a form of general absolution was used if there were not enough priests present to hear individual confessions. *The Song of Roland*, written *c.*1100, describes this practice, which it anachronistically attributes to the time of Charlemagne: before the battle of Ronscevalles archbishop Turpin makes the Frankish warriors kneel and make an act of contrition; he then absolves them and imposes as their penance that they should fight hard against the enemy.

Relatively few people went to confession in peacetime, presumably because they were deterred by the long canonical penances. Alan of Lille (†1203) wrote, no doubt with some degree of exaggeration, 'there is scarcely a single layman or cleric who makes his confession once in a year'. This changed in 1215 when the Fourth Lateran Council enacted that all men aged fifteen and over and all women aged twelve and over should make their confession and receive holy communion once a year at Eastertide. In theory it was only necessary to confess mortal sins. People who had only committed venial sins might fulfil their obligation by declaring to their parish priest that they had done nothing worthy of penance in the past year. In practice this distinction was not observed, and for the first time the sacrament of penance began to be used for the confession of venial sins.

The mendicant orders took an important part in enforcing the new legislation. They had the pastoral skills needed in the confessional, which the parish clergy initially lacked. During the next 100 years bishops commissioned the writing of manuals of penance for the guidance of secular priests, and by the fourteenth century confession had become a regular part of Catholic practice. Some people, of course, never went to confession, but a high proportion of the population did so at Easter, while some devout laymen went more often. The sacrament, if skilfully used, enabled priests to give spiritual counsel to lay people about the practice of the Christian life, and in this way a rudimentary kind of spiritual direction was made available to all lay people for the first time.

Many people had only venial sins to confess and received correspondingly light penances, normally consisting in the private recitation of certain prayers, but harsh penances continued to be imposed for mortal sins. Thus the early fifteenth-century Castilian penitential of Cuidad enacts that:

> A falsifier of money, or of measures, or of [legal] instruments, or of agreements, shall abstain on bread and water as long as he lives.

As confession became more frequent, so did holy communion. Many people in the later Middle Ages made their communion at Easter, and a few devout laymen did so about once a month, but more frequent lay communion was very rare indeed. The laity received only the consecrated Host and not the chalice when they communicated. This practice was defended on the theological grounds that Christ was wholly present under the species of both bread and wine, a doctrine known as concomitance. The reason for lay communion in one kind is uncertain, but may simply have been the persistence of a long-standing custom: for centuries before 1215 laymen had normally only made their communion when dying, and had done so from the reserved sacrament, and for practical reasons only the consecrated Host was reserved in churches for the communion of the sick and dying.

Fasting and abstinence

The laity were obliged to keep the fasts ordained by the church. The eastern churches kept three main fasts each year, but although some western monasteries in the early Middle Ages adopted that practice it never became general. The western church kept one main fast only, that of Lent, which began on Ash Wednesday and lasted for forty days until Easter. There were also single fast days, on the eve of great feasts, which were scattered throughout the year, and all Fridays and Saturdays were days of abstinence, on which meat and animal products should not be eaten.

On all days of fasting and abstinence people were forbidden to eat meat or any other animal product, eggs, milk, cheese, butter, or cooking fat, although fish was allowed. On days of abstinence, like Fridays, they could eat as often as they liked, but on fast days there was a limit on the number of meals. In the early Middle Ages the rigorous fasting laws of the early church were still in force: people might not eat or drink until sunset and then they might have only one, meat-free meal. The Middle Ages witnessed a gradual relaxation of this austere regime, and this caused grave scandal among eastern Christians, who claimed that the west was abandoning the traditions of the apostolic church. In an age when there were few clocks, time was measured by the monastic Office, and by the tenth century western people had begun to eat the only meal of the day during Lent after Nones had been sung, that is at about three o'clock in the afternoon. As attitudes to fasting became more relaxed, monks began to sing Nones earlier during Lent, until in the later Middle Ages they were sung in the late morning and people ate their Lenten meal at about midday. They then, of course, began to feel hungry in the evenings, and from the thirteenth century permission was given to eat an additional light collation of bread and fruit, or vegetables, after sundown on fast days. The ban on drinking was relaxed completely: St Thomas Aquinas expressed the opinion that drink of any kind, including wine, did not break the fast.

Some groups of people were exempted from fasting, though not from abstinence: the sick, the destitute poor, and old people in weak health were exempt. Although it was generally agreed that fasting was unhealthy for young children, opinions varied about the age at which they should begin to fast. Some theologians placed it as early as ten, but Aquinas recommended twenty-one, because that marked the end of growth and this ruling was subsequently incorporated in canon law. It was always recognized that it was difficult for peasants, who performed heavy manual labour, to keep the fast, and from the ninth century they were allowed to eat eggs and cheese during Lent. In 1440 Eugenius IV ruled that:

> Artisans performing manual work, together with peasants, irrespective of whether they are rich or poor, are not bound under pain of mortal sin to keep the fasts.

By the later Middle Ages the western church had in effect abandoned fasting and merely observed days of abstinence. These must have been penitential for the nobility, who customarily ate a great deal of meat and regarded vegetables as food fit only for peasants, but the poor, who ate little meat normally, may not have noticed much difference. During Lent everybody abstained from meat, and failure to do so was in itself popularly thought to be evidence of heresy. The nobility and the middle classes also observed fairly strictly the prohibitions against eating eggs and milk products, for when, in the later Middle Ages, it became possible to obtain papal dispensations from those requirements, quite large numbers of people were anxious to take advantage of this. There is also some evidence that most people tried to keep the Friday abstinence throughout the year, though not that of Saturday, but it is difficult to determine how widely lay people kept the lesser fasts. No doubt it was easier for the prosperous to keep them because they cooked separate meals, whereas the poor tended to live from the contents of a constantly replenished stewpot. At most they may have tried to avoid adding meat to the stew on fast days, without necessarily trying to avoid eating the previous day's meat stock.

On fast days married people were supposed to abstain from sexual intercourse. In the later Middle Ages, when parish registers began to be kept, few children whose baptisms are entered appear to have been conceived during Lent, which suggests that church law may have succeeded in creating a social climate in which such conceptions were frowned upon. From the late tenth century the church also tried to dissuade warriors from fighting on fast days, and clearly met with some success. Chrétien de Troyes (†1191) in his *Perceval*, when wishing to portray his hero as completely distraught, makes him go riding fully armed on Good Friday, whereupon passers-by remonstrate with him because he is committing a terrible social solecism.

The last rites

When a man was dying a priest might be summoned to administer the last rites. He would hear the dying man's confession and give him the *viaticum*, or 'provision for the journey [to the next life]', that is, holy communion from the reserved sacrament. He would then administer extreme unction. The purpose of this sacrament is explained in the Epistle of James:

> Is there any sick among you? Let him call for the presbyters of the church: and let them pray over him, anointing him with oil in the name of the Lord. And the prayer of faith shall save the sick, and the Lord shall raise him up; and if he have committed sins they shall be forgiven him. (Jas., 5, 14 15)

Although instituted as a sacrament of healing, unction was, from the tenth century, used exclusively for the dying, to give them spiritual healing so that the Lord should 'raise them up' to eternal life. The words of St James were understood to mean that unction conferred the forgiveness of sins, and that dying men who were unconscious, or who had lost the power of speech, and were unable to make their confession, would nevertheless be absolved from their sins by virtue of this anointing. Children who died below the age of fourteen were not allowed to be anointed since it was believed that they could have committed no mortal sin and could need no spiritual healing.

Where possible the prosperous always received the last rites, but poor people frequently did not, because priests often charged fees for administering them which the poor were reluctant to pay. The church, while considering the devout reception of the last rites desirable, did not suppose it was essential. It taught that a dying man might make his confession to a layman if no priest were available, since although a layman had no power to absolve, God would in such a case grant absolution as a special dispensation of grace. If a man died suddenly, having had no opportunity to confess to anybody, the church assumed that he had made his peace with God unless there was manifest reason to believe otherwise. Excommunicates could be reconciled by any priest if in danger of death and, although suicides were considered to have damned themselves by self-slaughter, some theologians argued that they might enjoy God's mercy and could therefore be prayed for if there was any evidence that they had repented before they died. It was very rare indeed for the church to refuse Christian burial to a baptized member.

Funerals and requiem masses

The bodies of noblemen and rich burgesses were received into church on the night before the funeral and placed on a catafalque, surrounded by tall candles of unbleached wax, while clergy and kinsmen kept vigil beside them all night. In many parts of Europe older customs were followed by the common people: the body remained in the house overnight and a wake was held in honour of the dead.

A requiem mass was invariably said at every funeral to plead Christ's sacrifice for the repose of the dead man's soul, but most people wanted additional masses to be said to help that soul on its way through purgatory. In the early Middle Ages monasteries were the chief intercessors for the dead: there was then no limit on how many masses a priest could say each day and, as most monks were priested, monasteries could undertake to celebrate an almost indefinite number of requiems. This changed in the thirteenth century when priests were forbidden by canon law to say more than one mass on most days, while at the same time monastic vocations declined, so that communities were unable to accept many new mass obligations.

For this reason laymen began to endow chantry chapels, served by one or more priests who were bound to offer the mass and recite the Office of the dead every day for the souls of those listed in the deed of foundation. A huge number of chantries was founded all over western Europe in the later Middle Ages, some of them in existing churches, but some as separate foundations, and although a few were endowed only for a limited period, the majority were founded to say mass in perpetuity.

The multiplication of prayers for the dead became a prominent feature of late medieval piety. People living in towns, who could not afford to endow a chantry, often joined religious confraternities, one of whose functions was to organize regular masses for the souls of dead members, and even the very poor usually arranged for a mass to be said on the year's mind, the anniversary of the death, of close kinsmen. Those who had no family to perform this duty for them had to rely on the masses offered in all churches on 2 November, All Souls' Day, for all the faithful departed.

It is arguable that medieval people valued the institutional church above all else as intercessor for the dead. The laity could at need baptize their own children; they did not have to get married in church; some of them rarely if ever went to mass or received the sacraments; some did not even receive the last rites because they knew that their salvation was not contingent upon doing so; but everybody recognized that the church alone could pray them out of purgatory.

13
Religious Observance II: Popular Devotions

Once the age of persecutions had ended and Christianity had ceased to be the faith of a small group of committed believers and become instead the religion of a continent, a variety of forms of religious expression developed within a single church. The learned clergy were concerned not only with preserving the traditional faith but also with finding new ways of expressing it, but lay people too evolved new forms of devotion. There was not necessarily any conflict between the faith of the hierarchy and lay piety, since the learned clergy were themselves influenced by popular devotions and were prepared to sanction them provided that they were compatible with orthodox belief.

Popular movements which were contrary to traditional teaching were labelled heretical (see chapter 18) and from the twelfth century were liable to prosecution. Yet it would be wrong to suppose that the church, even after it had acquired coercive powers, always succeeded in imposing its interpretation of the faith on the laity. When, for example, the church taught that war against fellow Christians was a sin, the military class largely ignored this; when the church condemned usury as a mortal sin this was ignored by all ranks of society. Christianity developed in the way it did during the Middle Ages because of the interaction between learned orthodoxy and lay piety, and both sides contributed equally to this. A number of practices became extremely popular which, although sanctioned by the church, were not considered obligatory parts of the Christian life. Some attention needs to be given to them in order to understand medieval Catholicism fully.

Votive masses

There was complete agreement between clergy and laity that the mass was the most powerful form of intercession which could be offered to God and it was customarily pleaded for the needs of the entire congregation. There were, however, always exceptions: funeral masses were said for a personal intention, the repose of the soul of the deceased. This practice was extended during the Middle Ages and masses were then said for a whole range of private intentions. These were known as votive masses and became extremely popular. They could be offered for any intention compatible with orthodox Christian teaching. Lay people paid priests to say them, and they were normally celebrated privately, with only a server and sometimes the donor in attendance, although the donor felt no obligation to be present and frequently stayed away. This reflected the medieval attitude of lay people towards their clergy: the chief function of the priesthood was not to lead prayers, but to offer prayers and masses on behalf of the whole of society.

The cult of the saints

The church taught that all its members had direct access to God through Christ, but medieval laymen found it difficult to approach God directly. They experienced Christ's presence among them at mass in the Elevation of the Host and this filled them with awe. They were very conscious of Christ's divinity, but found difficulty in accepting that he shared their humanity. In times of great need they arranged for priests to offer mass on their behalf, but in their private prayers they turned for help to the saints rather than to Christ. The saints had once been ordinary men and women, but had become members of the court of heaven, where, like members of any earthly court, they enjoyed positions of patronage and power. They were more approachable than God because they were less awe-inspiring.

It is sometimes said that the newly converted peoples of western Europe, who had formerly worshipped many gods, remained polytheists beneath a thin Christian veneer and worshipped many saints instead, some of whom were pagan gods with new names. Such a view is insufficiently nuanced. The laity on the whole seem to have accepted the church's ruling that God alone might be worshipped, whereas the saints might be venerated and invoked, while failing to grasp fully the absolute distinction which the church made between the godhead and any created being.

The saints were popularly held in great reverence, but they were not worshipped. When the consecrated Host was carried through the streets people knelt because they were in the presence of God, but they did not kneel when statues of the saints were carried in procession. Moreover, the laity never attempted to confess their sins to the saints, recognizing that they were powerless to forgive them.

Nevertheless, the saints were regarded by the laity as having power in their own right. Some kinds of prayer encouraged this belief. Normally lay people were taught to invoke the saints in the form, 'St X pray for us', which reminded them that the saints depended on God's help just as they did themselves, but some prayers asked the saint directly for help, for example, 'Holy archangel Michael defend us'. Similarly the Hail Mary, the invocation of the Virgin which everybody knew, was said in the Middle Ages in a purely Biblical form (see chapter 11), and therefore consisted in the praise of the Virgin Mother, in association with her divine Son, but contained no obvious reference to Mary's subordination to God. It was therefore possible for poorly instructed laymen to think of the saints as minor divinities, even though they did not merit the worship owed to God alone and were powerless to forgive sins.

The saints were universally credited with the power of working miracles in their own right. This was a simplification of the church's teaching that miracles were only performed by God, but that God sometimes acted in response to the prayers of a saint, or sometimes empowered a saint to act as his minister in performing a miracle. The medieval church found much the same difficulty in explaining this distinction to its members as the Apostles themselves had done when they were empowered to work miracles during their earthly lives (e.g. Acts, 14, 8–18).

The saints were popularly credited with almost unlimited powers. They could cure diseases, save their petitioners from natural disasters like shipwrecks and earthquakes, preserve women from sexual assault, defend the poor from oppression, and ward off the temptations, and sometimes the physical assaults, of the powers of evil. In the popular mind the saints represented the forces of divine order in a very insecure and hostile world: they afforded protection against natural disasters, they were an incorruptible court of appeal from the inadequacies of human justice and they were a spiritual police force which protected men against diabolical malice.

The saints were very real to medieval people. They moved through the world and could, if they wished, manifest themselves to the faithful. Thus St Odo of Cluny called one day in 936 on an elderly recluse who lived near his abbey and found that the old man had just received a visit from St Martin of Tours, who had told him:

> I come from Rome and I am going to France and as my journey brought me near to you, I turned aside to visit you. . . . Today is the coronation of Louis, king of the Franks, and I am hastening to be present at the anointing, so I am unable to delay.

The popular and learned traditions were in complete agreement about regarding Mary, the Mother of Jesus, as the greatest of all saints. An extensive range of miracles was attributed to her and she occupied a central place in the religious life of the entire west. It is worth noting that the rosary, which is now considered one of the chief Marian devotions, was not so important in the Middle Ages. Its use is first securely attested in twelfth-century Cistercian monasteries, where it was said by the lay brethren as an alternative to the choir Office, for the rosary has 150 beads, the same number as the psalms, so that the lay brethren who knew no Latin were able to substitute a Hail Mary for a psalm. The rosary was made popular among the laity through the work of the Dominican preacher, Alan de la Roche (†1475), but until the fifteen mysteries became fixed in *c.*1500 it could only profitably be used as a method of meditation as part of public prayers directed by a priest. Its widespread use as a form of private meditation belongs to the early modern period.

In the early Middle Ages saints were chosen by popular acclaim, although bishops always reserved the right to veto a new cult (see chapter 8). In most cases there was no disagreement between the bishop and the laity, for most saints were well-attested historical figures, venerated either for the sanctity of their lives or the manner of their deaths. Yet some popular cults needed to be justified in orthodox terms to the church hierarchy, and this was achieved by inventive hagiographers.

An example of this is the cult of the well which gave its name to Holywell in north Wales. Its sanctity was attributed to St Winifred, a seventh-century virgin, who was said to have been beheaded by a local nobleman, Caradoc of Hawarden, who was enraged that she had rejected his advances. A spring miraculously gushed from the ground where her head fell, and this became the source of the holy well, but this did not mark the end of St Winifred's career on earth: St Bueno miraculously joined her head on to her body again, and she was thus able to spend the remaining fifteen years of her life as abbess of a Celtic double monastery. Her *Life* was not written until some 500 years after these events are alleged to have occurred and it is reasonable to infer that the account of her beheading was inserted to justify the veneration of this well as a Christian shrine in terms which the hierarchy would accept.

When the papacy assumed control of canonization in the twelfth century it became more difficult to sustain popular cults which had no historical foundation, but it was still possible to do so provided that local commitment to such cults was strong enough. Thus shortly before 1261 the Dominican inquisitor, Stephen of Bourbon, discovered that women in the Dombes, in the diocese of Lyons, venerated St Guinefort as a child healer. Stephen was much edified by this until he was told that this saint was not, as he had supposed, a holy man, but a greyhound. A legend was associated with this hound, which is common to most Indo–European peoples: he had defended his master's child against a wild beast (in Guinefort's case a huge snake), but had been suspected by his master of killing the child and had been wrongfully stabbed to death by him. On learning this, Stephen of Bourbon went to the cult centre in a local wood and there disinterred and burnt the dog's bones.

Stephen does not record how old this cult was, nor does he explain why the greyhound was named after a saint who was venerated as a martyr in the diocese of Milan. The cult of St Guinefort in the Dombes may represent the survival of a pagan cult in Christian form, analogous to that of the dog-headed St Christopher in the Greek church, but it is impossible to be sure about this. What is significant is that despite the disapproval of the institutional church represented by an inquisitor, the holy greyhound Guinefort continued to be venerated in the Dombes area until the present century.

The church did not approve of the veneration of animals: the only non-human creatures which it held lawful to invoke were the angels. Prayer might be addressed to any member of the nine choirs, but the most popular cult was that of the archangel Michael, commander of the hosts of heaven, who was venerated by warriors, particularly by the Normans, and whose chief shrines were at Monte Gargano in Apulia and the Mont Saint-Michel in Brittany.

The cult of relics

The spiritual powers of a saint were believed to inhere in his relics, both in his primary relics, that is his physical remains, and in his secondary relics, his personal possessions or the places in which he had lived. A desire to collect relics is common to all ages: in our own society it takes the form of acquiring autographed photographs and other memorabilia of sportsmen and pop stars. But medieval people felt more than a sentimental attachment to relics: they believed that they put them in contact with the wonder-working saints in heaven. As Peter Brown has persuasively argued, far from being a perpetuation of pagan religious practices under a Christian veneer, the cult of relics was a Christian innovation, viewed with horror by the pagans of late antiquity, who regarded its chief manifestation, a reverence for corpses, as a pollution.

In origin the cult of relics was a popular devotion, but it was one which the institutional church was able to assimilate. It accepted that God might work miracles by means of relics, because he had allowed the sick to be healed and demoniacs to be cured in the first century at Ephesus with handkerchiefs and aprons brought from the body of St Paul (Acts, 19, 12). The early church had, in a decorous way, shown its respect for relics by celebrating mass on the tombs of the martyrs on the anniversaries of their deaths. The church therefore licensed the cult of relics, but did not make it an obligatory part of Christian devotion. The hierarchy reserved the right to authenticate relics and to destroy those which were spurious.

The most revered relics were those associated with Christ, the greatest of which was the holy cross, excavated at Jerusalem in 330 under the auspices of the empress Helena, mother of Constantine the Great. The cross was lost to the Christian world in 1187 when Saladin captured it at the battle of Hattin, but for some centuries previously fragments had been detached and sent to the west, like the one which the emperor Justin II (565–78) presented to the convent of the Holy Cross at Poitiers. Greater contact with the eastern Mediterranean in the time of the crusades resulted in the west's acquiring other relics of the Passion. In 1239 St Louis of France purchased the crown of thorns from the Latin emperor of Constantinople and built the Sainte Chapelle in Paris, perhaps the most beautiful shrine in the Gothic world, to house it; while both Trier cathedral and the parish church of Argenteuil claimed to have the seamless robe which Christ had worn to his crucifixion.

There could be no primary relics of the Virgin, who was believed to have been bodily assumed into heaven, but the places where she had lived on earth, together with her empty tomb outside Jerusalem, were shown to pilgrims to the Holy Land, while the church of Constantinople claimed to possess her cloak. In the west a painting of the Mother of God, said to have been made during her lifetime by St Luke, was shown at Sta Maria Maggiore in Rome, and was credited with the same miraculous powers as a relic; while in 1470 the claim was made that after the Muslim conquest of the Holy Land in 1291 the Holy House of Nazareth had been moved by angels, first to Yugoslavia and finally to Loreto near Ancona, where it might still be seen.

Relics were universally revered but unevenly distributed. Rome, the city of martyrs, had the greatest collection in the west, and a brisk trade was conducted in them during the early Middle Ages, bodies being dismembered so that their graces might be shared more widely. John the Scot (†877) commented:

> Rome, when the saints were alive you wounded them and cut them down;
> And now that they are dead, you cut them up and sell the assorted parts.

There was a ready market for saints' bones and most people were not over-scrupulous about how they were obtained. Anybody of substance who visited Rome or the Holy Land was expected to bring back relics for the local churches, and enterprising travellers stole relics with the same degree of panache with which nineteenth-century visitors to the Levant stole classical works of art. Thus in 1087 the merchants of Bari in Norman south Italy presented to their cathedral the relics of St Nicholas which they had looted from his shrine at Myra in south-eastern Asia Minor.

Some people were willing to go to bizarre lengths to satisfy their passion for relics. St Francis was considered a saint during his lifetime and, when he fell sick at Cortona in 1226 and expressed a wish to die at Assisi, the council of that city had to send an armed escort to accompany his litter, in order to prevent other cities on his route from forcibly detaining him so that they might possess his relics when he died. These relic hunters were at least prepared to let St Francis die naturally, but some 200 years earlier the peasants of Cuxa in the Pyrenees had attempted to murder their local hermit, St Romuald, when he told them that he intended to return to his native Italy, in order to be certain that his relics would remain in their village.

It was, of course, comparatively easy for the unscrupulous to impose on the credulity of the simple by faking relics. Boccacio tells of a friar who used to exhibit to the astonished gaze of the people a feather shed by the archangel Gabriel at the Annunciation, and how some students sought to embarrass him by secretly burning it and leaving the ashes in the reliquary. The friar proved equal to this, for when he discovered the substitution, at the climax of his sermon, he claimed that a miracle had taken place and that the feather of St Gabriel had been transformed into the ashes of St Lawrence, burned to death on a gridiron.

Although the cult was open to abuse, most people, both learned and simple alike, took relics very seriously. The church treasuries and museums of Europe are now full of medieval reliquaries, fashioned in gold and silver and embellished with cabuchon jewels and Limoges enamels, which were made to house saints' bones. Moreover, the entire west is full of great shrine churches and chapels which were built to house the more important of these relics.

Pilgrimages

Although pilgrimage was sometimes enjoined as a penance, it was not an essential part of Christian practice. Nevertheless, a large number of medieval people undertook long and difficult pilgrimages at least once in a lifetime. Jerusalem and the Holy Land were the greatest pilgrimage centres and never lost their pre-eminence, although after the fall of the crusader kingdom in 1291 the Mamluk rulers restricted western pilgrims to certain seasons of the year and normally only admitted parties who came by sea to the port of Jaffa. The most difficult pilgrimage was that to the Mount Sinai monastery, but there were always some western Christians throughout the Middle Ages who were prepared to make the desert journey there by camel.

The chief pilgrimage centre of the west was Rome, the burial place of Sts Peter and Paul, but from *c.*1200 three other shrines came almost to vie with it in importance, those of Compostella, Canterbury and Cologne. The relics of the Apostle James were 'discovered' at Compostella in the ninth century and the fame of this inaccessible Galician shrine grew steadily thereafter. Canterbury achieved fame all over western Europe with remarkable speed in the years immediately following the martyrdom of St Thomas Becket in 1170. Cologne owed its eminence to the translation there in 1164 of the bones of the Magi, who had visited Christ at Bethlehem, which had been discovered during the demolition of a church in Milan six years before. The Magi were credited with occult knowledge and it was thought that they could protect their votaries against witchcraft and this made their shrine at Cologne extremely popular.

Many shrines possessed considerable importance in a particular region, like that of Our Lady of Rocamadour in central France, famous for its image of the Virgin, or that of Our Lady of Walsingham, in Norfolk, which contained a chapel modelled on the Holy House of Nazareth. This cult, introduced it would seem by a local nobleman who had visited the Holy Land in the twelfth century, made Walsingham the most revered Marian shrine in England in the later Middle Ages. There were also a countless number of small shrines which enjoyed only a local reputation, but were focuses of piety at parish level.

Pilgrims were inspired by a wide range of motives. Some sought help for themselves or for others; some wished to fulfil pilgrimage vows which they had made in times of crisis; some went to give thanks for blessings received, while others went to do penance for their sins; and there were always those like friar Felix Fabbri of whom Hilda Prescott has written so engagingly whose primary reason for going on pilgrimage was a love of travel.

The best known medieval pilgrimage to most English speaking people is that described in the *Canterbury Tales*, but it would be misleading to consider that as normative. The distance from London to Canterbury is only about sixty miles and the route in Chaucer's day lay through peaceful and prosperous countryside. Such favourable conditions did not obtain in the case of more distant pilgrimages. Journeys of that kind were always slow: a rich man could travel as fast as a good horse could ride, a poor man as fast as he could walk. It was impossible to estimate how long a distant pilgrimage might take because there were too many imponderable factors, so all those who undertook such journeys knew that they were leaving their families and friends for an indefinite length of time. The rich arguably sacrificed more by going on pilgrimage than the poor did, for although they could afford to travel in more comfort, they had to delegate the management of their affairs to others for long periods of time and to jeopardize their careers by long absences from their native land.

Pilgrimages could also be very hazardous. Even in Europe brigandage was common, while those who went to the Holy Land were in danger of being captured by Muslim pirates and sold into slavery if they travelled by sea, or of being caught up in warfare between Christian and Muslim states if they went by land. Natural hazards, like storms at sea and epidemic diseases to which the traveller had no immunity, combined to make the death rate among pilgrims high.

Yet people were not deterred by these hardships. The roads of medieval Europe were thronged with pilgrims of all ages and social classes. The rich could afford to pay their expenses, but poor pilgrims had to beg. This was easier in medieval society than it would be now, because people were more conditioned to the presence of beggars and considered it a meritorious act to help some poor person to make a pilgrimage.

Shrines were conceived as places where earth and heaven intersected and at which spiritual forces were focused. Christianity, whose central doctrine is the Incarnation, belief in the physical presence of God in the created world, could accommodate the popular cult of pilgrimage without any sacrifice of principle.

Indulgences

The first offer of a general indulgence was that made by Urban II in 1095 to those who were willing to support the first crusade, and it owed its popularity in part to the fact that it combined pilgrimage to Jerusalem with the idea of holy war. Those who took the cross then admittedly had mixed motives, but any attempt to interpret the popularity of crusading in terms which exclude religious motivation has to be formulated without regard to the evidence, which shows conclusively that religious considerations were central to the thought of a high proportion of crusaders. The general indulgence of 1095 was not a soft option offering salvation on easy terms to lukewarm Catholics: a high proportion of those who took part in the crusade were killed in battle or died as a result of the rigours of the journey, while many of the survivors suffered long-term damage to their health. Men took the cross partly because the crusade was a congenial substitute for canonical penance (see chapter 4), but also because they valued the opportunity of performing a religious act on their own terms, by risking their lives for Christ, who had given his life for them.

Each new crusade was accompanied by the offer of a plenary indulgence and the movement remained popular until 1396 when the last great crusade to leave the west was decimated by the Ottoman Turks on the field of Nicopolis. Abuses had by then crept into the system, in that some men took the cross merely in order to enjoy the legal privileges which it conferred, but with no intention of fulfilling their vow except, if pressed, by paying somebody else to act on their behalf. Nevertheless, the majority of crusaders remained ready to risk their lives in battle in order to prove their devotion to the faith.

Crusades were designed primarily to appeal to the military class but there were many other people who would have liked the opportunity to obtain a plenary indulgence. Partial indulgences did exist, but these were merely a traditional method of commuting penance. Early medieval penitentials had, for example, sometimes permitted the substitution of a stated number of lashes with a flail for a period of fasting on bread and water. From the twelfth century the papacy began to attach indulgences of this kind to devotional acts, such as reciting certain prayers, or listening to a sermon. The performance of such an indulgenced act was reckoned equivalent to a stated number of days of traditional penance: thus listening to a sermon might be accounted as penitential as fasting for 100 days on bread and water. In the later Middle Ages this spiritual currency was attacked by inflation, so that it became possible to collect thousands of days of indulgence by playing the system correctly. By that time the old system of penance was seldom used, so that lay people were unclear about the meaning of the time factor involved in indulgences and commonly thought that it conferred a reduction of the time that they would have to spend in purgatory, which was a misconception since purgatory is a timeless state. Partial indulgences were intended to help the lukewarm to make good the deficiencies in their religious practice, but they were sought after chiefly by the devout who, presumably, did not need them.

The lukewarm were interested in obtaining plenary indulgences, so that when in 1300 pope Boniface VIII inaugurated a Jubilee year and offered a plenary indulgence to all those who made the pilgrimage to Rome this proved very popular. Unlike the crusade indulgence the Jubilee indulgence was not directed to the members of a single profession. It was particularly attractive because confessors in the city of Rome were granted faculties to absolve reserved sins (even those which were reserved to the pope) and to dispense from all vows except those of marriage and the monastic life. People flocked to Rome from all over the western world to obtain the indulgence and to make the pilgrimage of a lifetime to the chief shrine of the Latin church. Even Dante, who hated Boniface VIII, hailed the Jubilee year as a great religious event. Boniface had intended that a Jubilee should only be celebrated every century, but in 1343 Clement VI reduced the period to fifty years and in 1470 Paul II reduced it to twenty-five. This increase in frequency is an indication of the popularity of Jubilee years, for each generation wished to be able to participate in one of them. All the Jubilees were well supported, even that of 1350 which took place when the pope was resident in Avignon so that there was only a cardinal to preside over the ceremonies.

Because indulgences were so popular they became more widely available in the later Middle Ages. Some were offered in return for almsgiving and this looked dangerously like simony, the sale of holy things. In 1457 Calixtus III ruled that indulgences might be applied to the needs of the holy souls in purgatory: that is, those who obtained indulgences might offer them to God for the use of the faithful departed. It was the issue by Leo X of a plenary indulgence, applicable to the dead and obtainable in return for almsgiving, which led Luther to make his initial protest against traditional Catholic practice.

That dispute lies beyond the scope of this book, but what Luther was protesting against was less the official text of the indulgence than the popular understanding of it. The official wording of grants of indulgence was normally extremely cautious and theologically unexceptionable, for those documents were drafted by expert canon lawyers, anxious to avoid any suspicion of heresy. From the beginning indulgences had been hedged about with strict conditions: the crusade indulgence of 1095 had specified that its benefits would be received only by those who sincerely repented their past sins and had been absolved from them in sacramental confession, and who undertook the journey to Jerusalem from unmixed motives, out of a desire to honour God and to save their own souls. The problem with this and with later grants was that few people read the text of the indulgence; they knew only what preachers told them about it. Preachers tended to oversimplify the issues and, like good salesmen in any age, not to draw their audience's attention to the small print in the agreement. This had the effect of making indulgences more popular because they were made to seem an easy means of obtaining grace.

The abuses to which indulgences gave rise in the late Middle Ages should not be allowed to obscure the positive contribution which they made to the life of the western church. They were introduced as a way of helping lay people who were unwilling to perform traditional penances and who were thereby effectively cut off from the practice of the Christian life. A plenary indulgence had two effects: it allowed men to substitute an indulgenced act for other kinds of penance, and it restored them to the communion of the church as soon as they made their confession, which they were required to do in order to be eligible for the indulgence. If people did not meet the very high conditions which grants of indulgence stipulated only the first of those two effects was invalidated. In such a case the indulgenced act could not be guaranteed adequate as a substitute for other kinds of penance, but this could not, of course, be known for sure until the next life. The second effect of the indulgence was not affected by this: a man who went to confession and received absolution in preparation for acquiring an indulgence was undoubtedly restored to the communion of the church. In that sense the system of indulgences arguably did achieve its purpose as an instrument of pastoral care.

14

The Practice of the Christian Life

The Virtues and Vices

The church's founder defined the aim of the Christian life as perfection. This could not be achieved by observing moral precepts, for as he pointed out in the parable of the Pharisee and the publican, upright public behaviour might be totally valueless in the sight of God if wrongly motivated, and he also taught that there is no value in refraining from immoral acts if one consents to them in one's heart. In Christ's view virtuous behaviour was a consequence of holiness not a cause of it.

The church could not therefore exhort its members to observe some ethical code, such as the Ten Commandments, but had to train them in the life of perfection. Christians needed to be given a spiritual framework of reference against which they could measure their own motivation and behaviour and that framework needed to be flexible enough to be used by the learned and simple alike. Two formulae were devised in the patristic age which met this need, the seven virtues and the seven deadly sins.

St Paul had defined the three chief virtues as love, which was the nature of God himself, hope and faith. The Fathers called these the three theological virtues, because they were not natural to man in his fallen state but were implanted in him by God at his baptism. Classical Greek thinkers had considered that the most important virtues were prudence, temperance, courage and justice. The Fathers called these the cardinal virtues which, they held, were natural to all men, pagan and Christian alike.

Theologians took longer to reach agreement about which were the most serious sins, but Gregory I (†604) argued that there were seven deadly sins and his computation has been accepted ever since, partly, no doubt, because it balances the list of seven virtues. The sins, in order of importance, are pride, envy, anger, sloth, avarice, gluttony and lechery. They were called deadly because each of them, if practised persistently, could damn the soul by destroying its capacity to love. Their order was determined by the degree to which they offended against love. Thus lechery is a wrong love of other people, gluttony a wrong love of pleasure, avarice a wrong love of material possessions. These sins are the least serious because they involve some attachment to God's creation, however misdirected it may be. Sloth is more serious because it is produced by an absence of love for God or for his creation. The three most serious sins are those which replace love by hate or contempt. Anger is the least serious, for though inspired by hatred of others it does not dispute their right to exist, whereas envy is resentful of the existence of other people who have gifts which it lacks. Pride is the most deadly sin of all because it scorns all other creatures and wishes to be like God.

Lay knowledge of the virtues and vices

Throughout the Middle Ages the hierarchy emphasized that all lay people should be taught about the seven virtues and the seven deadly sins. These instructions were sometimes disregarded completely, and some priests supposed that they had done their duty if they made their parishioners learn the lists of the virtues and vices, but some people were given quite detailed teaching about them. This groundwork of knowledge could be reinforced by spiritual counselling provided throughout the life of an adult Catholic in the confessional. Numerous penitential manuals written after 1215, and even some which were written earlier, advised priests about the kinds of guidance which they should offer penitents who had committed particular sins. This system was only fully operative in the case of devout lay people, like those influenced by the *Devotio Moderna*, who went to confession frequently, always used the same confessor and were willing to spend time in examining their consciences. Most people received little spiritual direction in the confessional, since they went only at Easter, when there were long queues and priests were too busy to do more than make a few perfunctory remarks.

Manuals of instruction and manuals of penance drew on an enormous and continually growing literature about the spiritual life. That they did succeed in making some parts of the learned tradition available to lay people cannot be doubted. Gerson in his *ABC des simples gens* lists the seven contrary virtues as something which all lay people should be taught. These derive from the *Psychomachia*, or 'Battle for the Soul', an epic poem written by Prudentius (†410) in which he discussed which virtues were most effective in countering the deadly sins. He argued that chastity was the best defence against lechery; abstinence against gluttony; liberality against avarice; diligence against sloth; patience against wrath; brotherly kindness against envy; and humility against pride. These are the seven contrary virtues which Gerson thought everybody should know about.

Many lay people may not have been as well instructed as Gerson would have wished, and most of them may have had little skilled counselling in the confessional, nevertheless, most of them must have become aware, through going to confession, that the gravity of a sin depended less on what was done than on the reasons for its being done. The church was concerned to determine whether a sinner could plead what would now be called diminished responsibility and the penance enjoined varied accordingly. An eighth-century penitential, sometimes ascribed to Bede, has this to say about abortion, for example:

It makes a great deal of difference whether a poor woman [has an abortion] on account of the difficulty of supporting [the child] or whether a prostitute does so for the sake of concealing her wickedness.

In this way most people must have become aware that right and wrong conduct did not consist in doing some things and refraining from others, but was contingent on a man's interior disposition.

It is impossible to tell how far the people of western Europe practised the kinds of spirituality which the church advocated. Except in the case of some monastic clergy, the materials for a study of that kind do not exist for the medieval period. But the social consequences of the church's teaching can be examined and these do provide some measure of the impact which Christian spirituality had made on the lives of western people.

Society and the seven deadly sins

The church did not have to impose a completely new set of ethical standards on the peoples of western Europe, for there was much common ground between Christians and pagans over matters of morality. Nevertheless, there were also important points of difference, and it is in those areas that the degree of success which the church achieved in securing the adoption of Christian values can best be assessed. These issues of public morality will be considered under the headings of the seven deadly sins, because in the church's view every kind of immoral behaviour was an expression of one of those sins.

Pride

The church considered that pride was the gravest sin and it took many forms. For example, heresy was caused by pride, and that will be considered in Part III. The church had great difficulty in persuading the warrior class that pride was a sin at all, for in all the pagan societies of the west warriors had considered it a virtue and that attitude persisted long after their conversion. The concept of chivalry developed chiefly as a result of the church's attempts to persuade the knightly class to adopt Christian standards of conduct (see chapter 8) but it did not entirely fulfil its desired purpose. Knights were prepared to accept, at least in theory, that they had a duty to defend the church of God and to protect the weak from oppression. What they refused to accept, because it ran counter to their entire training, was the desirability of 'turning the other cheek'. They were quick to take offence if they considered that their honour had been impugned, often for the most trifling reasons, and to challenge their opponents to duels which frequently ended in death. It is clear from the large body of courtly romances written from the twelfth century onwards, which portray an idealized society living in accordance with the chivalric code, that the concept of honour formed an integral part of that code, and that the church had failed to persuade the knightly class of the merits of humility.

Envy and anger

The chief expressions of the sin of envy are jealousy and malice, which lack glamour and are a source of social discord. On the whole public opinion was broadly in agreement with the church's teaching about them.

Many of the sins of anger proved more controversial. It was universally agreed that wilful murder was wrong but no consensus existed about revenge killings. In pagan Germanic and Scandinavian society the kin of a murdered man were allowed to refuse to accept monetary compensation and instead to take vengeance on his killer. The church regarded revenge killings of this kind as murder and gradually succeeded in persuading rulers to amend the laws so that such practices were forbidden. Yet even after this had been done the vendetta persisted in many parts of Europe and was even viewed with some indulgence in cases of *crime passionelle*. The church was equally unsuccessful in its attempts to convince soldiers that it was a sin to kill fellow Christians in battle.

It did succeed in ending the custom of child exposure. It had been common in imperial Rome and in the barbarian societies of the west before the conversion to expose unwanted, newborn children, particularly girls, to the elements. The church regarded this as murder and persuaded rulers to amend the laws so that children were given legal protection from the time of their birth. This effected a revolution in the status of children, who were no longer regarded as chattels over whom their parents had absolute power, but as baptized Christians with guaranteed legal rights.

Abortion was also considered one of the sins of anger. Some theologians took the view that the foetus was not a living soul during the first six weeks after conception and that although abortion during that time was blameworthy, in as much as it prevented the growth of potential life, it was a less serious sin than a later abortion when the foetus was potentially human. All women who confessed to having abortions were given severe penances, but only those who had abortions after six weeks were considered guilty of the sin of murder, and their penances were correspondingly more severe.

Sloth

Although in theological terms sloth is as deadly a sin as any of the others, it was not, during the Middle Ages, regarded with the same degree of disapproval as the rest by society at large. Neglect of one's duties was censured by the church, but, except in some austere monasteries, work was not considered meritorious for its own sake in the Middle Ages. There were two reasons for this: one was that because conditions of life throughout most of the period were very harsh for almost everybody, including the nobility, they did not need to be reminded of Adam's curse, 'In the sweat of thy face shalt thou eat bread' (Gen., 3, 19). Indeed, anybody who could eat without working was regarded as in some measure blessed by God. Sloth was also regarded with tolerance because of the church's teaching about the deadly sin of avarice, for the slothful were, by temperament, little concerned about material possessions.

Avarice

Avarice consists in an inordinate attachment to possessions. It encompasses theft of other people's property, the miserly hoarding of one's own goods, and a refusal to share one's goods with others. It engenders a meanness of spirit, an unwillingness to give oneself to others and, in extreme forms, a reluctance to die because one is unwilling to give one's life into the keeping of God.

The church and society were at one in condemning theft, but the church also condemned miserliness and, indeed, carefulness about worldly goods. One of the counsels of perfection was Christ's injunction to the rich young ruler, 'Sell that thou hast and give to the poor and thou shalt have treasure in heaven' (Matt., 19, 21). The vow of personal poverty was taken by all monastic clergy, whose way of life was the model to which lay piety aspired (see chapter 8). It is true that the corporate ownership of property by religious communities tended to make nonsense of the avowed aim of monastic poverty, but society saw this as an abuse of a valid ideal. Critics of the monasteries did not question the principle of poverty but the failure to implement it.

The aristocracy shared the church's attitude towards avarice. A nobleman should not be parsimonious: he should reward his followers generously and show his disregard for material possessions by ostentatious expenditure. Such attitudes among the warrior class had been considered praiseworthy in the poetry of the heroic age, before their conversion, and continued to be praised in the courtly literature of the later Middle Ages. The church taught that liberality was the contrary virtue to avarice, but it did not understand liberality in the same way as the nobility. Aristocrats were concerned to spend lavishly in order to prove that they were indifferent to wealth, whereas the church encouraged the liberal use of wealth to help the poor. Nevertheless, the two ideals influenced each other as may be seen from the apocryphal life of the Apostle Thomas. This relates how he visited India and, being an architect, was commissioned by the king to build a palace for him. Thomas built nothing, but gave all the money he had received to feed the poor, and would have been executed had not the king been told by his dead brother in a dream how a wonderful palace (that of good works) was waiting for him in heaven, built by the Apostle. This story was read with approval and is often depicted in medieval religious art, and it shows St Thomas as displaying a truly aristocratic contempt for somebody else's money.

The combined opinion of church and aristocracy led medieval people to regard thrift and the accumulation of wealth as spiritually dangerous and therefore socially undesirable. Giving alms was considered praiseworthy and the support of beggars was rated highly as a good work: indeed, many stories were told of how the saints had appeared disguised as beggars to test the generosity of men. Although it was laudable to share one's wealth during one's life, it was essential to bequeath part of one's goods to charity, because posthumous good works would aid one's soul in purgatory. It would have been considered wrong for a rich man to bequeath his entire property to his natural heirs.

The acquisitive instinct is strong and many medieval people shared it, but medieval society seems to have viewed it rather as Victorian society viewed sex, as something which was unavoidable but distasteful. It was not until the values of the Florentine renaissance began to permeate the west in the fifteenth century that men began to regard the acquisition of wealth as virtuous provided that it was used for the benefit of one's fellow citizens.

Usury

The most controversial aspect of the church's teaching about the sin of avarice concerned usury. This is categorically forbidden in the Old Testament (Deut., 23, 19–21) and the church followed this ruling and condemned as sinful the charging of interest on loans of any kind. Its concern was at first the same as that of the legislator of Deuteronomy: to protect a predominantly rural society against exploitation by money-lenders who charged high interest rates and caused the peasantry to mortgage their futures.

The prohibition became a serious obstacle to the development of the western economy from the eleventh century, since it hindered the free circulation of money on which commerce and manufacturing depended. Ways were therefore found to circumvent the usury laws and when the banking system developed in the thirteenth century those laws were in practice disregarded. The church itself began to use banking facilities and in the fifteenth century the Medici of Florence opened a branch in Rome and became official bankers to the Holy See. Throughout this time the usury laws remained in force and the church never changed its official teaching. Pope Leo X (1512–21) admitted, albeit reluctantly, that loans made to the poor by licensed pawnbrokers at very low rates of interest were not sinful, but this was the church's sole concession to commercial opinion. Nevertheless the church's silence does not obscure the fact that it was defeated by public opinion in its attempt to classify commercial usury as a sin.

Gluttony

The deadly sin of gluttony in theory applied to the immoderate love of all kinds of pleasure, but in practice was understood to refer chiefly to the pleasures of the table. These vices were a regular source of temptation only to the rich, for the mass of the population could only afford to eat and drink too much on certain great feasts such as Easter. Gluttony was considered spiritually dangerous at all times because it lowered resistance to other kinds of sin, notably those of lechery and anger. It was only considered a serious sin in itself if it reached addictive proportions. The church did succeed in making the whole population eat moderately each year during the forty days of Lent, but during the rest of the year the rich customarily overate and rich men, though not rich women, tended to drink heavily. Equally, the poor were unwilling to be temperate in their eating and drinking habits on those rare feast days which enlivened years of near subsistence living.

Lechery

Lechery was the least serious of the deadly sins, but was the one about which there was at first the greatest divergence between the church's teaching and pagan practice. Everybody condemned rape: the church considered it a sin and it was also treated as a criminal offence and one which entailed the death penalty in most medieval states. But in other areas of sexual morality the church faced an uphill task when it tried to impose its ethic on society. In Christian tradition sex is legitimate only in monogamous and lifelong marriage and all other sexual activity of any kind is sinful.

The church had initially to fight quite hard in order to suppress polygamy among the nobility, but it won this battle when church courts secured control over cases of marriage law in the eleventh century (see chapter 2). Thereafter a nobleman might have only one lawful wife at a time, and only the children of such marriages were legitimate and had the right to inherit property. The church met with little opposition about monogamy from the peasantry, who made up the bulk of the population, since most of them could not afford to support more than one wife.

All pagan societies in the west had had incest taboos, but the church had more extensive ones. At first marriages were forbidden between fourth cousins, but in 1215 the prohibition was reduced to second cousins, although it was possible to obtain a papal dispensation from this ruling in some cases. The church succeeded in creating a social climate in which these rules were observed: common-law marriages between cousins met with social ostracism and people were therefore forced to make exogamous marriages, which led to complaints that it was difficult to keep family lands united.

The church also met with difficulties over the question of divorce, which had been allowed in all pagan societies. In effect the church compromised on this issue: divorce in a modern sense was forbidden, but marriages might be annulled if proof could be adduced that they had been invalidly contracted (for example because the couple were related within the prohibited degrees). Only the rich could afford to bring annulment proceedings, and they were not always successful: Philip Augustus of France, for example, could not obtain an annulment of his marriage to Ingeborg of Denmark.

Although all sex outside marriage was considered sinful the church recognized that this was a counsel of perfection for most men. When formulating penances for sexual sins the church used a double standard: although men and women who committed the same offences were considered equally guilty in the sight of God, women received severer penances. In this regard the church was accepting the standards of lay society, which placed a higher value on fidelity and chastity among women than among men. If a married woman was unfaithful to her husband this was regarded as a serious sin both on the part of herself and of her lover, but if a married man was unfaithful to his wife his sin was treated lightly, unless he had slept with another man's wife.

Fornication between two unmarried people was treated simply as a fact of life. All towns of any size had brothels and in parts of southern Europe in the later Middle Ages some of them were licensed by the town councils. There were even brothels in Rome: the Holy See deprecated this but admitted that there was no alternative.

The church strongly disapproved of homosexuality. It was inevitable that it should do so, since that was the kind of sexuality most readily available in monasteries, whose members were bound by rules of perpetual chastity. Canon lawyers equated homosexuality with the sin of Sodom and labelled it as one of the four sins which cry aloud to heaven for vengeance. Nevertheless, some churchmen viewed this sin more leniently when it was practised by adolescent boys among themselves. Archbishop Theodore's penitential says laconically: 'As for boys who mutually engage in vice . . . they should be whipped'. This sin is unique in Theodore's penitential in that no penance is prescribed for it: the author clearly considered it a common, if undesirable, feature of growing up in a single-sex school.

Good works

The practice of the Christian virtues found social expression in good works. The medieval church took very seriously Christ's discourse on the Last Judgement in which he explained that men's salvation or damnation would depend on the works which they had performed in this life (Matt., 25, 31–46).

This part of the church's teaching is extremely easy to understand. The way in which simple people were impressed by the need to do good works is seen in the

Lyke-Wake Dirge, an English ballad of the fifteenth century, which graphically describes the journey of the soul through purgatory:

> If ever thou gavest meat or drink,
>   Every nighte and alle,
> The fire shall never make thee shrink;
>   And Christe receive thy soule.

> If meat or drink thou ne'er gav'st nane,
>   Every nighte and alle,
> The fire will burn thee to the bare bane;
>   And Christe receive thy soule.

The seven corporal works of mercy

The church, with its love of mystical numbers, drew up a list of the principal good works, the Seven Corporal Works of Mercy, and this was included in late medieval catechisms so that everybody might learn it. The first six were drawn from the Gospels, the seventh from the book of Tobit: they were; to feed the hungry, to give drink to the thirsty, to give shelter to strangers, to clothe the naked, to visit the sick, to minister to prisoners and to bury the dead.

It was within everybody's capacity to perform these works, irrespective of income. Indeed, it was spiritually more meritorious for the poor to share what little they had with others than for the rich to give generously from their superfluity. One of the things which most endeared the early Franciscans to their contemporaries was their readiness to share their frugal belongings. In their founder's lifetime they observed a very strict rule of personal and corporate poverty and lived as beggars, dependent for their next meal on the generosity of others, yet this did not prevent them from being liberal within their means. The story is told of how, when St Francis and his early followers were living in small wooden shacks at the foot of Assisi hill, a poor widow came asking for help. The brethren reported that they had nothing to give her except the New Testament from which they read the lessons in chapel. Francis said, 'Give the New Testament to our mother that she may sell it to take care of her needs. I believe indeed that the gift of it will be more pleasing to God than our reading from it.'

It is impossible to quantify how far individuals regularly practised the corporal works of mercy, though the ease with which comparatively large numbers of poor pilgrims travelled through Europe suggests that private generosity must have been quite common. There was less opportunity to be charitable to strangers in the predominantly rural society of western Europe in the early Middle Ages where care of the needy was chiefly the responsibility of the kin-group and the village community, although monasteries, by the terms of their rule, had an obligation to give food and shelter to travellers.

The growth of urban life from the eleventh century onwards created new social problems which could not be dealt with solely on a personal level, because the poor and sick in cities were numerous and often had no kin on whom they could rely for help. A large number of hospitals was founded to meet this need and by 1500 few towns of any size in western Europe were without one or more of these institutions. They were endowed by laymen, but they were usually administered by clergy with the help of a salaried lay staff. Medieval hospitals did not simply care for the sick, but also distributed food and clothing to the poor and looked after orphan children and the aged and infirm. There were also charitable foundations which undertook more specialized work. Lepers were cared for in separate hospitals because of the fear of infection, and special foundations were also endowed to care for the mentally sick. In the late Middle Ages almshouses were also founded for the able-bodied old, who had no kin to provide them with a home.

Some of the works of mercy could not be performed by institutions. Sick visiting had to be carried out on a personal basis, as had the duty to bury the dead. The latter work of mercy often took the form of paying the costs of a proper funeral and requiem mass for a pauper. Ministering to those in prison did find institutional expression in the work of the Trinitarian Order, founded by St John of Matha in the early thirteenth century, whose members arranged the ransoming of Christian prisoners held captive by Muslims, particularly those captured during the wars in Spain.

It would be wrong to suppose that the medieval church tried to create a Christian welfare state, for it relied on personal giving and lacked the financial resources and administrative skills to do anything so ambitious. It was universally assumed that the kin-group would care for its own members, and the greater number of poor, sick, old and destitute people was cared for in this way. The church's concern was with those people who either had no kin or had become separated from them. It succeeded in creating a social conscience about such people in western society. A Viking proverb had said, 'A man without lord or kindred is like a lonely fir-tree, naked on a windy hill'. By the end of the Middle Ages a man similarly circumstanced would not have been able to say this of himself, for western Europe was covered with a network of charitable institutions.

True charity

Christ had said that good works done to the least of the brethren were done to himself, and the church tried to impress on its members that the poor and the sick, the homeless and prisoners, were not objects of pity but channels of grace, since it was through them that Christ manifested himself to his followers and in them that he might be served. The church set out this teaching symbolically in the liturgy of Maundy Thursday, during which the celebrant washed the feet of twelve poor men, as Christ had washed the disciples' feet at the Last Supper, while the choir sang the anthem: 'A new commandment I give unto you, that ye love one another as I have loved you' (John., 13, 34). This sentiment inspired the charitable work of the Order of St John of Jerusalem: its statutes enacted in 1181 state, 'The brethren are to serve the sick poor with zeal and devotion as if they were their lords'. The Hospitaller brethren were for the most part of noble birth, but they treated their patients as though they were their feudal lords because they believed that Christ was present in the poor and the sick.

Social pressures, if strong enough, may force people to act in ways which are considered virtuous, but there is no means of making them think in such ways. Medieval people who regarded the poor and sick as channels of grace were probably exceptional; nevertheless, there does seem to have been an awareness among all people then that a saint from heaven, if he appeared among men, would be more likely to manifest himself as a beggar than as a respectable citizen, and this was accompanied by a belief that the poor and the weak were specially favoured by God. Consequently it was not considered socially acceptable to adopt a patronizing attitude towards the poor and destitute, for that would have been taken as evidence of retarded spiritual growth. This, perhaps, is the best measure of the church's success in making people understand what the virtuous life, as conceived in Christian terms, was about.

Part III

Varieties of Religious Response

15

Contacts with Other Religions

The medieval west was not hermetically sealed off from all contact with the other great world religions and some consideration must therefore be given to what was known about them by the Catholic church, how widely that knowledge was disseminated and what impact it had on western religious attitudes.

Judaism

There had been Jewish colonies in parts of the west during Roman times and they spread beyond the old imperial frontiers during the Middle Ages. Almost all Jews in the west lived in cities. They were granted religious toleration and were allowed to build synagogues and to run rabbinic schools, but they were subject to certain kinds of civil disability, notably they were not allowed to exercise authority over Christians and therefore could not own estates or employ Christian labour. Mixed marriages were forbidden both by their own religious law and by Christian canon law.

From the late eleventh century Jews were subject to serious but intermittent bouts of persecution in the course of which some of them were forcibly baptized. The church deplored this but nevertheless ruled that such baptisms were valid unless the victim had expressly voiced his dissent during the ceremony. Despite this decision the church did not itself pursue any policy of forced conversion, although it welcomed voluntary conversions.

Throughout much of the Middle Ages Jews and Christians lived peaceably together in many western cities. For example, the rabbi Benjamin of Tudela has this to say about the situation in Rome in the pontificate of Alexander III (1159–81):

> Rome . . . contains about 200 Jews who occupy an honourable position and pay no tribute, and among them are officials of the pope Alexander . . . Great scholars reside here, at the head of them being rabbi Daniel, the chief rabbi, and rabbi Jechiel, an official of the pope. He is a handsome young man of intelligence and wisdom, and he has the entry of the pope's palace, for he is the steward of his house. . . .

Western churchmen sometimes held religious discussions with Jewish scholars. Gilbert Crispin, abbot of Westminster, debated the meaning of the Old Testament revelation with a Jew, each appealing to human reason to resolve their differences in interpretation. Gilbert, who published these conversations in the form of a disputation in 1092–3, was convinced that he had won the argument , but admitted that he had failed to persuade the Jew. Debates of this kind were not always conducted so courteously. One held at Cluny in St Louis's reign (1226–70) was attended by a sick knight, who was convalescing in the infirmary, and who wrecked the proceedings by asking the chief rabbi whether he believed that Mary was the Mother of God and by hitting him with his crutch when he answered no. Even when such debates were well conducted neither side expected to be convinced by the other's arguments, yet such exercises were not without value for they showed both Christians and Jews that each other's beliefs could be rationally defended and did not simply rest on blind prejudice.

Christian Biblical scholars regularly enlisted the help of rabbis in their study of the Old Testament and this sometimes caused them genuine intellectual problems because Jewish commentators interpreted certain key texts very differently (see chapter 20). Christian scholarship was also greatly enriched by the learning of some converts from Judaism, like Peter Alfonsi, friend of Peter Abelard and Peter the Venerable, who introduced the western church to the Talmud.

Christian theologians did not consider that Judaism was a serious intellectual challenge. The Jews were God's chosen people to whom the Old Testament revelation had been given in order to prepare them for the coming of Christ. Although Christ had been born of a Jewish mother and his earliest followers had been Jews, most other Jews had refused to accept him as the Messiah, and consequently the Christian church, which did accept him, had become the new Israel and would receive all the blessings promised by God to the old Israel. God's displeasure with his chosen people for their rejection of Christ had been shown in the destruction of the Jerusalem Temple in 70 AD and the dispersal of the Jews throughout the world. Although the Jews continued to worship the true God and to reverence his revelation, they read the Old Testament without understanding, and whenever the Synagogue, symbolizing contemporary Jewry, was shown in medieval Christian art, it was portrayed as a woman with a veil drawn over her face. The Jewish expectation of a Messiah who would return to restore the kingdom of David was, in the view of the church, a vain hope, since the true Messiah had already come.

Jews were forbidden to proselytize, a prohibition which they observed, but there were a few, rare cases of Christians who embraced Judaism, having become convinced that it was the true faith. Conversions of that kind were acts of apostasy, punishable by death in the law of all western countries, and in order to live in peace such men had to flee to Jewish communities in Islamic states.

It was not fear of prosecution alone which hindered conversions to Judaism, otherwise there would have been no heretics in medieval Europe. The question did not arise for the majority of Catholics, for they lived in villages and never met Jews, who were found only in towns. Urban Catholics, however, could mix with Jews quite freely since they were not segregated in ghettos. Nevertheless, the Jews were set apart by social and linguistic barriers: they did not intermarry or work with Christians and their liturgy was in an unknown tongue. Thus although Catholics living in towns quite often met Jews they knew little about their religion and did not seriously consider it as an alternative to their own faith.

Islam

From *c.*700 Catholic Christendom shared a common frontier with Islam. Contact between the two civilizations was not restricted to people living in the frontier zones, for throughout the Middle Ages western pilgrims visited the Holy Land

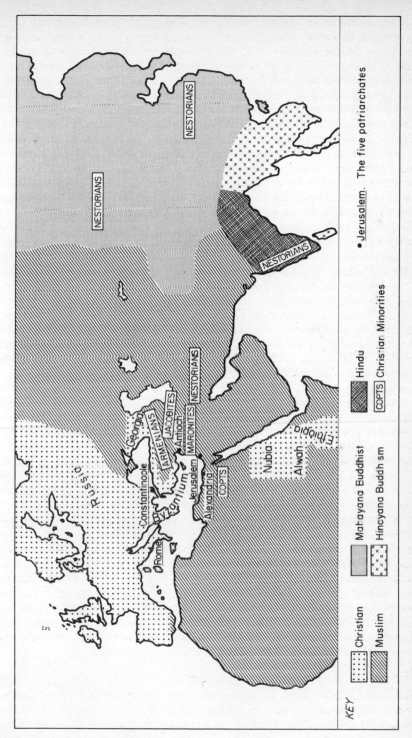

Map 2   Christianity and other world religions in c. 1300.

when it was in Muslim hands and western merchants traded with the Islamic rulers of Egypt and north Africa, while from the eleventh century crusades against the Muslims drew support from all over the western world. Consequently Islam made a considerable impact on the imagination of the Christian west, for a substantial minority of Catholics had direct experience of Muslim lands, while a high proportion of western people must have known somebody who had visited the Islamic world.

As a result of the Christian wars of reconquest large groups of Muslims were brought under western rule from *c*.1100 in the Spanish peninsula, Sicily and the Crusader States. They were granted religious toleration and forced conversions were forbidden although evangelization by peaceful means was allowed. The latter policy met with some success: in Sicily the entire Muslim population had become Christian by *c*.1300, and urban Muslims in the Spanish kingdoms had been converted by the fifteenth century. No serious attempt was made to convert the Muslims in the Crusader States during the 200 years of Frankish rule, while significant enclaves of Muslim peasantry remained in Castile until 1502 and in Aragon until 1526, at which times they were offered the choice of conversion or expulsion. These Spanish Muslims remained unconverted for so long, it would seem, because the Catholic rural clergy were unwilling to learn Arabic.

The presence of large numbers of Muslims in the Christian frontier kingdoms after 1100 made it possible for churchmen to study Islam in a more systematic way than had before been possible. As B.Z. Kedar has recently pointed out, although a reasonable amount of fairly accurate information about the origins and teachings of Islam did reach the Christian west in the early Middle Ages, little interest was shown in it. A literary convention emerged there which portrayed the Muslims as polytheist idolaters, and J. France has shown how this tradition remained dominant at the time of the first crusade. The authors of crusader chronicles and *chansons de geste* often had first-hand knowledge of Islam, they had been into mosques and knew that they did not contain idols, yet they continued to write about Muslims as polytheists in order to denigrate them.

A change occurred when Peter the Venerable, abbot of Cluny (†1156), commissioned Latin translations of the Koran and of other Muslim theological works. This was carried out in Toledo by a team of Christian and Muslim scholars among whom an important role was played by the Englishman, Robert of Ketton. This was the first time that the Koran was translated into any other language, for Muslims accord to their scriptures the same dignity which Christians accord to Jesus, each is accounted the uncreated Word of God. For that reason devout Muslims did not think it possible to translate God's Word which had been revealed to men in Arabic.

The detailed knowledge of Islamic theology which Catholics acquired in the twelfth century was put to use in the thirteenth, when attempts were made by members of the mendicant Orders to evangelize the Muslim world. St Francis initiated this process by expounding the Christian faith to al-Kamil, sultan of Egypt, in 1220, and some Islamic rulers were prepared to license formal debates between Christian and Muslim theologians. In order to make use of such opportunities Christian missionaries needed to learn eastern languages and study Islamic theology. Ramon Lull (†1315), the *doctor illuminatus*, or 'enlightened doctor', believed that it was possible to demonstrate the truths of the Christian religion by rational argument alone, starting from empirical evidence about the natural world on which Muslims and Christians would be in complete agreement, and reasoning from those premises to first principles. He put this idea into practice by going to Morocco and ingeniously forcing public debates to be held by announcing that he was a Christian who was willing to embrace Islam if he could be convinced of its truth by rational argument. Although this enabled him to use his method of demonstration he gained no converts because he was not allowed to evangelize in the normal way. Other missionaries in Muslim states fared no better.

Christians attributed this lack of success to the intolerance of Muslim rulers who would not let them preach freely, but when, in the second half of the thirteenth century, pagan Mongol rulers did allow Christians full freedom to evangelize their Muslim subjects, their success was negligible. Christianity clearly had little appeal for most Muslims and conversions occurred in appreciable numbers only among those who were living in Christian states, who were offered not merely a new religion but also a new culture. The only Muslims who were genuinely interested in Christian beliefs were the Nizarite Ismailis, a Shi'ite sect better known as the Order of Assassins. When St Louis's envoy, Yves le Breton, visited the Master of the Syrian Assassins, he found that he read Christian apocryphal books and speculated that God might operate through all faiths, including Christianity. This Gnostic outlook, which considered that all religions were symbolic expressions of the same ineffable mystery, was incomprehensible to the Christian clergy with whom the Ismailis discussed it, and who supposed, wrongly, that the Nizarites were expressing an interest in orthodox Christianity with a possible view to conversion.

Although the speculations of some Islamic philosophers caused intellectual difficulties for Christian scholars (see chapter 20), the Islamic religion was not considered a challenge to Catholic Christianity. The two faiths had much in common: both were monotheistic, both accepted the same overall picture of world history from the Creation to the Flood, and both believed that Moses was a prophet sent by God. They disagreed over the role of Jesus: the Koran taught that he was a divinely inspired prophet, and a specially privileged one, because he had been virgin-born of Mary his mother, and had not died, but had been taken up bodily into heaven from whence he would return to prepare the world for the Last Judgement. Nevertheless, Muslims denied that Jesus was God, and they also claimed that Mahomet was a prophet sent by God to the Arabs.

Christians could not accept the denial of Christ's divinity or Mahomet's claim to prophetic status, for if, as they believed, God had become man in Christ, then there was no need for a further revelation. Byzantine theologians tended to view Islam as a Christian heresy, for this enabled them to explain why some, though not all, of Mahomet's teaching was true. The western church never accepted that opinion, but considered that Mahomet was an impostor who had falsely claimed divine inspiration for his teaching.

Pope Innocent IV (1243–54) once considered the hypothetical question whether Muslims should be allowed to preach their faith freely in Christian lands, and decided that they should not, because they taught error. Any Muslim religious leader at the time would have held exactly the same opinion about the rights of Christian preachers in Muslim lands. In both Islamic and Christian states apostasy was a capital offence, yet there were men in both cultures who were attracted to the other religion and who changed their faith. Like political defection in our own age, this involved a complete cultural break, for the only way of achieving one's aim was to go to live in the land of one's adopted faith. The Moorish traveller Ibn Jubayr met a merchant from the Maghrib, when he visited Acre in 1184, who had not only become a Christian, but also a monk, 'thereby hastening for himself the pains of hell'. But Christians also fled to Islamic territory and became Muslims, in sufficiently large numbers for thirteenth-century popes to find it necessary to arrange for those who decided that they had made a mistake to be received back into the Catholic church. This presupposes that there were many more who had no wish to return.

Gautama the Buddha

The west came to know about the Buddha before it knew about his followers. In 1048 an anonymous western visitor to Constantinople read a Greek book which intrigued him so much that he translated it into Latin. Its title page read:

> An edifying story from the land of the Ethiopians, called the land of the Indians, thence brought to the Holy City by John the monk of the monastery of St Sabas, wherein are the lives of the famous and blessed Barlaam and Ioasaph.

It tells how Ioasaph, son of an Indian king, renounced the world and, guided by the ascetic Barlaam, became a Christian monk. The story enjoyed an immense success in the Catholic west and was translated into Old French, Anglo-Norman, Middle High German and even Norse, while James of Voragine included it in his *Golden Legend*. Barlaam and Ioasaph were venerated as saints because of their outstanding holiness of life, churches were dedicated to them, and in the sixteenth century cardinal Baronius added their names to the Roman Martyrology for 27 November.

Modern scholars have established that prince Ioasaph is, in fact, prince Gautama, the Buddha, and have traced the process whereby he was transformed into a Christian ascetic. The religion which the Buddha founded became divided into two main schools before the Christian era: the southern, Hinayana school, which flourished in Ceylon and south-east Asia, and which revered him as their founder and chief teacher; and the northern, Mahayana school of central Asia and China, which developed very differently.

Western travellers were not able to visit south-east Asia and Ceylon until the thirteenth century, but they then brought back accurate, though fragmentary, reports about the life of prince Gautama, whom they did not, of course, identify with St Ioasaph. Marco Polo, who called at Ceylon in 1292, records the reverence paid to the tooth and begging bowl of the Buddha which were preserved there and gives an accurate, brief account of his life, which concludes: 'For assuredly, had he been a Christian, he would have been a great saint with our Lord Jesus Christ.'

The Catholic world found no difficulty in reverencing the Light of Asia. When they heard his life story couched in Christian terms, western people immediately deemed him a saint; when travellers told the same story of a pagan teacher, he was seen as an example of 'a naturally Christian soul', and it did not seem scandalous that the people of Ceylon should reverence him and his relics. In so far as it was understood, his teaching posed no intellectual challenge to Christianity, for the Buddha appeared to have taught asceticism and world renunciation which the Catholic tradition regarded as the highest form of the Christian life.

Mahayana Buddhism

For a brief time during the Mongol ascendancy, from 1245 to *c.*1350, western travellers were able to visit central Asia and China, which they called Cathay. These regions were the home of Mahayana Buddhism, which differed so greatly from the Buddhism of Ceylon that western observers supposed that it was a separate religion. Prince Gautama does not occupy a central place in Mahayana theology, but is merely one among many enlightened beings who share the qualities of Buddhahood and have deferred their entry to Nirvana in order to help suffering souls to escape from the wheel of being. Western travellers called Mahayana Buddhists idolaters, and their temples certainly created that impression, for they were filled with statues and representations of many families of Buddhas, together with a pantheon of gods and tutelary demons, to all of whom religious reverence was paid. Catholic observers made no distinction between gods and Buddhas and this was a serious misapprehension, for the Mahayana schools taught that gods and demons were, like men, part of the world of illusion, that like men and animals they had souls which were subject to reincarnation, and that they needed the enlightenment which only a Buddha could provide. Buddhas were therefore superior to gods, but they were not gods.

Christians could not conceive of a religion in which gods were not important and this caused misunderstandings from the beginning. One of the earliest western visitors to central Asia was the Franciscan Friar, William of Rubruck, who stayed at the court of the Great Khan Möngke in 1253–4 as an envoy of St Louis of France. The khan, who was a pagan, organized a religious debate between Buddhists, Muslims and Christians, who appointed William as their spokesman. Although he had to speak through an interpreter, he had an advantage over his opponents in that he had been trained in the university of Paris and was more skilled in public debating than they were. The Buddhists spoke first and wished to discuss the creation of the world and the fate of the soul after death: they saw these as the central issues, because, unlike either the Muslims or the Christians, they believed that the created world was an illusion and that the soul at death was reincarnated. William objected that these were secondary issues and that they should first consider the nature of God, which was more important. This proposition was self-evident to a Christian, but it did not seem an important issue at all to the Buddhists, so the problem was referred to the Mongol arbitrators who upheld William's objection, because they too believed in one God, symbolized by the eternal heavens.

The debate lasted most of the day. The Buddhists, who believed in many gods but considered them all ephemeral, became involved in arguments about their relationship to each other and finally admitted that they did not consider any one god to be omnipotent. In the opinion of the spectators this was an admission of defeat, because the omnipotence of God was a matter about which all the non-Buddhists present were in complete agreement.

Later in the thirteenth century Catholic missionaries were allowed to work in parts of the Mongol empire and established dioceses in Persia and also in China. It is not known whether they converted many Buddhists, but they certainly became much better informed about Mahayana Buddhism than the early western travellers had been, not least because they were able to speak oriental languages. Friar Odoric of Pordenone, who travelled in the far east between 1318–30, met

Buddhist monks in China who told him that they regularly fed animals because they believed that through reincarnation they shared the same souls as men; and fragments of information of this sort allowed the west to form a more accurate picture of northern Buddhism. The most coherent account of it is contained in *The Book of the Estate of the Great Khan*, compiled in *c*.1330 at the request of pope John XXII by the Catholic archbishop of Sultaniyeh in Persia. This relates that the emperor of Cathay (China) has established an idolatrous religion whose clergy are red-hatted monks, subject to a pope, but it praises the monks as celibates who observe high moral standards and are well disciplined. This part of the report is quite accurate: the Mongol emperors of China patronized the Sakyapa Order of Buddhists from Tibet, who were red-hatted monks under the supreme authority of the Grand Lama of Sakya (the 'pope' of the account), and the Order had a high reputation for learning and for its celibate observance.

The report then gives an account of Buddhist beliefs:

> They be idolaters and worship divers idols. And over these idols they say that there be four gods; and these gods they carve in gold and silver, so as to stand out entire before and behind. And above these four gods they say that there is a greater god who is over all the gods, great and small.

This appears to be based on a genuine, though unsuccessful, attempt to understand Sakyapa iconography. Five Buddhas were singled out for representation in mandalas, each regarded as the head of a Buddha family, and they were positioned one at the centre of the composition and the others at the four main compass points of the circumference. Clearly the Catholic priests who supplied this information had been asking the same question as William of Rubruck eighty years before: which of the numerous gods in their temples did the Buddhists consider the chief god. They were not able to understand the answer, that the Buddhas were important but that the gods were not and that representations of the relationships between the Buddhas were made for purposes of meditation and not as statements of theological truth. When shown mandalas of the five Buddhas, and statues of those Buddhas in the temples, they not unnaturally thought that the Buddha of the centre must be more important than the rest, but they were wrong.

Mahayana Buddhism is a very difficult religion to understand: it encompasses a wide variety of schools of interpretation, it has a large canon of sacred writings and a huge body of exegetical literature, and it uses a technical theological vocabulary. The first western scholar to master its subtleties was the Jesuit, Ippolito Desideri, who lived in a lamasery at Lhasa from 1716–21 where he could receive expert training. No medieval missionary was prepared to treat northern Buddhism so seriously. Catholic observers were favourably impressed by the high standards of monastic life which they found in the Mongol empire. They could grasp the importance which the Buddhists attached to reincarnation, since that was a concept with which they were familiar through the descriptions given in classical writers and the church Fathers of the teachings of the Pythagoreans. But they did not understand either the central Buddhist teaching about the need for enlightenment, or the lack of significance which learned lamas attached to the existence of gods. Although they made some attempt to gain an accurate picture of Buddhist theology, their interest was superficial, for they seem to have considered that because the Buddhists were idolaters they would have nothing of interest to say about matters of faith. Mahayana Buddhism therefore presented no intellectual challenge to Catholicism because its main teachings were not known to the western church.

Hinduism

The west knew of the other great religion of Asia, Hinduism, from accounts in classical writers of Alexander the Great's campaign to the Indus valley, where he had met brahmins and a wise ascetic, or gymnosophist, who had accompanied him to Babylon. It was not until the thirteenth century that western Christians were able to visit the Hindu kingdoms of south India. Men like Marco Polo and Odoric of Pordenone give a good deal of picturesque information about Hindu practices. They have an eye for the sensational and describe the ghats on which the bodies of the dead are cremated, the reverence shown to sacred cows, the self-immolation of widows on their husbands' funeral pyres, and the way in which devotees fling themselves beneath the wheels of juggernauts on the feasts of Siva. They also speak favourably about the integrity of character of high-caste brahmins and admire the austerities practised by *yogis* which, they were told, were conducive to long life and good health. Beyond saying that the Hindus are idolaters, they say nothing about their religious or philosophical beliefs, of which they would seem to have known nothing.

Prophets outside Israel

The self-confidence of the west in the truth of its own religious values is expressed tersely in the *Song of Roland*, in which archbishop Turpin leads a charge against the Muslim host shouting:

Paiens ont tort et Chrétiens ont droit
(Pagans are wrong and Christians are right).

That was undoubtedly the view of unsophisticated clergy and laity alike, but learned clergy were not so dismissive of other faiths.

On the third mass of Christmas Day in the medieval Roman rite the first lesson was taken from the Epistle to the Hebrews:

God who at sundry times and in divers manners spake in time past unto the fathers by the prophets, hath in these last days spoken unto us by his son. (Heb., 1, 1–2).

Medieval churchmen did not suppose that all the prophets had been in Israel: they recognized that the gentile world had also been enlightened by prophetic utterances, as evidenced by the Sibylline writings and the Fourth Eclogue of Virgil which foretold the birth of Christ. They were therefore prepared to admit that other pre-Christian religions might contain elements of revealed truth, although, for reasons explained above, they were certain that no new revelation could have been given after Christ's coming and that therefore nothing could be learned from Islam.

The church believed that the purpose of all prophecy had been to prepare mankind for the coming of Christ. It therefore followed that there was no real parity between Christianity and other religions. The prophetic revelations given to the gentiles might enrich the way in which Christians understood their own faith, but of their nature could not contradict or add to any part of Christian teaching. It was profitable to study other religions, because this enabled one to see God's providence at work in history, it sometimes strengthened the proofs of the Christian revelation and it enabled the church to evangelize more successfully. Since Christ was the 'desire of all nations', Christianity was the fulfilment of all other religious aspirations.

The Christian laity was offered no religious choice because proselytizing of all kinds was forbidden in the west. Nevertheless they knew that other religions existed and a few men in each generation availed themselves of that knowledge and crossed the frontier to become Muslims.

16
Relations with the Eastern Churches

The Orthodox eastern churches

In the early Middle Ages the Catholic church of the west was in full communion with the Orthodox churches of the East which, like itself, held the faith of the first seven General Councils (see chapter 4). The Orthodox owed obedience to the patriarchs of Antioch, Alexandria, Jerusalem and Constantinople, of whom the latter was the most influential, for he was the head of the Byzantine church and also of the Slav churches of the Balkans and Russia which were converted in the ninth and tenth centuries by Byzantine missionaries. His colleagues of Antioch, Alexandria and Jerusalem, by contrast, had few adherents and after c.650 when they came under Islamic rule could take little regular part in the affairs of the rest of Christendom. The Orthodox churches, while sharing a common faith with the Catholic church, used different liturgical forms, conducted public worship in Greek or Old Slavonic rather than in Latin and observed a different code of canon law which, for example, allowed secular priests to marry.

Greek influence in the western church before 1050

Orthodox influence was widely felt in the western church in the early medieval centuries. Rome was part of the Byzantine empire until 751 and no fewer than eleven Greek popes were appointed in the last century of Byzantine rule. The Byzantines continued to rule southern Italy until the mid-eleventh century: there were substantial enclaves of Greek Christians in Apulia, while Calabria was almost exclusively Orthodox in religion. When Sicily was conquered by the Muslims in the ninth century Orthodox monks from Calabria began to migrate northwards to escape from Islamic raiders and they reinvigorated the Greek monasteries of Rome and its environs which had survived from the Byzantine period.

Greek influence was likewise experienced in many other parts of the western church. Monasticism had first reached the west from the eastern Mediterranean and western monks remained conscious of their origins. For that reason they welcomed Byzantine monks as representatives of an austere and primitive observance. Thus when the Greek ascetic, Nilus of Rossano, visited the Benedictines of Montecassino in c.980, the entire community descended the hill to escort him to the abbey with lighted tapers and smoking censers, 'as if', says his biographer, 'the mighty Benedict himself had risen from the dead'. Orthodox monks, mainly, though not solely, from Calabria, travelled widely in the west in the years 900–1050 and were received with general goodwill. A Greek monk called

Constantine settled at Malmesbury abbey in Wiltshire in *c.*1030 where he impressed the brethren by his holy and ascetic life. The activities of his contemporary, St Symeon of Trier, were more spectacular, for he was a monk of Mount Sinai who settled in the west and was at his own request walled up as a recluse in a small cell near the Black Gate of Trier, where he was attacked by demons who howled like wolves, and where he lived solely on a diet of bread and water until 1035 when he offered his life to God to stay a plague which had struck the city.

A few Orthodox churchmen were promoted to high office in the western church. An outstanding example of this is St Theodore of Tarsus, a Byzantine Greek, appointed archbishop of Canterbury by pope Vitalian in 668, who was an exceptionally gifted administrator and succeeded in creating a unified system of church government in England at a time when political power there was fragmented. Even more privileged was the Orthodox priest, John Philagathos of Rossano, who began his career as a chaplain to Theophano, the Byzantine wife of the emperor Otto II (†983), was appointed abbot of the great Lombard house of Nonantula and subsequently promoted to be archbishop of Piacenza. In 997–8 he set himself up as antipope, with the title of John XVI, and has the distinction of being the last Greek to occupy the Roman see, albeit irregularly.

Individually, Orthodox monks, prelates and even popes did not exercise any very decisive influence on the western church, but at most contributed to some local development. They were not numerous enough to affect the way in which the western church evolved. Yet they were important in a more general way, because they preserved in the west an awareness of the universality of the church. For they not only spoke a different language and used a different liturgy, but they had a distinct ascetic tradition and interpreted the common faith in ways which Latin Christians found illuminating. So long as such men were present in the west in any numbers it was impossible for people there to identify the Catholic church entirely with the church of the Latin rite.

The eastern schism

Tensions existed throughout the early Middle Ages between the churches of Rome and Constantinople and surfaced from time to time. There were disagreements about matters of usage and discipline: thus the western church celebrated mass in unleavened bread and in theory had a celibate priesthood, while the Orthodox used leavened bread at mass and required all secular priests to marry. The Orthodox also objected to the unilateral addition by western Catholics of the word *Filioque*, 'and from the son', to the statement of belief in the Holy Spirit contained in their common profession of faith, the Nicene Creed (see text p. 40). This practice appears to have originated in the Spanish church, to have spread to the Frankish kingdom in the ninth century, and to have been adopted at Rome only in 1009 when pope Sergius IV included the *Filioque* in the profession of faith which he sent to his colleague at Constantinople announcing his election. The patriarch refused to allow prayers to be offered for him in the churches of the empire and from that time a formal schism existed between Rome and Constantinople because all subsequent popes used the same form of the creed.

Some solution to this problem might nevertheless have been found had the situation not been aggravated by the papal reform movement of the mid-eleventh century. Since the fifth century papal authority had been differently understood by the churches of east and west. They all agreed that the pope was the successor of St Peter, but whereas the west supposed that this conferred on him powers which were different in kind from those of any other bishop and which extended to the whole church, the eastern churches considered that it conferred only primacy of honour in the universal church and patriarchal power in the western church. In 451 the council of Chalcedon had granted to the church of Constantinople within its own sphere equal rights and privileges to those of the Roman see, although the papal legates had refused to ratify this canon. This did not become a major source of controversy during the early medieval centuries because the papacy did not seek to exercise a dynamic role in the church during most of that time, but this changed after 1046 when the reformed papacy attempted to assert its claims to primacy of jurisdiction in ways which were unacceptable to the patriarchs of Constantinople. This led to a quarrel which culminated in the excommunication of Michael Cerularius, patriarch of Constantinople, by the legates of pope Leo IX in 1054. This used to be reckoned the beginning of the definitive schism between east and west, but scholars like Runciman and Every have argued that it was not understood in that final way at the time and that the schism developed more gradually as a result of worsening relations between east and west during the next 150 years.

Political and commercial rivalries between the western powers and the Byzantine empire during that period did nothing to make ecclesiastical relations between east and west any easier, but it is arguable that it was the crusades which caused the irretrievable breakdown in relations between Rome and Constantinople. The crusaders appointed Latin patriarchs at Jerusalem and Antioch, a policy which was unacceptable to the Byzantine emperor and the patriarch of Constantinople, who appointed titular patriarchs to those sees, who lived at Constantinople until political circumstances should allow them to be enthroned. Thus a formal schism came into being between Rome and two of the Orthodox churches.

Twelfth-century popes considered that the church of Constantinople was the chief obstacle to Christian unity because of its obstinate refusal to acknowledge the papal primacy. Thus when in 1203–4 the fourth crusade, for reasons not germane to the present argument, was diverted to attack Constantinople, pope Innocent III, while condemning the savagery of the attack, condoned its success and sanctioned the appointment of a Latin patriarch there. From a papal point of view the crusade was not successful enough, for although the crusaders overran Greece and their Venetian allies subdued the Greek islands, a Byzantine emperor and patriarch established their courts in exile at Nicaea in Asia Minor and from that base were able to recover control of much of central and northern Greece and in 1261 of Constantinople itself.

The thirteenth century thus witnessed a decline of papal influence in the Orthodox churches. Orthodox patriarchs were restored by the Muslim authorities, when they conquered those cities, to Jerusalem in 1187 and to Antioch in 1268 and, of course, the Byzantine reconquest of Constantinople in 1261 led to the restoration of an Orthodox patriarch there also. Pope Gregory X sought to secure recognition of the papal primacy by the Orthodox hierarchy, but although Byzantine delegates, acting under political pressure from their emperor, Michael VIII, who needed the pope as a political ally, attended the Second Council of Lyons in 1274 and signed an act of union with the western church, most of their fellow countrymen refused to honour it. The events of 1204 were too recent a memory and the union of Lyons remained a dead letter.

Orthodox Christians in communion with Rome

Although relations between the Orthodox churches and the western church deteriorated badly after 1050, large numbers of Orthodox Christians continued to live under Latin rule. At first the greatest number was found in the former Byzantine lands of south Italy, which were conquered by the Normans in the second half of the eleventh century and held by their rulers as fiefs of the Holy See. The Normans placed their dominions under the ecclesiastical authority of the pope and initially attempts were made to force the Orthodox clergy there to conform to western usages. Urban II made a more generous settlement at a council held at Bari in 1098, which enacted that Greek bishops should remain in office if they would acknowledge the papal primacy and should have authority over all the clergy in their dioceses, both Greek and Latin. Greek clergy were to keep their own rites and customs in so far as these did not infringe Catholic principles. They might celebrate the liturgy in Greek in their traditional rite; they might continue to have married, secular priests; they might celebrate mass with leavened bread; and they might even recite the Nicene creed in the traditional way without the inclusion of the *Filioque* provided that they did not criticize the Latins for using it.

Although the Greek bishops of south Italy were mostly replaced by Latins when they died, Greek parish clergy were left undisturbed, while the Norman rulers, Roger I (†1101) and Roger II (†1154), founded a number of important Greek abbeys for the benefit of their Byzantine-rite subjects. Paradoxically this combination of peace and royal patronage in southern Italy led to the virtual disappearance of Greek monks from the rest of western Europe. Before 1050 such men had come chiefly from Byzantine south Italy and they had no reason to emigrate once the Normans had established peaceful government there. The former Greek abbeys of Rome and its environs passed to Latin observance with the sole exception of Grottaferrata, founded by St Nilus the Young just before his death in 1004, which remained Greek throughout the Middle Ages.

The rulings of the council of Bari acted as guidelines which were followed elsewhere by Catholic governments with Orthodox subjects. In the Crusader States the south Italian model was adopted with one significant modification: all diocesan bishops were Latin Catholics, but, in areas where there was a large Orthodox population, Orthodox coadjutor bishops were appointed. A similar practice was adopted in Cyprus, which had an entirely Orthodox indigenous population, after its capture by Richard I in 1191. In Frankish Greece after 1204 the majority of Orthodox bishops resigned their sees rather than acknowledge the papal primacy, but most parish clergy and some monastic communities continued to serve under the authority of Latin bishops and were allowed to preserve their rites and usages provided that they accepted the papal primacy.

The Crusader States were lost to the Muslims by 1291 and the mainland territories of Frankish Greece were eroded first by the Byzantines and then by the Ottomans, so that few were left by 1400. Nevertheless, many of the islands remained in western control into the modern period, and in places like Cyprus, Crete, Corfu and Chios there were substantial communities of eastern-rite

Christians in communion with the Holy See throughout the later Middle Ages. Many of these islands were ruled by Venice and consequently there was a Greek religious presence also in the mother-city after 1204.

Separated eastern churches

In addition to the Orthodox churches of the east there were also churches which did not accept the faith of all of the first seven General Councils but which had separated from the rest of Catholic Christendom in the early Middle Ages. There were four main groups of separated Christians.

The Monophysites were divided into two main groups: those in Syria called themselves Jacobites after their first patriarch, Jacob Baradaeus. They worshipped in Syriac and their patriarchs claimed to be lawful bishops of Antioch. The Monophysites of Egypt called themselves Copts, for they worshipped in Coptic and owed allegiance to the Coptic patriarch of Alexandria. He was recognized as ecclesiastical superior by the church of Ethiopia (whose primate, the Abuna, was always appointed by him), and also by some, but not all, of the churches in the Christian kingdoms of the Sudan.

The Armenian church is sometimes described as Monophysite, but it denies this and has never been in full communion with either the Jacobites or the Copts. It worships in Armenian, has its own distinct rites and canon law and is subject to a prelate called the Catholicus. This church was established throughout the middle east in the early Middle Ages by Armenians driven from their homeland in the Caucasus by successive invasions.

The Maronites of Syria broke away from the Orthodox church in the seventh century and by the tenth century most of their adherents had sought refuge in the Lebanon where they are still to be found. They had their own patriarch and were the most nucleated of the eastern churches, for they had no diaspora.

The greatest of the churches of medieval Asia was that of the Nestorians. They worshipped in Syriac and had a patriarch who lived in Baghdad. Though forbidden to proselytize Muslims, no restriction was placed by the Islamic authorities on their evangelizing the peoples of Asia outside the Arab empire. In this they met with considerable success, establishing churches in China, converting the khan of the Keraits, a tribe of the Mongol confederacy, and bringing under the control of their patriarch the Christians of the Malabar coast of India who claimed that their church had been founded by the Apostle Thomas.

The west knew that these churches existed, for papal legates had been present at the councils which had condemned the various heresies which the separated churches of the east professed. Very occasionally a member of one of those churches would come to western Europe, but effectively the western church had no links with these churches before the first crusade.

Uniate churches

The foundation of the Crusader States brought large numbers of separated eastern Christians under western rule: most of them were Armenians, Jacobites and Maronites. They were treated differently from the Orthodox because they were not considered to be members of the Catholic church. Separated eastern Christians were not made subject to Catholic bishops but were allowed complete religious freedom under their own hierarchy. This tolerant policy led to the development of friendly relations between them and the Franks and this caused some eastern prelates to wish to form closer links with the western church.

In c.1182 the Maronite patriarch entered into union with Rome and, although this initially met with strong opposition from some conservative members of his church, the union lasted until the end of Frankish rule in Syria in 1291. The details of the Maronite union were worked out in Innocent III's reign (1198–1216): the Maronite hierarchy was not subject to Catholic bishops, but their patriarch was directly responsible to the pope and his legate; the Maronites accepted Catholic doctrine, but preserved their own liturgy, ritual and canon law except if these contravened Catholic principles. They thus became the first uniate church, preserving their own identity while entering into corporate reunion with the Holy See.

In 1198 a similar union was negotiated by the Catholicus of Armenia, but this was dictated partly by the political interests of the Armenian ruler of Cilicia and proved more difficult to implement. The Armenians had a large diaspora, many of whom lived under Muslim rule and did not favour closer relations with the western church, and they were unwilling to fulfil the conditions which the papacy had stipulated when the union was discussed. Yet although the agreement was fraught with difficulties, some Armenians remained in communion with Rome until the independent kingdom of Armenian Cilicia was overrun by the Egyptian Mamluks in 1375.

Although they were on excellent terms with the Jacobites the Catholic clergy in the Crusader States did not succeed in negotiating an act of union with them, perhaps because so large a number of them lived under Muslim rule that a move of that kind might have split the Jacobite church.

Prester John

The west was dimly aware that there were Christians living in further Asia beyond the Islamic lands and they received proof of this when an Indian archbishop named John visited the court of pope Calixtus II in 1122. There is no reason to suppose that he was an impostor, for Indian Christians certainly reached Jerusalem in the time of crusader rule, so that there is no reason why one of them should not have travelled on to Rome. The archbishop told exaggerated stories about the wealth and power of the Christian rulers of the Malabar and, although the pope was sceptical about this, most people in the west who heard these stories believed them. This gave rise to the legend of Prester John, a powerful Christian ruler in further Asia who would one day attack Islam from the east. Consequently whenever reports reached the Crusader States about wars on the eastern frontiers of Persia, it was supposed that the armies of Prester John were on the march.

When news reached the fifth crusade in Egypt in 1221 of Genghiz Khan's attack on the Khorezm Shah, ruler of the most easterly lands of Islam in central Asia, it was thought that this was another instance of Prester John's power. The Mongol attack on Catholic eastern Europe in 1241–2 showed that they were not the west's hoped-for Christian allies, but this did not lead to the abandonment of the belief in Prester John's existence. In the late Middle Ages he came to be identified with the Christian emperor of Ethiopia, although this ruler of an embattled and backward kingdom seemed to western observers, when they finally reached his court, to have lost much of his former glory.

The Mongol mission

The Franciscan friar, John of Piano Carpini, sent as an envoy to the Mongol court by pope Innocent IV in 1246, was the first of a series of western visitors who brought back accurate information about the Mongols. They reported that the Mongol rulers were pagan, but that there were Nestorian Christians among their subjects, who enjoyed complete religious toleration. The papacy therefore had hopes both of converting the Mongols to Catholicism and of reconciling the Nestorians to Rome.

The first of these hopes proved illusory. The Mongol leaders in south Russia and Persia were converted to Islam and the Mongol emperors of China to Buddhism. Nevertheless, they were prepared to allow Catholic missionaries, drawn from the mendicant Orders, to work in their territories, and Catholic bishoprics were founded in many parts of the Mongol empire, including China. John of Montecorvino, the first Catholic archbishop of Peking, died in 1328, having rooted Catholicism firmly in China, for in 1338 a delegation of Chinese Christians came to Avignon to inform pope Benedict XII that all the Catholic clergy in China had died and to request replacements. A mission led by John of Marignolli was sent to reorganize the church in China, which accomplished its purpose and returned to the west in 1352, and it would appear that Chinese Catholicism collapsed less because of the problems of communication with its European headquarters, than because the seizure of power by the xenophobic Ming emperors in 1368 led to the closing of China to all foreign influence for a further 200 years.

Papal dealings with the Nestorians were inconclusive. In 1286–8 Arghun, Il-Khan of Persia, sent as his ambassador to the rulers of the west the monk Rabban Bar–Sauma, a friend of the Nestorian patriarch. Bar–Sauma had been born in Peking and was probably the first Chinese visitor to leave a description of western Europe. He visited Paris, Bordeaux, where he met Edward I of England, and Rome, where he celebrated mass in the Nestorian rite in the presence of the Franciscan pope, Nicholas IV. According to Bar–Sauma's own account he was examined by the cardinals about the faith of his church, which was pronounced orthodox, and the pope then issued a diploma for the Nestorian patriarch, authorizing him to exercise religious jurisdiction over 'all the children of the east'. This diploma is not recorded in the papal registers, so Bar–Sauma may have misrepresented the contents of a letter which the pope sent to the patriarch with a gift of relics, but if Bar–Sauma's account is true, it would mean that the Nestorian church was accorded uniate status by the pope.

The Nestorian church fell into a sad decline after the conversion of the Mongol Il-Khans of Persia to Islam in 1295. The Nestorians had been favoured by the pagan Il-Khans at the time of the Mongol conquests and this had been greatly resented by the Muslims of Persia. When the Il-Khans became Muslim this resentment found expression in a savage persecution of the Nestorians, and during the later Middle Ages their church declined in numbers and influence although it was not completely destroyed. Closer papal relations with the Nestorians were made impractical by the collapse of the Mongol empire in the course of the fourteenth century into a number of independent, mutually hostile states. This effectively ended the west's first contacts with Asia beyond Islam and precluded further evangelization, or the further reconciliation of eastern Christians living in those regions.

The Council of Florence

By 1400 the Catholic church in communion with the pope was once more almost conterminous with the Latin church of western Europe. Missionary activity in Asia had ended, the Maronite and Armenian unions had collapsed, and the only traces of a wider Catholicity were those Byzantine-rite churches in southern Italy, Cyprus and the Greek islands which acknowledged the papal primacy.

A fresh opportunity for establishing closer relations with the Orthodox churches occurred when the Byzantine emperor John VIII, anxious to secure western aid against the Ottoman Turks, opened negotiations with pope Eugenius IV about the possibility of church unity. This led to the emperor's attending the council of Ferrara/Florence in 1438–9, together with the patriarch of Constantinople and a distinguished group of Orthodox clergy. After prolonged discussion, agreement was reached about all matters of controversy and the decree of union, ending the schism between the Catholic and Orthodox churches, was sung in Greek and Latin from the pulpit of Florence cathedral.

The council continued to sit for another five years and negotiated with the separated eastern churches: the main groups of oriental Christians, Jacobites, Copts, Ethiopians, Armenians, Maronites and Nestorians, all sent representatives to Florence and signed acts of union. For the first time in a thousand years all the main branches of the Great Church were officially in communion with each other.

The long-term achievements of the council were less impressive. Most Orthodox clergy and laity repudiated the union and those churchmen who remained faithful to it had to flee to the west after the Ottoman conquest of Constantinople in 1453. The most distinguished of them were Isidore of Kiev, head of the Russian church, and John Bessarion, archbishop of Nicaea. Both were created cardinals, and Bessarion took a leading part in promoting Greek studies among Italian humanists and at his death in 1472 bequeathed his library of Greek texts to the Venetian republic.

The accords reached at Florence with the separated eastern churches proved equally ephemeral in many cases, because some of the delegates had not been empowered to reach agreements of a binding kind on behalf of their churches. But the union made on behalf of the Maronites of Lebanon proved enduring, for they welcomed the diplomatic protection which submission to Rome might afford them. The detailed provisions of the union were not finally worked out until the eighteenth century, but since the council of Florence Maronites have been eastern-rite Catholics in full communion with the Roman see.

Eastern-rite Catholicism

The council of Florence had little significance for most Catholics in the west. Eastern-rite Christians in communion with Rome no longer travelled frequently in the west as they had done before the mid-eleventh century. Most westerners, including some educated people, would have been surprised to know that there were any eastern-rite Catholics and would have supposed that all eastern Christians were in schism.

Nevertheless, the council of Florence had reaffirmed an important principle: it was not necessary for anybody who wished to join the Catholic church to become a Christian of the Latin rite. This was an admission by the papacy that the eastern churches, although in schism and in some cases guilty of heresy as well, had nevertheless been granted certain kinds of divine insight into the meaning of the Christian faith and the conduct of the Christian life which the western church lacked. These gifts of the Holy Spirit needed to be preserved as part of the fullness of Catholic experience.

This was more than an academic issue. Already while the council of Florence was in session the voyages of discovery were underway and within a century the trade routes of the world would be dominated by the fleets of Spain and Portugal, both Catholic powers. These discoveries made possible the greatest period of missionary activity in the history of the Christian church, and it was important that before this happened a decision should have been reached that, whereas non-Christian converts should become Catholics of the Latin rite, the separated Christians of Africa and Asia should, if they made their submission to Rome, become eastern-rite Catholics.

17

Witchcraft, Ritual Magic and the Cult of the Magus

I. Witchcraft

The survival of folk magic

> Some wicked women . . . seduced by illusions and phantoms of demons, believe and profess themselves in the hours of night to ride upon certain beasts with Diana, the goddess of the pagans . . . and in the silence of the night to traverse great spaces of earth, and to obey her commands as of their mistress, and to be summoned to her service on certain nights. . . . An innumerable multitude, deceived by this false opinion, believe this to be true. . . . Wherefore the priests . . . should . . . preach to the people that they may know this to be in every way false and that such phantasms are imposed upon the minds of infidels and not by the divine but by the malign spirit.

This enactment, known as the Bishop's Canon, dates from the ninth century and describes the continuing practice in northern Europe of a pagan fertility rite, the wild hunt. The Canon dismisses the hunt itself as illusory, while attributing belief in it to demons who exploit human gullibility. By the eleventh century paganism had died out in most of western Europe, except in very recently converted areas, and it is likely that surviving pagan rituals and beliefs, like that of the wild hunt, would have been allowed to degenerate into folklore had it not been for the persistence of *maleficium*, witchcraft.

The attempt to harm others by supernatural means had been treated as a crime even in pagan times. The church viewed such offences equally severely because of the Biblical injunction, 'Thou shalt not suffer a witch to live' (Exod., 22, 18), and witchcraft was made a capital offence in most Christian law codes. The church did not doubt that crimes of *maleficium* were performed with the help of demons. The rituals which witches used might have had pagan forms, but they could not be relegated to the realm of folkore because the harm which was attempted by those means was real and so, in the church's view, were the demons who were invoked to procure it.

Incubi and succubi

The church taught that the invocation of spiritual beings was always addressed to demons unless it used specifically Christian forms, because there were no beneficent spirits except the angels and the saints. It was essential to use Christian rituals, because demons were capable of deceiving men about their true nature. Like the saints, they could appear to men, and , as St Paul had warned, they could look like angels (II Cor., 11, 14–15). Medieval people credited demons with considerable powers in human affairs, as can be seen from the widely held belief in the existence of incubi and succubi, demons who appeared in male and female form and had intercourse with mortals. This belief seemed to be confirmed by various reputable authorities: the Bible related how the sons of God had once married the daughters of men (Gen., 6, 2), while classical legend told of heroes like Aeneas, born of unions between mortal men and pagan goddesses whom the church regarded as demons.

The hold which this belief had over the imagination of the west can be seen in the late twelfth-century romance, Robert de Boron's *Merlin*, in which the seer is said to be the son of a human mother and a demonic father, possessing the innocence of his mother and the supernatural knowledge of his father. But the belief also appeared to be validated by the testimony of women tried for witchcraft who claimed that they had slept with incubi.

Pacts with the devil

In the later thirteenth century the church began to rationalize its attitude towards folk magic. Although it had previously held that all kinds of magic, whether beneficent or malefic in intent, were diabolically inspired, it had not considered that beneficent magic was consciously directed towards the devil by its operators, but rather that the devil took advantage of human ignorance. During the thirteenth century educated opinion came to accept the Aristotelian concept that every effect must have a cause, and theologians then argued that all kinds of magic must be based on an open or tacit pact with the devil since otherwise their effectiveness could not be logically explained; for non-Christian rituals must be seeking to achieve results through the help of non-Christian spiritual powers, which could only be diabolical.

Thus in the later Middle Ages all folk magic was labelled black magic. Those accused of such offences confessed that they had invoked the aid of demons: they may not, of course, have done so consciously, but may simply have performed traditional pagan rituals, but they were Catholics like their judges and had no other way of rationalizing their actions except in terms of diabolism, which their judges proposed; for there was no neutral ground in the supernatural world as they understood it on a conscious level.

Yet although beneficent magic was technically considered an act of diabolism by the church, its practitioners were rarely brought to trial; the majority of cases of magic heard by the church courts concerned *maleficium*. Those accused were delated to the bishops by their neighbours in the traditional way. The church did not seek out witches, for the only tribunal competent to do so was the Inquisition and pope Alexander IV had in 1258 licensed it to deal only with those cases of witchcraft which were related to heresy. It was not until 1398 that the theology faculty of the university of Paris defined all witchcraft as heretical because it involved a pact with the devil, thus bringing it within the jurisdiction of the Inquisition. Some attempt was made in fifteenth-century Italy to seek out witches and bring them to trial, but on the whole little use was made by the inquisitors of their extended powers over witches during the Middle Ages.

The Malleus Maleficarum

A great deal of information about witchcraft, part of it derived from the depositions of those tried for *maleficium*, became known to the church authorities in the later Middle Ages. This was synthesized in a comprehensive digest, the *Malleus Maleficarum*, or 'Hammer of Witches', published in 1486 by the Dominicans, Henry Kramer and Joseph Sprenger. The following extract gives some idea of the intellectual capacity of the authors:

> The following procedure is practised against hailstorms and tempests. Three of the hailstones are thrown into the fire with an invocation of the Most Holy Trinity, and the Lord's Prayer and the Angelic Salutation are repeated twice or three times, together with the Gospel of St John, 'In the beginning was the Word'. And the sign of the cross is made . . . towards each quarter of the world. Finally, 'The Word was made flesh' is repeated three times, and three times 'By the words of this Gospel may this tempest be dispersed'. And suddenly, *if the tempest is due to witchcraft* [italics mine] it will cease. This is most true and need not be regarded with any suspicion. For if the hailstones were thrown into the fire without the Divine Name, then it would be considered superstitious.

The final phrase appears not a little disingenuous. The *Malleus* is, indeed, an outstanding example of the way in which people grow like what they fear. The authors became so obsessed with the prevalence and malice of witches that they came to see the Christian faith primarily as a kind of white magic affording protection against diabolical attack.

The authors had been appointed to make inquisition for witchcraft in parts of Germany by pope Innocent VIII, and his standard letters of appointment were prefaced to the printed text of the *Malleus*, making it appear that the pope approved the contents and considered witchcraft as important as the authors did. There is no reason to suppose that this was so, but clearly other people shared the authors' views, for the *Malleus* went into fourteen editions by 1520. This was a symptom, not a cause, of the obsession with witchcraft which was to lead to extensive witch-hunts in Protestant and Catholic Europe and America in the sixteenth and seventeenth centuries in a way which had been unknown in the Middle Ages.

The absence of Satanism

The church authorities in the later Middle Ages were convinced that there were Satanists in western Europe who paid religious worship to the devil instead of to God. The wild hunt, denounced in the Bishop's Canon as an illusion, had become a reality in the minds of some churchmen, having been transformed into the witches' sabbath, at which the devil or his minister presided and at which plans were made to undermine the Christian faith.

The church could cite what appeared to be good evidence for such practices, the confessions of those who had taken part in them. This evidence does not seem so convincing now, because what such depositions describe are rituals rooted in pagan folklore but rationalized by an educated clergy. There is no doubt that people who performed acts of *maleficium* invoked demons to accomplish their ends; but there is no evidence known to me that those who practised folk magic of a traditional kind worshipped the devil. The rites which they practised were not diabolical, but pagan ceremonies whose religious origins had been forgotten. Yet logically such rites had no place in the life of Christian people. Ecclesiastical judges were able to convince suspects of the truth of this and get them to agree to swear to depositions about diabolical practices, thereby reinforcing the church's belief that such things really happened.

Medieval people undoubtedly regarded the devil and his legions as sources of power, but they did not apostatize from the Christian faith in order to worship Lucifer in place of God, perhaps because they were conscious that, though he might reward his followers in this life, the prince of darkness could offer them nothing in the next life except hell, which was not attractive. The black mass and other trappings of modern Satanist ritual cannot be traced earlier than the seventeenth century and had no place in the medieval world.

II. Ritual magic

Ritual magic formed part of the learned tradition. It was closely linked to the study of astronomy and was therefore not much practised in western Europe before the twelfth century, when classical Greek scientific texts and Arabic commentaries on them became available in Latin translation for the first time.

Astrology

The new understanding of astronomy affected the study of all natural sciences, for it was believed that all heavenly bodies affected life on earth and that an important part of science was the study of the correspondences between earthly and heavenly things. Such a world view encouraged a belief in astral determinism: that the entire course of events on earth, including the lives of individuals, was 'written in the stars', and that it should therefore be possible for the learned to decipher the writing and foretell the future.

The church accepted the belief in astral correspondences as a matter of scientific fact, but condemned astral determinism. Theologians accepted that God sometimes sent messages to men through the stars (cf. Gen., 1, 14), as when he guided the Magi to Bethlehem by that means, but they denied that the stars could inhibit human free will. The Magi, for example, did not have to go to Bethlehem because they saw the star, it merely gave them information. It therefore followed that, if men had free will, the future could not be foretold by astrological study and it was heresy to claim that it could be.

The church lost this battle. Astrologers proliferated in the later Middle Ages, many of them highly educated men like Michael Scot (†1235), the adviser of the emperor Frederick II. Such men cast horoscopes and advised rulers about the propitious times to conduct state business, and they were rarely disciplined by the church, partly because they had powerful protectors, but chiefly because they did not use forbidden means to gain their knowledge.

Star demons

Many of the astronomical treatises translated from Greek and Arabic in the twelfth and thirteenth centuries gave instructions about how to invoke and command the aid of spiritual beings who controlled the planets and the stars. The church held that any beings which could be commanded must be demons, for, although angels might have sidereal ministries, they would only take orders from God. Demons certainly inhabited the material heavens, for St Paul had warned men about 'spiritual wickedness in the heavenly places' (Eph., 6, 12).

Some of the ritual invocations were clearly directed to maleficent spirits, because they required sacrifice. For example, one spell recommended for use in hydromancy (the art of seeking a reply to a question by gazing into a mirror or a bowl of water) involved the Latin invocation of the demon Floriget by a seven-year old girl, acting as the sorcerer's assistant, and the offering to that spirit of a dead man's bone. Sorcerers trained in ritual magic were sometimes employed to procure acts of *maleficium* by the invocation of demons: a number of cases of this kind, involving members of the French court, occurred in the early fourteenth century.

Many scientific treatises urged scholars to fashion talismans from materials known to be under the influence of particular stars to act as astral magnets to focus the powers of those stars. The church did not object to this unless the talisman was inscribed, since that pre-supposed that it was addressed to an intelligence capable of 'reading' the inscription and an intelligence willing to do so could only be malign. The church's prohibitions were widely disregarded but those who used engraved talismans were not normally prosecuted unless they were accused of *maleficium*.

Alchemy

Among the experimental sciences which the west learned from the Arabs in the Middle Ages was alchemy, the study of chemical transmutation. Aristotle had speculated that all matter was formed from a *prima materia* and that each substance owed its specific form to being impressed by some combination of the four elements, earth, air, water and fire. It should therefore be possible, if the right agent could be discovered, to transmute any substance into any other, and alchemists normally tried to transmute base metals into gold.

The church had no objection to scientific alchemy. The Dominican scholar, Albertus Magnus, the *doctor universalis* (†1280), assayed gold which was claimed to have been produced by alchemical methods on three occasions and on all of them succeeded in reducing it to ashes. He concluded that the experiments had been wrongly conducted, but supposed that gold could have been produced had the right method been found.

Alchemists had a reputation for practising ritual magic, although it is difficult to be sure whether this was justified. Sherwood Taylor argued that most of them were concerned with practical experiments and that the air of magic which surrounded their work derived at least partly from the fact that, lacking a received terminology, they had to use imagery which sounded magical in order to describe empirical experiments. Thus 'the sun was devoured by a green dragon' means that gold containing copper was dissolved in hydrochloric acid which was tinged with green as a result. Against this view it might be urged that alchemists needed to represent their work as practical in order to escape ecclesiastical censure, but that the correspondences which were believed to exist between the heavenly bodies and the metals with which they experimented must have tempted them to resort to astral invocation.

III The cult of the Magus

The Gnostic view of man

Ritual magicians were interested in knowledge and in power but they did not question the orthodox Christian definition of man's capacity and its limitations. That became possible after the discovery of a body of Gnostic writings by the Florentine humanists in the second half of the fifteenth century.

The early church had considered the Gnostics its most dangerous enemies. They claimed to have inherited the secret teachings of Jesus, and they dismissed the Gospels as a mere shell, of interest only to the uninitiated. As Frances Yates pointed out, they did not accept Christian teaching about man's place in the universe:

> The dignity of Man as Magus . . . having within him the divine creative power and the magical power of marrying earth to heaven, rests on the gnostic heresy that man was once, and can become again through his intellect, the reflection of the divine *mens*, a divine being.

The church's willingness to receive texts which taught this doctrine resulted from a complete misconception about the date at which they had been written

Hermes Trismegistus

In 1459 Cosimo de' Medici obtained from his agent in Macedonia a text of the treatises attributed to Hermes Trismegistus and commissioned Marsilio Ficino to prepare a Latin translation. Thrice-great Hermes was the ancient Egyptian god Thoth, but the Florentine humanists supposed, on the authority of St Augustine, that he had been a mortal man, a younger contemporary of Moses, and had been deified. One part of Hermes' work, the *Asclepius*, had been known throughout the Middle Ages in a Latin translation wrongly attributed to Apuleius, the author of *The Golden Ass*. This was an ambivalent treatise from a Christian point of view, for although the author showed evidence of genuine prophetic insight by foretelling the end of Egyptian paganism, he also gave instructions about how to animate idols by drawing demons into them.

The newly discovered Hermetic works contained no hint of occult practices, for they were entirely speculative. In part they were consonant with orthodox Christian teaching, for they spoke of the creation of the world by God, of man's need for spiritual regeneration, and even implied knowledge of the Incarnation of God's Son. In view of this evidence it was argued that the idolatrous passages in the *Asclepius* had been inserted by the translator, Apuleius, a self-confessed sorcerer, and did not form part of Hermes' own teaching.

There was no accurate method of dating the Hermetic writings and they were taken as evidence that the gentile world had received intimations of the truths of Christianity centuries before the Incarnation. While humanists like cardinal Bessarion saw in the *Hermetica* an imperfect understanding of Christian orthodoxy, which must be received with discretion, other scholars were less discriminating. For Florentines, with their great reverence for classical scholarship, were very ready to be impressed by this early work which showed that the ancient world had understood so well the principles of the Christian religion.

Yet the Hermetic works were in fact Gnostic writings of the early Christian centuries. Any knowledge of Christianity which they might display was not prophetic, but was simply knowledge of current affairs; although scholars now tend to think that they were influenced by Jewish rather than Christian ideas. Moreover, the view of man which they taught was a Gnostic view. The *Hermetica* considered that man could perfect himself and that, by understanding and entering into communion with the spiritual principles which informed the heavenly spheres, he could realize the divine potential within him. The Florentines of Ficino's day did not attempt to use the work in this magical way, but they made it available for a later group of scholars who would seek to use it in that way.

The cabala

Ficino's pupil, Pico della Mirandola, inherited his master's respect for the Hermetic writings which he believed bore witness to the truths of Christianity. He also found additional confirmation of Christian truth in the cabala, which he would appear to have been the first Christian scholar to study.

The cabala was a form of Jewish mysticism which had developed among the Sephardim of medieval Spain. It was claimed that Moses had taught this esoteric tradition to the initiated. Fundamental to cabalistic thought is the belief that Hebrew is not merely the language of the Old Testament but the language of creation: that the Word of God which brought the world into being was spoken in Hebrew and that mastery of the true meaning of Hebrew can therefore give men insight into the creative process itself. In Hebrew each letter has a numerical equivalent and it is possible to transpose letters into numbers and then calculate those numbers into a different series of letters. When this art of sacred cryptography is applied to the Old Testament a new text can be produced, containing the esoteric teaching of Moses and his successors. The cabala attached great importance to the significance of the names of God, the ten most common of which form stations on the Sephirotic Tree, the symbol used in meditation to enable the soul to ascend to God. But a special branch of cabalistic number symbolism, known as *gematria*, enabled the practitioner to convert the names of God into numbers and by that means to investigate the secrets of creation. This method could produce very precise results, as, for example, the computation that the hosts of heaven numbered 301, 655, 172. This was important because the heavenly host and their demonic counterpart occupied a central place in cabalistic thought, and each had a name and could be invoked if the initiate could discover what that name was.

Pico della Mirandola believed that the cabala confirmed the truths of the Christian religion far more precisely than the literal prophecies of the Old Testament did. He also believed that the cabalistic teaching about angels conformed to the Christian teaching on this subject attributed to St Paul's pupil, Dionysius (see p. 87 above). Pico accepted the attribution of the cabala to Moses and considered that he and Thrice-great Hermes, who had been near contemporaries, had given clear intimation to the Jewish and gentile worlds of the future Christian revelation.

In 1486 Pico offered to defend in public debate in Rome 900 theses about Hermetic and cabalistic teaching. The most arresting of these is the statement that:

There is no kind of knowledge which gives us more certainty about the divinity of

Christ than magic and cabala. (Nulla est scientia que nos magis certificet de divinitate Christi quam Magia et Cabala.)

By *magic* Pico meant the kind of natural magic recommended in the Hermetic works.

The debate did not take place because pope Innocent VIII censured some of the theses as heretical, but in 1493 Alexander VI reviewed the case and exonerated Pico from any heretical intention on the grounds that he had always stated his willingness to submit all his opinions to the pope's judgement. Alexander did not make any pronouncement about the orthodoxy or otherwise of Pico's theses, but by taking the author under his personal protection he left him free in effect to publish them.

The Christian Magus

Like the rest of their contemporaries, Alexander VI and Pico della Mirandola were ignorant of the true dates of these works. Yet the cabala was post-Christian and represented a Gnostic form of Judaism just as the *Hermetica* were Gnostic writings of the early Christian era. Both taught that men could, by secret knowledge and by the help of supernatural powers, gain mastery of the universe and evoke the divinity within themselves. Neither pope Alexander nor Pico appears to have been aware of this danger, but when Pico published his theses and prefaced them with Alexander's bull, he made the study of Hermetic and cabalistic magic licit for Catholics. That study had considerable potential for producing very unorthodox practitioners as soon became apparent.

Henry Cornelius Agrippa wrote his *De Occulta Philosophia* in 1510, although it was not published until 1533. It gives instructions about how to practise ritual magic in an Hermetic context, which the author claimed was consonant with Christian orthodoxy. That this claim is misleading is evident from the third part of the work, which is concerned with religious magic. In this Agrippa claims that an ordained priest of Catholic faith can, by the use of magical formulae based on the Divine Names, obtain mastery over nature and perform such feats as raising winds, healing the sick and even raising the dead to life.

This approach to Christianity led some men to strive to become Christian Magi, by activating the divine power within themselves in order to obtain mastery of the created order. This magical Christianity was a form of Gnosticism. It never attracted many followers, but it had its roots in the late medieval period and was to persist into the seventeenth century when a new scientific model of the universe eroded the conceptual basis in which it was grounded.

18
A Tradition of Dissent

Once Arianism had died out in the west during the late seventh century (see chapter 1) there was no popular religious dissent there for some 300 years. The Adoptianist heresy, which arose in the Mozarabic church of Spain in the late eighth century, scarcely comes under that heading. It was a highly technical dispute about the relationship between the divine and human natures of Christ, which had little popular appeal and disappeared after the death of its chief protagonist, archbishop Elipandus of Seville.

Early dissenting movements

This religious peace was ended by the outbreak of a number of isolated, apparently unconnected, cases of heresy in Lombardy, France and Germany during the first half of the eleventh century. Some of these heretics are called Manichaeans in the sources and this has led to much scholarly controversy. Runciman, for example, concludes that these heretics were representatives of Bogomilism, a dualist movement founded in tenth-century Bulgaria, while R.I. Moore argues that the label Manichaean was used merely to describe the extreme asceticism of some of these dissidents. He considers that most of them were indigenous western reformers, concerned to purify the church, and points out that when the papacy assumed the leadership of the struggle for reform in the 1050s and called on all men of goodwill to help, heretical outbreaks virtually ceased for sixty years and started again only when the popes began to compromise about reform issues.

It may well be that there were both dualists and reformers among these early heretical groups, but no firm consensus has yet been reached on this subject. These outbreaks do not seem to have had any lasting effect on the development of heresy in the west, but they are important because they mark the beginning of a tradition of dissent within the western church.

Reforming heresies of the twelfth century

Eleventh-century papal reform made the church strong and in the process created a degree of vocal anti-clericalism which had been absent from the west in earlier centuries, even though the clergy had then been far more corrupt, but which never abated throughout the rest of the Middle Ages.

The bitterness felt in some circles about papal venality is expressed in satires like 'The Gospel According to the Mark of Silver':

And it came to pass that a certain poor clerk came to the curia of the lord Pope and cried, saying: 'Have mercy on me, ye doorkeepers of the Pope, for the hand of poverty hath touched me.' . . . But they hearing this had indignation among themselves and said: 'Friend, thy poverty go with thee to perdition. . . .'. And the poor man went away and sold his cloak and his tunic and all that he had and gave to the cardinals and the doorkeepers and the chamberlains. But they said: 'And what is this among so many?' And they cast him out, and he going out wept bitterly and could not be comforted.

But anti-clericalism is not necessarily a sign of hostility to the established faith. One need look no further than Ireland today to see that extreme anti-clericalism is not incompatible with the devout practice of Catholicism. Nevertheless, when anti-clericalism is widespread, dissenting preachers can be assured of a ready audience from which to recruit supporters. During the twelfth century a number of men appeared who began by seeking to reform the church but came into conflict with the hierarchy and were driven into schism with their followers.

A typical example of this kind was the gifted popular preacher, Henry of Lausanne. He was concerned with the problems of urban prostitution and in c.1116, with the consent of the bishop, conducted a mission in Le Mans which met with great success. Prostitutes repented and Henry arranged marriages for them, but his teaching about marriage brought him into conflict with the clergy and, although the common people sided with him (for clearly he had hit upon a volatile social issue), he was driven from the city. He spent the next thirty years in southern France, where he attracted a large following by preaching the need for church reform. He attacked the church's wealth and taught that only a worthy priest could validly celebrate the eucharist, and he denied the need for sacramental confession. Yet although he was condemned as a heretic he was obviously wishing only to reform the existing church, not to found a new one. His movement collapsed after his death because it lacked organization.

Other reform movements of the same period had a similar history. A forceful leader would attract followers but fail to give his movement any structure, so that it would fade away after his death. A change came about in the later twelfth century when the first reformed church was founded, that of the Waldensians.

The Waldensians

Their founder, Valdès, was the most orthodox of men. He was a rich merchant of Lyons who, moved by hearing the *Life* of St Alexius (see p. 82), gave all his goods to the poor, took a vow of apostolic poverty and, gathering lay adherents of both sexes, began preaching to the poor. In 1179 pope Alexander III praised him for his vow of poverty and gave him and his followers permission to preach provided that they obtained a licence from their bishop. It was perhaps inevitable that the bishop should only have been willing to grant a licence on conditions which the Waldensians found unacceptable, that they should have continued to preach without a licence, and that they should have been excommunicated and driven into schism.

The Waldensians spread over much of southern France and Lombardy. Although at first they had no quarrel with the theory of Catholicism, only with its practice, they needed to develop an organization of their own once they could no longer operate inside the church. They accepted what later ages would call 'the priesthood of all believers', allowing all instructed members of their church, women as well as men, to carry out the work of public ministry including preaching. They had no ordained clergy and preserved only three of the Catholic sacraments: infant baptism, marriage, and the eucharist, which they celebrated only once a year on the evening of Maundy Thursday. They confessed their sins to one another and condemned certain Catholic practices, notably the offering of masses for the dead, the practice of priestly blessing and absolution, the use of excommunication and the granting of indulgences. Yet, as many Catholic writers admitted, the Waldensians remained close to the church in their teachings about the central truths of the faith. They were the first dissenting group in the west to develop an organization which enabled its members to preserve their identity after the death of their founder.

The Cathars

Although there is considerable dispute about whether dualist heretics were present in the west in the early eleventh century, there is no doubt that they were there in the twelfth. These heretics called themselves Cathars, a name derived from the Greek word *Katharoi*, the pure, and it is now generally agreed that they were an offshoot of the Bogomil heresy found in the Balkans and Greece. Although contemporaries called the Cathars Manichaeans, the name of the adherents of the great dualist movement of late Roman times, it has proved impossible to establish with certainty an historical filiation between the two movements.

The Cathars are first securely attested in the west in 1143, when one of their bishops was put on trial at Cologne, although they may have been there much earlier. During the next sixty years they formed congregations throughout much of western Europe, but flourished particularly in southern France and Lombardy, and these western churches retained strong links with the Balkan Bogomils.

The Cathars brought an excellent organization with them to the west. They had territorial dioceses, each with a Cathar bishop at its head, who was assisted by two coadjutors, known as his Elder and Younger Sons. When a bishop died his Elder Son automatically succeeded him, his Younger Son became the new Elder Son and a new Younger Son was elected. This made the Cathar church very resilient in time of persecution. Each Cathar diocese was divided up into smaller units, rather like Catholic parishes, each with a Cathar deacon at its head, who had jurisdiction over all the professed Cathars there and was a liaison between them and the bishop. Unlike other heretical groups, the Cathars were not interested in reforming the Catholic church. They wished to abolish it, though not by force but by persuasion, because they believed that it was a counterfeit of the true church, which was their own.

The Cathars based their faith on the New Testament, and not merely used an entirely Christian vocabulary, but were undoubtedly followers of Christ. It is necessary to say this, because it is frequently argued that Catharism was not Christian at all. It is nevertheless true that Cathars understood the Gospel in a different sense from all other Christians, for they were Christian dualists, that is to say that they did not believe that the Good God had made the material heavens and earth. A variety of opinions existed among them on matters of theology, which makes generalization difficult. Some believed that the material universe had been created by an evil god, co-eternal with the Good God, while others attributed it to the work of an evil demiurge who had fashioned it from the four elements which the Good God had made. All were agreed that human souls belonged to the Good God and had been trapped by the power of evil in material bodies; while some Cathars also thought that all warm-blooded beasts and birds shared souls of equal status with those of men and that all those souls were kept imprisoned by a continuous process of reincarnation. All Cathars agreed that Christ had appeared on earth to accomplish the deliverance of the imprisoned souls, although they differed about the form which his intervention had taken.

Christ had founded the Cathar church to preserve his teaching and to administer the unique sacrament of salvation, the *consolamentum,* or strengthening, which could be conferred only by a fully initiated Cathar and which was normally granted only to adults who had undergone a lengthy period of training and instruction, although it could be conferred, without probation, on the dying. The central part of the rite consisted in the placing of a Gospel Book on the head of the candidate by the minister with the words: *perfecti.*

> Holy Father, receive thy servant/handmaiden in thy righteousness and send thy grace and thy Holy Spirit upon him/her.

This act had the sacramental power to free the recipient from sin, from the dominion of evil and from the round of re-birth. He became a 'perfect', a fully initiated member of the Cathar church, but his salvation was conditional on perseverance, for the perfect had to live perfectly. They had to renounce all property, to vow perpetual chastity, to undertake never to lie, to swear an oath or to take the life of any creature, even if in danger of death. They were bound by a strict rule of life which enjoined the recitation of set prayers at fixed hours, fifteen times each day and night, and total abstinence from meat and all secondary animal products such as eggs, cheese, milk and lard, although they might eat fish. In addition they had to observe rigorous fasts and to place themselves completely at the disposal of their bishop. Some of them were employed in the work of public ministry, but most of them lived in small communities which performed charitable work, or were organized as workshops in which the perfect earned their keep as weavers.

Although only the perfect were full members of the church, the Cathars also attracted large numbers of believers who were committed to their teachings with varying degrees of fervour. They were not bound by the rules of the church, but they hoped to be consoled when they were dying and thereby to achieve salvation.

The problem of toleration

When a group of Cathars from Flanders came to England in the 1160s, even though they only gained one convert, retribution was swift. Henry II summoned a synod of bishops to Oxford who tried the heretics and, when they refused to recant, handed them over to the king for punishment. He ordered them to be branded, stripped naked to the waist and turned out to freeze to death in the depths of winter, and inserted a clause in the Constitutions of Clarendon in 1166 forbidding any of his subjects to aid them.

This kind of prompt reaction to heresy did not occur everywhere. In southern France and Lombardy, where political and ecclesiastical authority were fragmented, it proved difficult to prosecute heresy when it first appeared. In those regions Cathars, and Waldensians as well, preached openly, held religious assemblies, and even ecclesiastical councils, with no attempt at concealment, and on occasion staged public debates with Catholic clergy about the relative merits of their respective faiths. After this had happened for thirty years a generation of people had grown up who accepted religious pluralism as normal. Members of the same family sometimes professed different faiths while remaining on amicable terms, and when in 1207 the bishop of Toulouse asked a Catholic knight why he and others like him did not drive the heretics out, the knight replied:

> We can't. We have grown up with them; we are related to them; and we can see what good lives they lead.

The medieval church did not consider religious toleration a virtue, for, believing as it did that it taught the truth, it did not doubt that dissenters were in error, nor that they endangered the salvation of those whom God had entrusted to the church's care. Church courts had the right to examine cases of heresy, but their powers were limited. Heretics had to be delated to the bishop by their neighbours, there was no machinery for seeking them out; and church courts had no penal authority, so that obdurate heretics could only be excommunicated and released. Lay authorities, it is true, could punish excommunicated heretics if they wished, but they were not required to do so. Yet in much of northern Europe this system worked reasonably well as heresy became more common in the course of the twelfth century: heretics were delated to bishops and rulers cooperated with the church in punishing those who refused to recant.

But in southern Europe the system broke down: most of the time heretics were not delated to bishops, and rulers refused to aid the church in the suppression of heresy, being apparently content to preside over a society in which religious pluralism was encouraged. This led Innocent III in 1209 to launch a crusade against the rulers of southern France. It was not envisaged as a means of suppressing heresy, but as a way of replacing men who tolerated heresy by princes of undoubted orthodoxy, who would give full support to the church. In the long term it was successful in this, for by 1229 successive crusades had brought southern France under the effective control of the very orthodox Capetian kings of France.

The Inquisition

In order to detect heretics in areas where the local population was sympathetic towards them and would not delate them to the bishop, pope Gregory IX in *c.*1233 set up the Inquisition. Its work is often misunderstood, for it was not a church court with penal powers, but a commission of inquiry entrusted with detecting those guilty of heresy and of taking depositions from them under oath. Inquisitors were appointed only in those areas where heretics were known to exist, and never operated, for example, in England or in medieval Castile. The inquisitors appointed in each district were an autonomous group, personally responsible to the pope, and there was no central coordinating committee in Rome to oversee the work of regional inquisitors comparable to the Holy Office set up for that purpose by Paul III when he reformed the Inquisition in 1542.

The medieval Inquisition was staffed by trained theologians drawn chiefly from the mendicant Orders. Although licensed to sanction the torture of obdurate witnesses, it seldom seems to have used that power during the main heresy trials of the thirteenth century. Indeed, the Inquisition was far less bloodthirsty and oppressive than it is often represented as being. The vast majority of those whom it found guilty were dismissed with canonical penances, and a substantial minority were detained in the Inquisition's prisons, but the number of unrepentant heretics handed over to the secular authorities and burned at the stake was small. That was the result of a deliberate policy, for the inquisitors were reluctant to allow heretics to be executed, because that removed any possibility that they could be converted. *–how holy of them.*

The Inquisition had a chequered career because initially it aroused considerable popular animosity, while secular governments were unwilling to give it their full support, but it gradually became an accepted part of the machinery of ecclesiastical justice. Within a century of its establishment the Cathars and Waldensians had been driven to the margins of western society, though not eliminated. It would be simplistic to attribute this result solely to persecution, which normally has the effect of disseminating proscribed movements more widely. Of course, the Inquisition had some part in the decline of heresy, but credit should also be given to the mendicant Orders, whose intensive evangelization of the west during the thirteenth century must also have helped in the erosion of support for heresy, as well as in giving new vigour to Catholicism.

Cathars and Waldensians after 1300

While it undoubtedly weakened the older heresies, the Inquisition did not eliminate them. The Waldensians withdrew from those areas where it was most active and settled in remote parts of Piedmont, south Italy and southern and eastern Germany. Since theirs was a reformist church, they were prepared to adopt a policy of occasional conformity towards Catholicism. They allowed their children to be baptized by Catholic priests and occasionally went to mass, although they would not communicate. Their own itinerant clergy ministered privately to them, but much of the time they looked like lukewarm Catholics. From time to time they were persecuted: in 1488 a crusade was even preached against those of Piedmont, but, although it caused much destruction and suffering, it did not succeed in stamping out the faith. The Waldensians survive to this day although, as Euan Cameron has recently shown, they had little in common with the Calvinists with whom they joined in the sixteenth century, and it was only Protestant historiography which created the myth of their being harbingers of the Protestant Reformation.

In 1325, as Catharism was disappearing in western Europe, pope John XXII reported that Cathars were flocking to Bosnia in large numbers. This remote region of northern Yugoslavia had been nominally converted to Catholicism before the twelfth century, but in *c.*1200 Bogomilism, the Balkan form of Catharism, took root there and from *c.*1250 displaced Catholicism as the established religion, although it should be noted that the evidence about this is interpreted differently by J.A.V. Fine. Catholic Franciscans established missions in Bosnia in the fourteenth century, but Catharism remained the dominant religion there until the Ottoman conquest in 1463 and survived in neighbouring Herzegovina until the Ottomans occupied it in 1482. Thereafter nothing is known about the Balkan Bogomils, but before that time any western European with Catharist inclinations could travel to Bosnia to receive instruction in the faith and to be professed as a perfect. There is evidence that a few people did so, but no serious attempt was made by the Bosnian church to re-introduce Catharism into western Europe.

The persistence of dissent

The Inquisition had authority to deal with all types of heresy and it continued to function, albeit with diminished zeal, even after the principal heresies, Catharism and Waldensianism, had collapsed in the western heartlands. Yet despite the use of religious coercion, it proved impossible to return to the religious situation of three centuries earlier when conformity had been the rule. Dissent had become part of the western tradition.

It took a wide variety of forms. The Spiritual Franciscans, who attempted to adhere to their founder's ideal of absolute poverty, were persecuted for their intransigence in the early fourteenth century and driven to take up an extreme position about the virtue of apostolic poverty. John XXII condemned those views as heretical and the Spirituals who refused to accept his ruling were driven into schism and persecuted as heretics. They became the Fraticelli, who survived until the fifteenth century as a dissenting minority, strongly opposed to the wealth and privilege of the established church, but not in other ways heterodox in belief.

The Lollards

In England a new dissenting movement developed among the followers of John Wycliffe (†1384), an academic theologian in the university of Oxford who attacked abuses in the church, including non-residence and pluralism, but also criticized established devotions such as pilgrimage and the invocation of saints. More radically, he objected to the ways in which papal power was exercised and, while asserting belief in the Real Presence of Christ in the eucharist, criticized the Catholic definition of transubstantiation on philosophical grounds, arguing that the substance of bread and wine remained in the consecrated elements, not merely the accidents. It was, perhaps, as well for Wycliffe that the church did not adopt his proposals about pluralism, since for many years he was rector of Lutterworth and canon of Westbury-on-Trym and resident in neither.

When some of his adherents were expelled from the university of Oxford in 1382 for refusing to abjure some of Wycliffe's teachings, they began to preach to the laity and to attract popular support. The movement received its distinctive character from the use by Wycliffite preachers of an English Bible. The work of translation would seem to have been initiated by Wycliffe though only completed after his death. His supporters became known as Lollards and initially were quite numerous. Although the Inquisition did not function in England, heretics fared no more leniently there than elsewhere, for in 1401 parliament enacted the statute *De Haeretico Comburendo*, which made burning at the stake mandatory for obdurate heretics. The number of Lollards who suffered that penalty was mercifully small, because most of them recanted when brought to trial. Though reduced in numbers by persecution, the Lollards survived until the sixteenth century. They took up more extreme positions than those which Wycliffe had held, rejecting clerical celibacy and the doctrine of indulgences, denying that sinful priests could validly say mass, and advocating that the church should renounce all its endowments. They completely rejected papal authority and regarded the Bible, as interpreted by themselves, as the final authority in religious matters. Yet for all their radical attitudes they had more in common with earlier medieval reforming movements than with the Protestant reformers by whom they were absorbed in the sixteenth century.

The Hussites

John Hus, the founder of a similar reform movement in Bohemia, was Rector of the university of Prague and was much influenced by Wycliffe's writings although by no means uncritical of them, rejecting, for example, Wycliffe's teaching on transubstantiation. Hus became leader of the pietist movement among the Slav population of Bohemia, but this brought him into conflict with the largely German episcopate and led to his being excommunicated. Hus appealed against this to the General Council of the church meeting at Constance in 1415 and went to it armed with a safe conduct from the emperor Sigismund and a certificate of orthodoxy from the inquisitor of Prague. At that time the Holy See was vacant and the Fathers of the council had just passed the decree *Sacrosancta* declaring that the authority of a General Council is superior to that of the pope (see chapter 4). Hus therefore timed his protest badly when he refused to retract some of his opinions which the council had censured unless it could be proved that they were contrary to the teaching of the Bible. By doing this he was denying the council's claim to be the final authority in the church, and was ranging himself not against papal authoritarianism, but against the most enlightened and reform-minded opinion in the western church in his day. Disregarding his safe-conduct, the council burned him for heresy, an act which appears to have been unjust in all senses, for the modern Catholic theologian, P. de Voogt, has argued that Hus's teaching was completely orthodox in intention.

His death led to a revolt in Bohemia, supported by two very dissimilar social groups. The Utraquists were drawn from the conservative circle of Slav pietists who sought moderate reform in the Bohemian church. They were mainly Czech noblemen, burgesses of Prague and members of the university, and their chief desire was to be allowed to receive holy communion in both kinds (*sub utraque specie*), which was refused to the laity at that time (see chapter 12). Their associates, the Taborites, were chiefly peasants, who resented the landed wealth of the Bohemian church, and who set up their headquarters on a mountain near Prague which they called Mount Tabor, believing that the Second Coming of Christ was imminent. The Taborites broke completely with the church, elected their own bishop, abolished all Catholic rites including the observance of Sunday, and recognized the Bible as their final authority.

These two groups allied in 1419 in order to prevent the emperor Sigismund, whom they held responsible for Hus's death, from succeeding to the Bohemian throne. They agreed a common programme, the Four Articles of Prague: no restrictions should be placed on freedom of preaching; the laity should receive holy communion in two kinds; the church should renounce all property; and the state should punish all those who had committed mortal sin. Sigismund tried to gain the throne with the help of armies recruited chiefly in Germany, and pope Martin V gave these expeditions the status of crusades against heretics, but they were roundly beaten by the Hussites in 1420, 1421, 1422, 1427 and 1431.

While they remained united the Hussites were invincible, but the Utraquists became alarmed by the social radicalism of some of the Taborites and withdrew their support from them, sending envoys instead to try to reach an agreement with the new General Council which met at Basle in 1431. Deprived of Utraquist help, the Taborite army was decisively defeated in 1434 and this marked the effective end of the radical wing of Hussitism. In 1436 the Council of Basle made concessions to the Utraquists which were of no practical significance except for the permission to receive holy communion in both kinds. The Utraquists, now without allies, settled for this compromise, and although pope Pius II attempted to revoke the faculty about holy communion in 1462, it was safeguarded by the Bohemian Diet. This was the only practice which by that time distinguished Utraquist Hussites from other Catholics. In 1467, however, a group of Utraquists broke away from the church and formed the Bohemian Brotherhood. They were world-renouncing quietists, who rejected oath-taking and military service, and disapproved of urban life and of personal property. They survived into the early modern period and later evolved into the Moravian Brethren.

Hussitism was the last dissenting movement of any consequence to develop during the Middle Ages. As will be evident from this brief survey, religious pluralism existed in the west from 1000 onwards, but during much of that time dissent could not openly be practised in most places. Nevertheless, a surprisingly wide range of clandestine alternatives to Catholicism did exist and it may, with some justice, be claimed that a dissenting tradition was established during the Middle Ages, with the result that religious pluralism has remained a permanent feature of western society to this day.

19

The Individual Quest for God

The Christian church is a community and the Catholic tradition places particular emphasis on the corporate nature of salvation and the communal nature of worship. Nevertheless, there have always been people who do not like taking part in group activities; they existed in the medieval west just as they do now, and a place had to be found for them in a church which claimed to be universal. Accommodation proved possible because the church is primarily a spiritual society: natural solitaries, with an aversion from human company, might nevertheless fulfil the conditions of church membership if they were willing to pray for the fellow Christians whom they did not wish to meet.

The solitary life was accounted a special vocation, and although it may be assumed that God does not normally call men to live in ways to which they are completely unsuited by temperament, it would be misleading to class all religious solitaries as by nature anti-social, for among them were to be found some gregarious people who had embraced the solitary life because it was the most austere kind of penance of which they could conceive. Solitaries were known as hermits, those who lived in the *eremia*, or wilderness. They took monastic vows and were accounted members of the regular clergy.

The first hermits

The first known example of a solitary Christian vocation is that of St Paul of Thebes who as a young man fled to the desert during the Decian persecution (250) and remained there for ninety years, being discovered only shortly before his death by the monastic founder, St Anthony. Although St Paul's *Life* may be largely mythical, St Jerome considered it authentic and translated it into Latin, and this set the seal of approval on the solitary life in the western church.

In the eastern churches the eremitical life sometimes took extravagant forms, producing stylites, who spent their lives perched on the tops of classical columns, and dendrites, who lived in trees from which they seldom if ever came down. The western climate may account for the fact that such extremes were not found there, although the eremitical vocation proved very popular.

The training of hermits

The *Rule of St Benedict* has this to say about hermits:

> They are men who have learned to fight against the devil because of the support they
> have received from many others in the daily round of monastic life. . . . Being well

instructed, they are able to leave the regiment of the monastic brotherhood and to undertake solitary combat as hermits, secure in the knowledge that without human help, but through God's grace and their own strength, they are capable of fighting the sins of the body and of the mind.

All monastic writers were aware of the spiritual dangers which lay in wait for a novice who entered upon the solitary life without any preliminary training. He had to come to terms with his entire personality and if he tried to do this by himself he was liable to suffer severe psychological disorders. Medieval monastic writers did not, of course, use that terminology but spoke of spiritual evil, but the symptoms which they describe are recognizable in terms of modern medicine. The aspiring solitary needed to be trained in self-discipline, self-knowledge and discernment (the capacity to distinguish between true and false experience) before he could live alone safely.

Most hermits therefore served a novitiate in a monastery before moving on to the solitary life. There was a very strong tradition in Celtic monasticism of experienced monks' becoming recluses and withdrawing from their communities completely to live in isolated places, difficult of access, such as small, rocky islands near the coast. Recluses were also found in the early Middle Ages in Benedictine monasticism, despite its far stronger emphasis on the importance of community life. Benedict himself, St Gregory relates, had spent his early life as a solitary at Subiaco, and throughout the early Middle Ages in many Benedictine houses there were brethren who followed his example: having been trained in community they withdrew to cells on the monastery estates and lived as recluses.

Rules for hermits

Although they were given their initial training in monasteries, recluses often received little guidance about the conduct of their daily lives after they withdrew into solitude. To meet this need Grimlaicus, a Rhenish or French recluse of the ninth or tenth century, wrote a *Rule for Solitaries* closely modelled on the Benedictine Rule. The Benedictine Rule had been designed for cenobites and it was arguable that hermits needed direction of a different kind. This was provided by St Romuald of Ravenna (†1027).

He was trained as a Benedictine, but felt a vocation to the solitary life and became the pupil of the hermit Marinus, who was self-taught. This experience may have influenced Romuald in his decision to provide a proper training for recluses. He founded a number of communities for solitaries in north and central Italy and was called by his disciple, St Bruno of Querfurt, 'the father of reasonable hermits . . . of those who live under a law'. Romuald gave no written rule to his followers and did not even form his foundations into a congregation, and Jean Leclercq has truly said of him that 'he did not rule an Order, but taught an ideal'. That ideal survived his death and his foundations grew into the Order of Camaldoli. The organization of the Order seems to have owed much to St Peter Damian, the cardinal-hermit, who entered the Romualdine community of Fonte Avellana in 1035, although the Camaldolese Rule did not achieve its final form until 1072 when it was licensed by pope Alexander II.

Although Romuald saw his foundations as Benedictine communities which truly reflected the intention of the Rule in the training which they provided for the eremitical life, yet they bore a strong resemblance to the *lauras* of the

Orthodox church. Romuald may have been influenced by Greek monks, of whom there was no shortage in north Italy in his day (see chapter 16), but there is no firm evidence to support this view, and it is possible that the oriental influences discernible in his teaching came from his reading the *Lives* of the Desert Fathers.

Camaldolese hermits were divided into two groups: one group lived in pairs, inhabiting cells near the chapel, and undertaking the administration of the community and the training of novices; while the other group was made up of fully-trained recluses, who lived singly, in cells situated at some distance from the chapel and took little part in community life. The brethren were required to recite the Divine Office each day, and in addition to recite two whole psalters, (i.e. 300 psalms), one for the living and one for the dead. Part of each day was spent in religious reading and part in manual labour, and there can have been virtually no time available for extempore mental prayer. Romuald clearly considered that the best safeguard against distraction in prayer was continual meditation on the psalms. The Camaldolese in their early years led a very austere life and ate very frugally as well. They also used corporal penance regularly, and practised voluntary flagellation as an aid to concentration while reciting the psalms.

The Carthusians

St Romuald is said to have wished to 'turn the whole world into a hermitage', but his Order was too austere to become popular. Nevertheless, he had drawn attention to a need in the western church, that of giving regular spiritual direction to the quite large number of men who wished to live as solitaries. This ideal was taken up by other religious reformers, most notably by St Bruno, a secular priest, who had been head of the cathedral school of Rheims and chancellor of the diocese, before entering the religious life at the age of about fifty and founding the Grande Chartreuse in 1084. This, and his later foundation of La Torre in Calabria, formed the nucleus of the Carthusian Order, whose *Rule* was drawn up after his death and approved by the pope in 1133.

The Carthusians resemble the Camaldolese in combining Benedictine monasticism with strict personal asceticism and solitude. Each professed brother lives in a separate cell, almost like a private house, within the monastic complex. The brethren attend chapel each day to recite the Divine Office and sing mass, but they only eat together on great feast days. They follow a common timetable, devoting part of each day to work and study and part to private prayer, and the Order has always been characterized by extreme austerity of life. Unlike the Camaldolese the Carthusians do not have a tradition of corporal penance, nor are they bound to meditate on the psalms, but are allowed freedom in the kind of mental prayer they use. The Order has never had a large number of houses, but it has always maintained a steady flow of vocations and preserved so high a standard of observance that it can with justice claim that it has never stood in need of reform.

Hermits in the later Middle Ages

Although these new Orders were founded to train hermits, this did not mark the end of the older custom whereby recluses lived as dependants of cenobitic monasteries. Most of the great houses of western Europe in the central Middle

Ages had some recluses living on their estates, and not all of them were drawn from the communities themselves. For secular clergy sometimes withdrew from the world to live as hermits, as did some lay people, and they tended to affiliate themselves to the nearest monastery. It should not be forgotten that some women also chose to lead the eremitical life, like Christina of Markyate, who became a recluse at the age of sixteen in order to avoid contracting a marriage which her parents had arranged for her, and lived until she was seventy on a property belonging to the Benedictines of St Albans.

There was clearly no shortage of men and women with vocations to the solitary life. A considerable number of new eremitical Orders was founded in the later Middle Ages: some were small and short-lived, while those which were successful tended in time to broaden their activities and undertake active work. This happened to the Hermits of Mount Carmel, founded in the Crusader kingdom of Jerusalem in the mid-twelfth century as a community of solitaries. The Order established communities in western Europe in the thirteenth century and was reorganized to become a mendicant Order, known popularly as the whitefriars, whose new constitutions were ratified by Innocent IV in 1250. Yet even after this had happened the late medieval Carmelites retained a strong love of the solitary life and some of them were allowed to live as recluses provided that they would agree to return to the world when required to do so.

True solitaries

St Peter Damian, the cardinal-hermit of Fonte Avellana, distinguished between hermits who lived in community and true solitaries who were attached to no foundation but lived completely alone in the wilderness, and remarked that 'in our time they are rarely to be found, if at all'. This may have been an exaggeration, but certainly when he wrote, in the mid-eleventh century, solitaries were less numerous than they had once been.

The church authorities had never been entirely happy about the existence of solitaries. This is evident from the very beginning in the way in which the church recounted the life of St Paul of Thebes. St Anthony was needed partly as a literary device in order to explain how anything was known about the recluse Paul at all, but Anthony also represented the institutional church, for he possessed a cloak which had been given to him by St Athanasius, patriarch of Alexandria and head of the church of Egypt. The *Life* relates that Paul requested to be buried in this cloak, and this symbolizes his acceptance of duly constituted ecclesiastical authority.

Not all solitaries were so orthodox. Although many of them had been trained in monasteries, they had little connection with the institutional church once they had left the community. Unless they were priests they could not receive the sacraments, and they never joined with other Christians in acts of worship. They normally had no service books and so could not recite the Divine Office or observe the feasts and fasts of the church's year. The religious activities of such men consisted of manual labour, in order to grow food to feed themselves, and mental prayer, but there was always the danger that their total separation from the institutional church could lead them to form very idiosyncratic opinions about matters of faith.

The movement pioneered by St Romuald to encourage recluses to live in community was intended to prevent situations of that kind from arising, but true solitaries were temperamentally men like Paul of Thebes, who were quite happy to live in the desert for ninety years without speaking to another soul, and a different kind of approach was needed to integrate them into the worshipping life of the church. In the central Middle Ages solitaries were encouraged to become anchorites and anchoresses.

Anchorites and anchoresses

Such men and women made their monastic profession to a bishop and vowed to spend the rest of their lives in a cell, or anchor-hold, in which they were ceremonially walled-up. This terminology creates a totally false impression of an anchorite's living conditions. Anchor-holds were normally situated in towns and, although they could be very austere, many of them seem to have been quite comfortable. The cell consisted of one or more furnished rooms in which the anchorite lived; there was usually a fireplace to give heat in the winter, and several windows, one of which opened on to the street so that the anchorite might converse with visitors. Cells were frequently built adjacent to churches, and an interior window was then pierced in the church wall so that the anchorite could follow the services. Some cells had courtyards and small gardens which formed part of the enclosure so that the anchorite might walk there. Arrangements were made by the church authorities for the regular provision of food and fuel, and although anchorites might not leave their cells, there was no restriction on the visitors whom they might receive at their windows. A priest would regularly bring the sacraments to them, and some anchoresses employed maids who brought them cooked food. Some anchoresses were also allowed to keep cats, who could enter and leave through the windows of the cell.

In many ways anchor-holds would have been ideal 'sheltered' housing for elderly, housebound people of a devout turn of mind, but the life was usually entered upon by men and women who were young and healthy and their chief enemy must have been boredom. They followed a variety of rules written specially for anchorites and their time was spent chiefly in reading and in mental and liturgical prayer. It might be supposed that it was psychologically damaging for healthy adults to choose a way of life which allowed no exercise and gave scope only for mental activity, but the evidence does not bear this out. For example, the English anchoress, Julian of Norwich, who lived in enclosure for some forty years, was, to judge from her writings, a woman possessed of considerable common sense and unusual serenity of mind, whereas her younger contemporary, Margery Kempe (who, like Julian, was a mystic) was a married woman with children, who had travelled through much of Europe, yet it was she who suffered from mental instability. Environment is not in itself a determinant of health.

St Francis of Paola

Anchorites were very numerous. Every sizable town in western Europe in the later Middle Ages would appear to have supported at least one, and some had several. Consequently the kind of wild solitary who had been quite common in the early Middle Ages had virtually ceased to exist in the western church by the end of the fifteenth century. This became clear when Louis XI of France (1461–83), fearing the approach of death, had to send to Calabria to fetch the

Franciscan hermit, Francis of Paola, to pray for him. Francis, founder of the Order of Minims, was a true solitary, with unkempt hair and beard, and was distinguished by his great austerity of life, for he would eat neither meat nor fish. Such a figure appeared totally out of place at the sophisticated Valois court, but the king regarded him with deep reverence as a true holy man. A few centuries before such a hermit could have been found in almost any part of western Europe, but by the late fifteenth century the church had brought almost all such men within the establishment, as licensed anchorites, members of eremitical Orders, or recluses attached to monasteries.

Holy tramps

In the later Middle Ages a group of men became classified as hermits who were not in any received sense solitaries at all, but men who were attracted to the monastic life but did not wish to live in a monastery. The phenomenon was as old as monasticism itself, and St Benedict had dismissed such men as *gyrovagi*, gadabouts, but in the later Middle Ages men of this temperament were able to obtain a bishop's license declaring them to be registered hermits. They often accepted employment, being made responsible for the upkeep of bridges, or the maintenance of beacons at river estuaries to help guide shipping by night, and in such cases they were given a cell in which to live.

Itinerant hermits of this kind were a very mixed group of men. Some of them, despite their monastic status, were medieval hippies, indistinguishable from tramps, while others were very distinguished indeed. The English mystic, Richard Rolle (†1349), was a man of that kind. A priest and a scholar, he had been trained at Oxford and in the theology schools of Paris, which should have qualified him for a successful career in the church, but he preferred to live as a hermit and to be itinerant. He wrote on the mystical life, composed works of Biblical commentary, translated the psalms into English and wrote devotional poetry. He also preached regularly, and he ended his life at Hampole in Yorkshire as spiritual director to a community of Cistercian nuns.

Monastic retreats

Many monks were attracted to the solitary life for short periods of time. This was particularly true in Celtic monasteries. Abbots regularly withdrew to hermitages to keep a retreat which lasted for the whole of Lent, while bishops trained in this tradition followed similar courses: St Aidan, when bishop of Lindisfarne, for example, used regularly to go into retreat on one of the Inner Farne islands. Even in the mainstream of Benedictine monasticism, which placed great emphasis on communal activity, the solitary life exerted a powerful attraction: John, abbot of Fécamp in Normandy (1028–78), wrote a lament for the loss of solitude which the duties of his office prevented him from enjoying. The same desire also moved some members of the active Orders: thus St Francis of Assisi made no fewer than six retreats to the solitude of Mount Alvernia in the last years of his life, and some of his later followers were likewise strongly drawn to the eremitical life.

Hermits and the life of the church

Hermits were regarded in the medieval west as the élite members of the church, men and women who had taken their religion so seriously that they had been prepared to sacrifice everything in order to wait on God. Dante reflects this opinion when, in the *Paradiso*, he places the contemplative saints, among whom the hermits are found, in the seventh heaven, where they are outranked only by the Virgin and the Apostles in the eighth heaven.

Because they were so highly regarded, hermits were much valued as counsellors by lay people, who credited them with a ready access to God. This was true of all classes. The young emperor Otto III, for example, when staying at Ravenna in 1001 and planning how to restore the Roman empire in the west, frequently consulted the hermit Romuald and his companions who lived in the nearby marshes. Indeed, so disruptive did these visits by the court prove to be to the peace of the hermitage that Romuald was forced to move to Parenzo in Istria to escape from his imperial guest. His experience was not unique: throughout the west hermits were consulted by poor men who wanted their help in tracing stray animals; by noblemen and noblewomen who were troubled in conscience and sought spiritual direction; and by the oppressed who sought the hermit's prayers to obtain divine justice. To some extent this kind of role was taken over by anchorites and anchoresses in the urban communities of the later Middle Ages.

Recluses devoted their lives to prayer. It is impossible to assess the effects of so personal an activity, but some of them wrote about their experience of prayer in ways which were of value to the rest of the church. The English anchoress, Julian of Norwich († post 1413), is an example of this, and certainly has an originality of approach in her religious writings. Some of her images are striking because they are cast in homely terms, unusual in treatises on the spiritual life, as when, in describing her vision of Christ crowned with thorns, she says of the drops of blood that 'their roundness as they spread out on his forehead were like the scales of a herring'. All Julian's images are vivid:

> And [God] showed me a little thing, the size of a hazel-nut, on the palm of my hand, round like a ball. I looked at it thoughtfully and wondered, 'What is this?' And the answer came, 'It is all that is made'. I marvelled that it continued to exist and did not suddenly disintegrate; it was so small. And again my mind supplied the answer, 'It exists, both now and for ever, because God loves it'. In short, everything owes its existence to the love of God.

It is difficult to find a parallel anywhere in Christian writing which so strikingly describes the difference between the Creator and his seemingly insignificant creation.

It is arguable that recluses wrote about prayer with a greater degree of originality and independence of mind than other religious writers. They were trained contemplatives, able to devote their lives to mental prayer of a very personal kind, unlike the monastic clergy who were chiefly occupied in liturgical prayer, or the secular clergy and the laity who had little time to spend in prayer of any kind.

It should not be assumed that all solitaries were adepts of contemplative prayer. There must always have been those among them who chose the solitary life for secular rather than religious reasons, because they found human relationships difficult, or felt an aversion from communal activities. By finding a place for such people within the religious community, the church achieved something which was of benefit to itself and to them. The church benefited because Christianity is not just a social club which holds religious meetings, but is concerned with the relationship between the individual believer and God, and the existence of recluses kept this aspect of the faith in the minds of all Christians. The recluses benefited because, however difficult some of them may have found life, society valued them. How important this was became apparent when the tradition of religious solitaries was lost in Protestant countries in the sixteenth century. For the solitary, who still existed as a psychological type, was then reduced to the role of being at best a tolerated eccentric and at worst a social misfit.

20

The Difficulties of Belief

Medieval people naturally experienced doubt about matters of faith, but the church did not regard such reactions as necessarily sinful. Pope Gregory the Great remarked that the doubt of St Thomas was more valuable than the faith of the rest of the apostles because it had led Christ to give proof of his bodily resurrection, which satisfied Thomas and was recorded in the Gospels for the edification of future generations. Rightly used, doubt would strengthen belief because it would pose questions which would lead men to examine and understand the faith more profoundly.

It would be mistaken to suppose that medieval people concealed their doubts through fear of persecution. The church's coercive powers have, in any case, been much exaggerated: although savage penal laws were enacted against religious dissidents, they were difficult to enforce because there was no system of public prosecution; while the Inquisition, which was created to circumvent that problem, only operated effectively for brief periods of time in restricted areas. People whose doubt was so extreme that they left the church in order to become dissenters or apostates were, indeed, liable to be prosecuted, but a Catholic who had doubts about his faith was very rarely disciplined provided that he remained in the church and did not attempt to teach unauthorized doctrine to others.

Atheism

In Christian terms the most extreme form of religious doubt is atheism. In a theological sense this seems to have been virtually non-existent in the medieval west, but there were undoubtedly some people who behaved as though they were not accountable to God. Dante described them as Epicureans and assigned their spirits to a plain filled with burning tombs in the sixth circle of hell. The choice of the name Epicurean is revealing, for the philosopher Epicurus (†270 BC) had not denied the existence of the gods, but had asserted that they were not interested in events in this world and that men were not answerable to them, because their souls were not immortal. The Epicureans whom Dante names were all well born Italians, like Farinata degli Uberti and Cavalcante de' Cavalcanti, but the attitude he criticizes in them existed among people of different social status in other parts of Europe. A few years after he wrote, Jacques Fournier, bishop of Pamiers in southern France, discovered in his diocese a peasant, Raymond de l'Aire, who did not believe in the immortality of the soul and asserted that heaven consisted of being happy in this life and hell of being miserable. It is not surprising that there should have been people who reacted against the whole ethos of medieval society by denying the importance of the church's teaching and by taking self-interest alone as a sufficient guide for their lives. Naturally the devout among their contemporaries were deeply shocked by the open avowal of such sentiments, but the church authorities on the whole accepted the situation, treated these men as lapsed Catholics who had a right to Christian burial, and did not seek to discipline them unless, like Raymond de l'Aire, they were suspected of associating with heretics.

Scepticism

Not only was genuine atheism almost unknown in the Middle Ages, so was agnosticism. The Renaissance scholar, Lorenzo Valla (†1457), is sometimes considered a sceptic in matters of faith. He certainly had a highly critical mind and little sympathy with traditional forms of theology: he proved that the Donation of Constantine, the written evidence for papal claims to temporal sovereignty, was a forgery (see chapter 2); he criticized St Jerome's translation of the New Testament by comparing it with the original Greek; he held up to ridicule the dialectical methods used by western theologians since the twelfth century; he denied that it was possible in terms of human reason to reconcile God's omnipotence with human free will; he criticized the ideals of the monastic life to which all medieval piety had aspired; and in 1431 he wrote *De Voluptate*, 'On pleasure', in which he discussed the relative merits of the Christian, Stoic and Epicurean views of life and argued that the pleasures of the senses were the greatest good. Nevertheless, although his writings might suggest that he was sceptical about all matters of faith, his life does not entirely bear out this supposition. In 1431, the year in which the *De Voluptate* was written, he was ordained priest and in later life he became an apostolic secretary at the court of pope Nicholas V. It is arguable that, if the *De Voluptate* is set aside as a youthful *jeu d'esprit*, Valla was a conventional Catholic who was extremely critical of much of the tradition of the church. The papacy's willingness to patronize him, together with the respect in which he was later held by so conservative a religious thinker as Luther, suggests that he was not considered an agnostic by his contemporaries.

Religious doubt

Yet if disbelief in the existence of God was rare, doubt about the other articles of the Christian faith appears to have been very common. John Busch (†1480), an Austin Canon and one of the leading figures in the *Devotio Moderna* movement, confessed that during his novitiate:

> I reflected how our founder Augustine and the other Fathers, who had lived nearly 400 years after Christ, had written and preached that Jesus was God: and I thought how strange it was that such learned men should forget their reason to the extent of asserting the divinity of a man they had never seen.

Other medieval religious leaders admitted to entertaining similar doubts in their youth and such experiences must have been quite common. Indeed, they wrote about them precisely because they believed that many young men training for the religious life felt doubts of that kind but were ashamed to talk about them.

Some people found certain articles of the church's teaching particularly difficult to accept. Friar Jordan of Pisa, when conducting a preaching tour in Florence in 1303–6, told his audience that they should not find it hard to believe that at the resurrection their bodies would be made up of the same elements as their present bodies, because God could do all things. That he needed to say this at all must mean that many people did find this doctrine difficult to accept and this is borne out by similar evidence from other parts of Europe. There was a universal belief in the immortality of the soul, but the church's teaching about the resurrection of the body was called in question by many people, presumably because it was contrary to observable fact: the bodies of the dead rotted in the churchyard, and it seemed impossible that they should be restored to their former state at the Last Judgement.

Many people in the later Middle Ages also had doubts about the doctrine of transubstantiation. It was difficult to convey to the unlearned the teaching of the Fourth Lateran Council about the nature of Christ's presence in the eucharist, couched as it was in terms of Aristotelian physics (for the text of the definition see p. 44). The impression was given that the consecrated bread and wine were turned into flesh and blood and men found this impossible to believe because it was demonstrably untrue. It is clear from the large number of late medieval miracle stories which relate how consecrated Hosts bled when sacrilegiously stabbed, thus demonstrating that they were indeed the flesh of Christ, how widespread was scepticism about transubstantiation, which needed to be allayed. Doubt about this doctrine did not in any way extend to belief in Christ's true presence in the Host and the adoration which was due to him then, which was the chief focus of medieval worship (see chapter 12).

The problem of evil

The origin of evil is a perennial problem in a Christian society, for the faith teaches that there is only one God who is entirely good. The Cathars owed a good deal of their popularity in the twelfth and thirteenth centuries to the fact that they were able to give a straightforward answer to this problem in simple terms which everybody could understand:

> God is very good. In this world nothing is good. It therefore follows that God did not make anything which is in this world.

For the Cathars taught that the material creation was evil and had not been made by the Good God at all, and he therefore could not be accounted responsible for such afflictions as human sin, natural disasters, disease and death.

The origin of evil was the subject of a lively debate between Catholic and Cathar theologians. The Cathars were divided about the ultimate origins of evil. Some of them believed that there was only one God, who was good and who had created the demiurge who became evil and fashioned the material creation from the four elements which the Good God had created. This view was not an intellectual challenge to Catholic thinkers because it was too close to their own cosmology. The Cathar demiurge, like the Christian devil, was conceived as a creation of the Good God, so the problem of the ultimate origin of evil needed to be explained in both cases.

One group of Cathars held a more radical belief: that there are two gods, existing from all eternity, one good and the other evil. They taught that each had creative powers and that each had created a universe peopled by intelligent beings, but that the evil god had attacked the realm of the good God, capturing some of the angelic spirits who lived there and imprisoning them in his creation where they were endlessly reincarnated in material bodies. The Cathars defended this opinion by appealing to their own interpretation of the Bible and by pointing out the illogicality of supposing that the Good God alone could be responsible for the state of the present world, in which evil is so powerful. Catholic theologians found little difficulty in refuting this view. They remarked that beings who became involved in a power struggle in time, as the Cathars envisaged the two gods doing, were, by definition, creatures and not gods, because they were subject to change. The only evidence that the Cathars could adduce to support their interpretation was the human situation in which good and evil struggled for man's soul, but it was theologically untenable to project that struggle from time into eternity as the Cathars attempted to do.

In the face of Cathar teaching the church had to formulate its own doctrine of evil and it had to be logically coherent. Thirteenth-century theologians argued that since there was only one creator and since he was good, evil must be negative in origin. Christianity taught that God is love and it therefore followed that all his creatures must have been given free will since freedom is inherent in love. The possibility therefore existed in all creatures of choosing to love something other than God, and that choice included self-love: all sin stemmed from that. Lucifer and his angels, who had made that wrong choice, persisted in their war against God and sought to enlist men's help. Men, through sin, had become estranged from God and had lost the capacity, originally proper to them, of controlling the world, which had therefore become hostile to them; through sin they had admitted the devil and his angels to that world and had thereby further disordered God's creation. Unrepented sin on the part of any creature brought hell into being, for that was the spiritual state from which God was absent, and consisted in the isolation of being in that nothingness which is the nature of evil. Creatures could exist in hell, because God would not overrule the free will which he had given them.

That was the intellectual answer to the problem of evil, but the church had a more powerful emotional answer to Cathar objections in the image of Christ crucified. The Cathars, who had an equal devotion to Christ, could not use that method, for they did not believe that Christ had come into this evil world with a physical body, but only with a spiritual body which could not suffer pain. Catholics, on the contrary, could point to Christ's humanity and say that, however difficult to understand the problem of evil might be, God was willing to suffer its effects alongside men in the person of his Son.

The problem of the origin of evil had not been resolved in terms which were universally acceptable: it remained what St Paul had described as 'the mystery of iniquity', but the medieval church had been forced by the Cathars to admit that there was a problem. For people in the Middle Ages asked the perennial questions: 'If there is a God, why does he allow war/disease to happen?'

Scholarly difficulties

The problem of evil was common to all people, but certain ranges of religious difficulty were only experienced by the learned. For example, Peter Abelard, the foremost dialectician in the schools of Paris at the beginning of the twelfth century, drew attention to the contradictions to be found in the western theological tradition in his *Sic et Non*, 'Yes and No'. This consisted of 158 propositions to which conflicting solutions had been given in different writers whom the church regarded as authoritative. These propositions covered the whole range of faith and practice, and Abelard's method was simply to set out the authorities in favour of each of them, followed by those which appeared to contradict them, without offering any resolution.

By drawing attention to the apparent contradictions in church teaching as it had evolved during the previous thousand years, Abelard showed that there was a need to place theological study on a systematic basis, using the new dialectical skills which had become available. Many of his contemporaries shared this wish and in time solutions were found to the problems raised by him as well as to other apparent contradictions in the western tradition. Although this was sometimes achieved only through acrimonious debate, the difficulties which surfaced during these discussions did not cause the Christian faith itself to be called in question, since all the disputants were agreed that that faith was true and were anxious to reach a common opinion about disputed points. These quarrels occurred entirely within the western Christian tradition.

It might have been expected that the application of logical techniques to the study of the Bible would have raised considerable problems by drawing attention to internal inconsistencies in the text. This did not occur, partly because it was accepted that, although the Scriptures were divinely inspired, the Holy Spirit had had to use human agents to set down the text and they had been conditioned by their time and circumstances. As Guibert of Nogent (†1124) expressed it:

> You must indeed be aware that many things are recorded in the Scriptures not as they truly are, but as they seemed to be [to the writers].

As has been explained in chapter 6 the Bible was not read merely in a literal way as an historical record, but in a fourfold sense as a spiritual document. This immediately removed certain ranges of problem. The Fathers had argued that 'absurdity is a sign of allegory', meaning that if some statement occurred which it was impossible to accept in a literal sense, then the divine author intended it to be understood in a spiritual way. But the most important factor was that the Bible entered the Middle Ages flanked by volumes of patristic commentary, because the Fathers had found solutions to many of the most difficult passages.

Biblical scholars faced no real intellectual challenge to their faith so long as they worked within the context of the western tradition, but difficulties arose when they stepped outside it. Andrew of St Victor (†1175), who studied Hebrew in order to discover more about the literal meaning of the Old Testament, found that the rabbis did not understand many of the prophetic passages, which the church applied to the coming of Christ, in a messianic sense, but saw in them prophecies of the restoration of the Jewish state after the Babylonian exile. Such knowledge could not be ignored and it became necessary radically to re-think the way in which the four senses of Scripture were understood. The problem was resolved a century later by St Thomas Aquinas, who distinguished between the literal meaning of a prophecy, which was what the prophet believed he was talking about, and its mystical meaning, which was the one which God intended to convey, but which could be understood only after the events to which it related had taken place.

The challenge of Aristotle

A far more serious challenge to the west's understanding of the Christian faith came from the rediscovery of the lost works of Aristotle and of Arabic commentaries on them. The medieval church had inherited from late antiquity a theory of the relation between faith and reason which was in essence Platonist. Plato's concept of the divine demiurge who fashioned the world was considered to approximate closely to Christian belief in a Creator, and Plato's theory of knowledge was compatible with Christian conceptions. Plato taught the existence of Ideas, the ideal forms of which all individual examples are copies. The Ideas can be recognized by the human intellect, which is thus enabled to make sense of empirical experience. The church equated Platonic Ideas with the Thoughts of God, of which the physical creation is an expression, and argued that knowledge of the ideal forms as they existed in God's thought was implanted by God in each human soul and enabled men to communicate with God and to understand the mutable creation.

These theses were unchallenged until, during the twelfth century, western scholars began to translate the works of Aristotle on philosophy and the natural sciences which they discovered in Arabic versions in the Moorish libraries of Christian Spain. Aristotle already enjoyed immense prestige in the western schools because his logical works were the chief text for the study of dialectic, the fundamental skill used in all branches of learning. Aristotle's theory of knowledge, revealed in his lost works, was very different from the dominant Christian Platonism of the west. He assumed that the only secure foundation of knowledge was empirical observation from which concepts might be abstracted. He concluded that there must be a First Cause, the source of movement in the universe, but although this concept was not incompatible with a Christian belief in God, it was very different from such a belief, for the First Cause lacked any attributes, including that of creator.

The challenge posed by Aristotle was compounded by the translation into Latin at the same time of commentaries on his works composed by Muslims and Spanish Jews. G. Leff has pointed out that those writers had an ambivalent influence on western thinkers: on the one hand Christians profited from the attempts which these other monotheists had made to achieve a synthesis between scientific pragmatism and revealed religious truth; while on the other hand, Muslim commentators in particular raised additional problems to those posed by Aristotle himself. This was specially true of Averroes (†1178), author of the fullest Arabic commentary on Aristotle, who made no attempt to harmonize reason and revelation and did not consider that reason should be subordinated to revelation if there was a conflict between the two. One important consequence of this approach was his conclusion that the universe existed from eternity in dependence on God, since, although this was contrary to the belief in creation enjoined by the Koran, it was more consonant with reason to postulate that nothing can happen to God who by definition is eternal and immutable.

St Thomas Aquinas

These challenges to traditional Christian modes of thought met with a variety of reactions. The new statutes of the university of Paris, promulgated in 1215, banned the study of Aristotle's writings on metaphysics and the natural sciences, together with commentaries on them. This was an unprofitable approach, not least because it proved impossible to enforce. The majority of scholars, of whom perhaps the most eminent was the *doctor seraphicus*, St Bonaventura (†1274), were prepared to accept those parts of the new learning which were compatible with traditional beliefs, but they continued to assert the paramountcy of revelation over reason and therefore rejected as erroneous all statements in the new writings which were contrary to revealed truth.

A far more radical approach was that of the *doctor angelicus*, St Thomas Aquinas (†1274), who was prepared to face the intellectual challenge to faith which the new learning posed. His primary concern was to come to terms with Aristotle's theory of knowledge. In order to do this he first prepared and edited, with the help of his colleague, William of Moerbeke, a new translation of the Aristotelian corpus, based directly on Greek texts and thus free from Arabic glosses and interpolations. Having established what Aristotle had in fact written, Aquinas applied Aristotle's method to an examination of Christian teaching. He expressed his arguments in terms of syllogistic logic derived from Aristotle, and he began by examining the natural world on the basis of empirical observation, just as Aristotle had done. Aquinas concluded that by extrapolating concepts from the evidence obtained in that way an inquirer would ineluctably be drawn to a knowledge of God in agreement with that contained in the Christian revelation. His arguments are set out in his *Summa contra Gentiles*, 'The Defence of the Faith against the Pagans', and his *Summa Theologica*, 'Compendium of Theology', which remained incomplete at the time of his death. His originality consisted in this: unlike earlier western theologians, who argued that men knew about God because of an intuitive knowledge implanted in their souls, Aquinas asserted that physical experience of the universe was the surest means which a man had of learning about his creator.

When writing these works St Thomas had to contend with similar problems to those which had confronted Islamic thinkers like Averroes, for, like them, he had to consider the relationship between human reason and divine revelation. Unlike Averroes he did not believe that the two were incompatible, but argued rather that they were complementary. In many areas of knowledge there was no conflict between faith and reason, but in other areas faith could complete the knowledge which reason could only apprehend in part. Thus whereas reason demonstrated the existence of a First Cause, revelation made known the nature of that Cause, the Triune God.

Like Averroes, St Thomas was faced by the problem of deciding priorities in the event of a conflict between revelation and reason. The chief instance of this was the same for them both: reason suggested that the universe had existed from all eternity in dependence on God, whereas revelation taught that it had been created *ex nihilo*. St Thomas concluded that although reason could not demonstrate that the universe had a beginning, it was equally unable to demonstrate that it did not have a beginning, and, given that lack of certainty, we should accept the revealed truth that the universe was created by God. In St Thomas's view faith would never be found to contradict reason, but if a choice needed to be made between two equally logical solutions to a problem, one of which was based on revelation and the other on reason, then the one based on revelation should always be accepted.

Averroism

While St Thomas was pondering the metaphysical problems raised by the new Aristotle, other scholars reacted to the new learning very differently. The prohibition on these works contained in the Paris statutes of 1215 had proved impossible to enforce, but they were studied chiefly in the Arts Faculty of the university, whose members had no theological training. Some of them became convinced that human reason should not be made subordinate to religious orthodoxy and because this was the distinctive mark of Averroes' teaching they were known as Averroists although their speculations were derived from a wider range of authors.

They flourished in the decade after 1265 under the leadership of Siger of Brabant and taught among other things that matter was eternal, and that therefore the world had neither beginning nor end. They denied that God was omniscient, or that his Providence guides the affairs of men, alleging instead that men's actions are determined entirely by the stars. They seem to have been as intoxicated by the premise that reason need not be subordinate to revelation as the men of Abelard's age had been by the discovery of dialectic, and some Averroists were willing to follow human reason to the point where they became free-thinkers. Some of them even asserted that 'the sayings of the theologians are based on myths', although none of them, it would seem, denied the existence of God.

It soon became apparent that the Averroists were not typical of western educated opinion as a whole. In 1277 the university of Paris condemned 219 theses as heretical, many of which were Averroist opinions, and within ten years of this prohibition the movement died out. This is not a testimony solely to the effectiveness of the 1277 condemnations for, had Averroism been at all widely diffused, those censures would have proved as ineffective as the 1215 ban on reading the new Aristotle had been. The decline of Averroism cannot either be attributed to the persuasiveness of the work of St Thomas Aquinas, for, although highly regarded by later generations, St Thomas made little impact on his contemporaries. Indeed, some of his theses were among the 219 condemned at Paris in 1277, notably his contention that the soul derived its knowledge of God partly through bodily experiences of the created world.

The separation between faith and reason

The lack of support for the Averroists seems to reflect the way in which western society instinctively recoiled from the prospect of allowing human reason to speculate about the final realities untrammelled by revelation. Certainly western thinkers in the first half of the fourteenth century came to make a rigid distinction between the spheres in which faith and reason might operate, restricting reason to the material creation alone. This had far-reaching implications. William of Ockham, the *doctor invincibilis* (†1349), broke with the tradition stretching back to St Anselm (see p. 43), by asserting that it was impossible to offer convincing proofs for the existence of God in terms of human reason.

This might be described as a Byzantine solution to the problem of the relation between faith and reason. In the Orthodox tradition a distinction is observed between the Inner Learning, which comprises man's knowledge of God and of theology and is the province of revelation alone, and the Outer Learning which deals with man and the natural world and is the province of human reason. There is no reason to suppose that Byzantine influence affected the thinkers of Ockham's generation, but by the end of the fourteenth century that influence is directly perceptible in the Florentine Renaissance which drew much of its inspiration directly from the Byzantine classical tradition and employed Greek teachers trained in that milieu, such as Manuel Chrysoloras. Consequently the views initiated by men like Ockham about the absolute separation between reason and revelation became reinforced by the Florentine humanists and firmly embedded in the thought of fifteenth-century Europe.

The demarcation of the relative spheres of reason and revelation did not, of course, mark the end of theological disputes. Theologians continued to argue fiercely between themselves about the interpretation of the Christian revelation and the correct practice of the Christian life, arguments which culminated in the Reformation controversies of the sixteenth century; but those arguments were not between the relative claims of revelation and reason but between different interpretations of revelation.

When considering medieval religion, it is worth remembering that some of the issues which made it difficult for people in modern times to accept Christianity first surfaced in the thirteenth century. Some churchmen at that time were quite prepared to face up to them and to rethink the whole Christian tradition in a radical way; but society as a whole instinctively recoiled from some of the questions which were raised then, and arguably created a severe problem for the church in later centuries by separating reason and revelation. Yet the very fact that society did recoil in that way is an index of how profoundly Christian the medieval west had become by the fourteenth century.

Conclusion

The Middle Ages lasted for more than a thousand years, half the lifespan of the Christian church. During those centuries Christianity ceased to be the faith of a minority and became what it has remained ever since, one of the great world religions. The secular consequences of the conversion of Europe cannot be ignored: it led to the formation of a western Christian civilization whose monuments and works of art surround us on all sides. Europe is full of medieval cathedrals and parish churches, mostly still in use; its museums contain great collections of medieval works of art; medieval creative writers like Dante, Wolfram von Eschenbach and Malory are still read, if only in translation; and the works of medieval composers are still regularly performed.

Attention is less often drawn to the religious consequences of the conversion of Europe, partly because the Protestant Reformers claimed, and no doubt sincerely believed, that they were returning to the faith of the church of the Fathers and breaking with the medieval past. In fact, of course, this proved impossible, for they were products of the medieval tradition and, although they could react against it, they could not throw off that heredity. The medieval church had had to deal with two particular areas of faith and practice. First, it had to decide how Christ's abiding presence manifests itself in the life of the church, and this led to the definition of the nature and effects of the sacraments. Secondly it had to deal with the pastoral problem created by post-baptismal sin, which reached huge proportions when the entire population was Christian. Most major theological controversies in the western churches since the end of the Middle Ages have been concerned with these two areas of teaching: how Christ manifests his presence in the church, and how sinful church members may be restored to grace.

A knowledge of medieval religion can therefore help to explain how twentieth-century western society and the modern western churches came to be shaped as they are. Yet arguably the chief interest of medieval religion consists in the fact that it enables us to study a civilization which has no parallel in the modern world and to see the Christian faith at an earlier stage in its evolution. To achieve that understanding it is important not to impose our own distinctions too firmly on the past.

We are tempted to do this because part of the religious experience of the Middle Ages is readily accessible to us, irrespective of whether we share its faith. We can take an aesthetic pleasure in the art and architecture of a medieval cathedral, or an intellectual pleasure in the method of argument used by a great medieval theologian. Other ranges of medieval experience seem opaque both to believers and non-believers alike: the most conventionally devout western

European today would not even consider walking barefoot to Jerusalem as penance for his sins; and I doubt whether any of my readers would be prepared to believe that the bones, or perhaps the spirit, of a dead greyhound would cure their sick children.

But in the Middle Ages not merely did both kinds of attitude coexist in society, they were to some extent shared by all members of society. It is a methodological necessity when examining certain kinds of evidence to distinguish between the 'learned' and 'popular' attitudes in medieval religion, but it should be borne in mind that the distinction is not absolute. The learned members of society were not insulated at birth from popular beliefs; their learning was only acquired later in life and coexisted with such beliefs. Conversely, uneducated people were not totally incapable of understanding the conclusions which the learned reached about matters of faith, even if they were not able to follow the arguments on which those conclusions were based. I have tried to show that the mass of the people understood many of the teachings formulated by the learned clergy a good deal better than they are sometimes credited with doing, and that the learned clergy in their turn shared many of the attitudes of the people, including an often uncritical enthusiasm for thaumaturgic bones. Medieval civilization was a unity and must be accepted in its often disconcerting totality.

Appendix:
The Vulgate Old Testament

The Vulgate accepted as canonical those Old Testament books contained in the Septuagint, the Greek translation of the scriptures made for the Jews of Alexandria, probably in the third century BC. The sixteenth-century Protestant reformers accepted as canonical only those books which were found in the Hebrew text of the Old Testament, and modern Protestant editions of the Bible normally follow this practice. In the Authorized Version of 1611 the books found in Hebrew were printed as the canonical Old Testament, while those which were found in the Septuagint alone were printed separately as Apocrypha.

The Council of Trent declared all the books of the Vulgate Old Testament to be canonical, with the exception of the Prayer of Manasses and the Third and Fourth Books of Esdras, which it accounted apocryphal. In modern Catholic versions of the Bible these are either omitted or relegated to an appendix.

In the following table the books of the Vulgate are listed in column 1 with their Latin titles; the books contained in modern Protestant Bibles are listed in column 2; and the books published as Apocrypha in the Authorized Version are listed in column 3.

Vulgate	Protestant Bibles	AV Apocrypha
I *Pentateuch* (Books of the Law)		
Genesis	Genesis	
Exodus	Exodus	
Leviticus	Leviticus	
Numeri	Numbers	
Deuteronomium	Deuteronomy	
II *Libri Historici* (Historical Books)		
Iosue	Joshua	
Iudices	Judges	
Ruth	Ruth	
I Regum	I Samuel	
II Regum	II Samuel	
III Regum	I Kings	
IV Regum	II Kings	
I Paralipomenon	I Chronicles	
II Paralipomenon	II Chronicles	
I Esdras	Ezra	
II Esdras	Nehemiah	
III Esdras		I Esdras
IV Esdras[1]		II Esdras
Tobia		Tobit
Iudith		Judith
Esther[2]	Esther	

III *Libri Didactici* (Books of Teachings)

Iob	Job	
Psalmi	Psalms	
Proverbia	Proverbs	
Ecclesiastes	Ecclesiastes	
Cantica Canticorum	Song of Solomon	
Sapientia		Wisdom
Ecclesiasticus		Ecclesiasticus

IV *Libri Prophetici* (Books of Prophecy)

Isaias	Isaiah	
Ieremias	Jeremiah	
Lamentationes	Lamentations	
Baruch		Baruch
Daniel[3]	Daniel	
Oratio Manassae		Prayer of Manasses
Osee	Hosea	
Ioel	Joel	
Amos	Amos	
Abdias	Obadiah	
Ionas	Jonah	
Michaea	Micah	
Nahum	Nahum	
Habacuc	Habakkuk	
Sophonias	Zephaniah	
Aggaeus	Haggai	
Zacharias	Zechariah	
Malachias	Malachi	

V *Libri Historici Novissimi* (Modern Historical Books)

I Machabaeorum	I Maccabees
II Machabaeorum	II Maccabees

1. IV Esdras did not form part either of the Hebrew or Septuagint canons, but was included in the Vulgate because it was attributed to Esdras (the Greek form of Ezra) and was widely cited by early Christian writers.
2. The Septuagint text of the Book of Esther translated in the Vulgate contains passages not found in the Hebrew. These are omitted in Protestant editions and printed in the AV Apocrypha as 'The rest of Esther'.
3. The Septuagint text of Daniel translated in the Vulgate contains the following passages not found in the Hebrew: The Song of the Three Children; The Story of Susanna; The Idol Bel and the Dragon. These are omitted in Protestant editions, but printed in the AV Apocrypha with those titles.

Further Reading

Works of Reference

The most detailed history of the medieval church and its institutions is A. Fliche, V. Martin, gen. eds., *Histoire de l'Église*, vols. 3–14 (I). A great deal of detailed, specialist information is contained in the articles found in five great Catholic encyclopaedias:

Dictionnaire d'archéologie chrétienne et de Liturgie, 15 vols (1924–51).
Dictionnaire du Droit Canonique, 7 vols (1935–65).
Dictionnaire d'histoire et de géographie ecclésiastiques, 19 vols (1912–in progress).
Dictionnaire de Théologie Catholique, 16 vols (1905–67).
Dictionnaire de Spiritualité (1932–in progress).

A useful, single-volume work of reference is *The Oxford Dictionary of the Christian Church*, ed. F.L. Cross, E.A. Livingstone, 2nd edn., Oxford, 1974.

Much information about all aspects of medieval church life is to be found in the enactments of councils and synods. This is given, with French translation or paraphrase, in C.J. Hefèle, ed. H. Leclercq, *Histoire des Conciles*, vols. I–VII (I), 1907–17. Vol. VII (I) deals with the Fifth Lateran Council of 1512–17.

Chapter 1   The Emergence of Christian Europe

E. Peters, ed., *Monks, Bishops and Pagans. Christian Culture in Gaul and Italy, 500–700*, Philadelphia, 1975, a selection of translated texts with commentary, which vividly convey the insecurity of life in the heartlands of the west during the early Middle Ages.

K. Hughes, *The Church in early Irish Society*, London, 1966, a masterly description of the unique character of Celtic Christianity.

H. Mayr–Harting, *The Coming of Christianity to Anglo-Saxon England*, London, 1972, deals with the fusion of the Celtic and Roman traditions.

A.P. Vlasto, *The Entry of the Slavs into Christendom*, Cambridge, 1970.

E. Christiansen, *The Northern Crusades. The Baltic and the Catholic Frontier, 1100–1525*, London, 1980. These works deal with the very different problems faced by the church in evangelizing eastern Europe, in which political and religious interests conflicted.

Chapter 2   The Church in Society

There are two excellent modern, general histories of the church in the west in the Middle Ages:

D. Knowles, D. Obolensky, *The Middle Ages*, vol. II of *The Christian Centuries*, London, 1969, adopts a chronological approach to this subject and can be used by readers with no prior knowledge. It has the merit of dealing also with the Eastern Orthodox church.

R.W. Southern, *Western Society and the Church in the Middle Ages*, Pelican History of the Church, vol. 2, Harmondsworth, 1970, is a brilliant study, accessible to the non-specialist, but presupposes a knowledge of the chronological framework.

G. Barraclough, *The Medieval Papacy*, London, 1968, is the briefest scholarly treatment of this subject in recent years.

For the late medieval period two works are helpful: H. Jedin, *History of the Council of Trent*, vol. I, London, 1957, contains a wealth of information about the state of the western church in the fifteenth century; J. Bossy, *Christianity in the West, 1400-1700*, Oxford, 1985. The opening chapters give a very lively account of late medieval religion.

A. Murray, *Reason and Society in the Middle Ages*, Oxford, 1978, is an important and original contribution to the understanding of medieval thought and belief.

Three more specialist studies.

W. Ullmann, *The Growth of Papal Government in the Middle Ages*, London, 1955, traces the way in which power became centralized in the western church. The author tends to read back the ambitions of eleventh-century popes to the Carolingian age.

G. Barraclough, *Papal Provisions*, Oxford, 1935, the classic study of the way in which centralization was experienced throughout the church.

W.E. Lunt, *Papal Revenues in the Middle Ages*, 2 vols., New York, 1934, translated documents with an introduction and commentary, remains a valuable initial guide to the church's sources of revenue.

Chapter 3   Monasteries and Religious Orders

D. Knowles, *Christian Monasticism*, London, 1969, one of the last works of the foremost historian of English monasticism.

C.N.L. Brooke, *The Monastic World, 1000-1300*, London, 1974, deals with the golden age of western monasticism and is beautifully illustrated.

C.H. Lawrence, *Medieval Monasticism*, London, 1984, the most recent scholarly survey of the field.

D. Knowles, *From Pachomius to Ignatius*, Oxford, 1966, a study of monastic rules, but also of the spiritual aims of monastic legislators.

J. Leclercq, *The Love of Learning and the Desire for God*, New York, 1962, a brilliant study of monastic scholarship.

The Rule of St Benedict is arguably one of the most influential writings produced in the Middle Ages. Controversy surrounds its relationship to the *Rule of the Master*. I have followed the solution offered by the only scholar who has edited both Rules, A. de Vogüé, *La Règle de Saint Benoît, Sources Chrétiennes*, vols. 181-7, 1972-77, *La Règle du Maître, Sources Chrétiennes*, 105-7, 1964-5.

Much has been written on the friars: J.R.H. Moorman, *A History of the Franciscan Order . . . to 1517*, Oxford, 1968, and W.A. Hinnebusch, *History of the Dominican Order*, 2 vols, New York, 1966, 73, both give full bibliographies. For those interested in the life of St Francis, the main sources have been translated in a single volume, M.A. Habig, *St Francis of Assisi, Omnibus of Sources*, London, 1972.

There is no satisfactory history of medieval nuns, but see B. Bolton, *The Medieval Reformation*, ch. 5, 'Religious Women', London, 1983.

Chapter 4   The Faith of the Church

An important study of this theme has recently been completed, J. Pelikan, *The Christian Tradition. A History of the Development of Doctrine*, vol. I, *The Emergence of the Catholic Tradition, 100–600*, vol. III, *The growth of medieval theology, 600–1300*, vol. IV, *The formation of Church and Dogma, 1300–1700*, Chicago, 1971–84. NB: Volume II is concerned with the Eastern Church. The merit of this author's approach is that it disregards conventional chronological divides, which enables him to look at the evidence in fresh ways.

J. Daniélou, A.H. Couratin, J. Kent, *Historical Theology*, vol. 2 of *Pelican Guide to Modern Theology*, Harmondsworth, 1969, although not a short-cut for those without stamina to read Pelikan, will give an understanding of the way in which doctrine developed during the Middle Ages.

T.G. Jalland, *The Church and the Papacy*, London, 1944. A scholarly discussion of the development of the theory of papal authority. It is not easy to find detached treatments of this emotive subject, but the author of this work is not a Catholic yet is sympathetic to the papal ideal.

R.W. Southern, *St Anselm and his Biographer*, Cambridge, 1963, a biography of one of the greatest medieval theologians.

J. Le Goff, *The Birth of Purgatory*, London, 1984, a persuasive, though controversial work about the development of the doctrine of the afterlife during the Middle Ages.

Chapter 5   Public Worship

On the architectural setting of medieval worship, H. Focillon, *The Art of the West in the Middle Ages*, 2 vols., London, 1963.

J.A. Jungmann, *The Mass of the Roman Rite*, 2 vols., New York, 1950–5, is the authoritative study of the eucharistic liturgy.

L. Duchesne, *Christian Worship, its origin and evolution*, 5th edn, London, 1919, remains important as a study of the liturgical forms used in other sacraments in the Middle Ages.

P. Batiffol, *History of the Roman Breviary*, London, 1898. Unlike the mass, the Divine Office has not attracted great attention recently.

N. Hunt, *Cluny under Saint Hugh, 1049–1109*, London, 1967, contains one of the best discussions of the arrangement of a liturgical timetable.

For the musical setting of the liturgy, A. Hughes, *The New Oxford History of Music*, vol. II, Oxford, 1954.

Chapter 6   Knowledge of the Bible

The pioneer work in this field was M. Deanesly, *The Lollard Bible*, Cambridge, 1920, which contains much useful, factual information, particularly about the Bible in medieval England, but it must be used in conjunction with *The*

Cambridge History of the Bible, vol. 2, *The West from the Fathers to the Reformation*, ed., G.W.H. Lampe, 1969. The following articles are useful: R. Loewe, 'The Medieval History of the Latin Vulgate', J. Leclercq, 'The Exposition and Exegesis of Scripture from Gregory the Great to St Bernard'; B. Smalley, 'The Bible in the Medieval Schools'; S.J.P. van Dijk, 'The Bible in Liturgical Use'; R.L.P. Milburn, 'The 'People's Bible': Artists and Commentators'; G. Shepherd, 'English versions of the Scriptures before Wyclif'; W.B. Lockwood, 'Vernacular Scriptures in Germany and the Low Countries before 1500'; C.A. Robson, 'Vernacular Scriptures in France'; K. Foster, 'Vernacular Scriptures in Italy'; M. Morreale, 'Vernacular Scriptures in Spain'.

The most important work in English on the way in which the Bible was studied and understood by the learned is B. Smalley, *The Bible in the Middle Ages*, 3rd edn, Oxford, 1983.

Those who are interested in the four levels of exegesis should read the definitive work of H. de Lubac, *Exégèse mediévale. Les quatre sens de l'Écriture*, 2 vols. in 4 parts, Paris, 1959–63.

The quotation on p. 66, is from Origen, *De Principiis*, IV, 1, trans. F. Crombie, *The Writings of Origen*, 2 vols., Edinburgh, 1871–2, pp. 315–16.

Chapter 7 Methods of Instruction

On preaching before the coming of the friars, M. Zink, *La prédication en langue romane avant 1300*, Paris, 1982; on preaching by the friars in their early years, D.L. d'Avray, *The Preaching of the Friars*, Oxford, 1985; on preaching by the Observant friars in the fifteenth century, I. Origo, *The World of San Bernardino*, London, 1963.

To understand why medieval art was not necessarily an ideal medium of instruction for the simple, see E. Mâle, *The Gothic Image*, London, 1913, reprinted 1961, which explains how the fourfold interpretation of scripture was translated into religious art.

E.K. Chambers, *The Medieval Stage*, 2 vols., Oxford, 1903, reprinted 1963, despite its age contains a wealth of detailed information which makes it a standard work of reference for liturgical drama and for mystery plays. G. Wickham, *The Medieval Theatre*, London, 1974, is vividly written and describes how plays were staged.

On p. 68 I cite Bede, *A History of the English Church and People*, III, 5, trans. L. Sherley–Price, Penguin Classics, 1955, p. 145, and on p. 68 *Njal's Saga*, c.101, trans. M. Magnusson and H. Pálsson, Penguin Classics, 1960, p. 218.

Chapter 8 The Quest for Perfection

A valuable study of the religious understanding of medieval kingship is, M. Bloch, *The Royal Touch*, trans. J.E. Anderson, London, 1973.

The ethics of the nobility, which were Christian but with a difference, can be gauged from a collection of studies ed. P. Contamine, *La noblesse au Moyen Age, XIe–XVe siècles*, Paris, 1976.

R. Barber, *The Knight and Chivalry*, New York, 1970, is a general introduction to this subject aimed at the non-specialist reader.

A great deal has been written about lay piety in the late Middle Ages, among which are recommended: R.R. Post, *The Modern Devotion*, Leiden, 1968, on the impact of the *Devotio Moderna* movement; C. Trinkaus, H.A. Obermann, *The Pursuit of Holiness in Late Medieval and Renaissance Religion*, Leiden, 1974, which deals with wider themes. One of the most characteristic and influential works of the *Devotio Moderna* school was Thomas à Kempis, *The Imitation of Christ*, which has been frequently translated into English, though often only in part; a complete translation was made by C. Bigg, London, 1898, and has been reprinted many times.

E.W. Kemp, *Canonization and Authority in the Western Church*, Oxford, 1948, is an authoritative study of the way in which canonization became centralized in Rome.

Benedicta Ward, *Miracles and the Medieval Mind*, Philadelphia, 1982, is an important study of the way in which medieval people understood and reacted to the cult of the saints.

The most typical collection of medieval saints lives is James of Voragine's *Golden Legend*, which has been translated in part in a single volume by G. Ryan, H. Ripperger, New York, 1969.

The theme of world-renunciation is central to Ramon Lull's novel, *Blanquerna: a thirteenth-century romance*, trans. E.A. Peers, London, 1925.

Chapter 9   The Christian World Picture

The cosmology of the pseudo-Dionysius is explained in D. Rutledge, *Cosmic Theology*, London, 1964. Modern theologians seem to think that angels are not a suitable subject for study. If my readers are interested in the Nine Choirs I would recommend to them the recent edition of the *Celestial Hierarchy*, Denys l'Aréopagite, *La Hiérarchie céleste*, ed. and trans. M. de Gandillac, G. Heil, R. Roques, 2nd edn, *Sources Chrétiennes*, No. 58 (bis), Paris, 1970.

For the Ptolemaic universe, J.L.E. Dreyer, *A History of Astronomy from Thales to Kepler*, New York, 1953, and the excellent article by O. Pedersen, 'Astronomy', in D.C. Lindberg, ed., *Science in the Middle Ages*, Chicago, 1978.

On medieval geographical knowledge the most comprehensive survey is still C.R. Beazley, *The Dawn of Modern Geography*, 3 vols., London, 1905–6.

Highly recommended for an easy approach to medieval natural history, T.H. White, ed. and trans., *The Book of Beasts*, London, 1956, a lively translation of a Bestiary, complete with line drawings of the illuminations.

The best brief account of the medieval 'mirror of History' is probably that of B. Smalley, *Historians in the Middle Ages*, London, 1974. This does not deal with the history of the future: to understand the hold which that had on the minds of medieval people, I recommend M. Reeves, *Joachim of Fiore and the Prophetic Future*, London, 1976, also, R.K. Emmerson, *Antichrist in the Middle Ages*, Manchester, 1981.

Chapter 10   The Legacy of Paganism

The influence and attraction of the pagan poets for medieval scholars and writers is conveyed well by F.J.E. Raby, *A History of Secular Latin Poetry in the Middle Ages*, 2 vols., 2nd edn, Oxford, 1957. The author assumed that all students would read Latin; as this is perhaps no longer realistic, I would suggest combining Raby's text with H. Waddell's *Medieval Latin Lyrics* (Penguin Classics) 1952, which contains a good English verse translation.

J. Seznec, *The Survival of the Pagan Gods*, New York, 1953, traces the strange transformations which the Olympians underwent in the art of the Middle Ages.

G. Turville–Petre, *Myth and Religion in the North*, 1964, examines the evidence for pagan Scandinavian religion as preserved in Christian written sources and interpreted in archaeological evidence.

Devils, like angels, have a bad press now: theologians avoid the topic and much non-specialist writing on the subject is drivel. The most recent scholarly work is that of J.B. Russell *Lucifer. The Devil in the Middle Ages*, Ithaca, and there are also useful essays in G. Bazin and others, *Satan*, London, 1951.

J.G. Frazer, *The Golden Bough*, 8 pts., in 12 vols., 3rd edn, London, 1914–27, remains the principal quarry for anybody interested in finding examples of pagan rituals surviving in western folklore. Mummers' plays, a specialized aspect of this, are considered briefly in Wickham, *The Medieval Stage* (see chapter 7 above).

The strange evidence about cenotaphs for departed spirits in southern France is contained in, J. Bordenave, M. Vialelle, *La mentalité religieuse des paysans de l'albigeois médiéval*, Toulouse, 1973. The pagan imagination of western Europe as exemplified in the Arthurian legends is examined by R.S. Loomis, *Celtic Myth and Arthurian Romance*, New York, 1927 and *The Grail from Celtic Myth to Christian Symbol*, Cardiff, 1963.

On p. 100 I cite Bede, *A History of the English Church and People*, I, 30, Penguin Classics, p. 87.

Chapter 11   Knowledge of the Faith

The reading for this chapter is the same as for chapter 7, which is dealing with the same range of evidence.

On p. 108, I cite *Anonymi Gesta Francorum*, ed. and trans. R. Hill, London, 1962, p. 21.

Chapter 12   Religious Observance I: The Sacraments

In addition to the items listed above under Chapter 5, J. Leclercq, F. Vandenbroucke, L. Bouyer, *The Spirituality of the Middle Ages*, vol. II of *A History of Christian Spirituality*, London, 1968, gives valuable insight into the practice of the Christian faith throughout the Middle Ages.

J.A. Jungmann, *Pastoral Liturgy*, London, 1962, despite its title, is concerned primarily with the history of the liturgy and with lay participation in it.

Interesting work has been done on marriage by G. Duby, *Medieval Marriage: two Models from Twelfth-Century France*, Baltimore, 1978 and *The Knight, the Lady and the Priest*, London, 1984. These show the church seeking to control marriage in France in the central Middle Ages in a way which does not agree with the overall picture of medieval marriage patterns which I have given in this chapter. Duby's evidence relates to one class in one period of the Middle Ages, when the church was seeking to impose Christian rules of marriage on the nobility. In society as a whole and over a longer period the pattern was rather different and ecclesiastical power less constricting.

J.T. McNeill, H.M. Games, ed. and trans., *Medieval Handbooks of Penance*, New

York, 1965, a useful source for the practice of penance but also for determining what sins the church considered most serious.

B. Poschmann, *Penance and the Anointing of the Sick*, London, 1964, examines the administration of last rites. J.N. Tentler, *Sin and Confession on the Eve of the Reformation*, Princeton, 1977, considers late medieval attitudes towards sin, as well as towards sacramental penance.

J.T. Rosenthal, *The Purchase of Paradise. Gift Giving and the Aristocracy, 1307–1485*, London, 1972, has good, detailed information on the endowment of chantries. P. Ariès, *Western Attitudes to death from the Middle Ages to the present*, Baltimore, 1974, is of interest for its treatment of the later Middle Ages.

On p. 115 I have cited, *The Lay Folks Mass Book*, ed. T.F. Simmons, Early English Text Society, London, 1879, p. 30, (I have modernized the spelling). On p. 119 I have cited McNeill and Gamer, *Medieval Handbooks of Penance*, p. 362. The translation of part of the hymn of St Thomas Aquinas on p. 116 is that of J.R. Woodford, *English Hymnal*, no. 331.

Chapter 13   Religious Observance II: Popular Devotions

C.N.L. Brooke and R.B. Brooke, *Popular Religion in the Middle Ages, Western Europe, 1000–1300*, London, 1984, is an excellent study of this field during the central Middle Ages.

E. Le Roy Ladurie, *Montaillou*, London, 1978, is the most accessible study of a medieval peasant community and its religious beliefs. It must be read sensibly: it gives evidence for the peasants of the Haute Ariège in the early fourteenth-century, and unsubstantiated wider inferences should not be drawn from it.

P.R.L. Brown, *The Cult of the Saints*, London, 1981, an important study of how this devotion began in the late Roman period.

J-C. Schmitt, *The Holy Greyhound*, Cambridge Studies in Oral and Literate Culture, 6, Cambridge, 1983, examines the evidence for the cult of St Guinefort and its survival into the twentieth century.

Much has been written about pilgrimage, but the practical details of travel and the atmosphere of devout globe-trotting has seldom been better described than by H.F.M. Prescott, *Jerusalem Journey*, London, 1954, and *Once to Sinai*, London, 1957. A lively discussion of pilgrimage in England is given by, R.C. Finucane, *Miracles and Pilgrims, Popular Beliefs in Medieval England*, London, 1979.

P.J. Geary, *Furta Sacra: Thefts of Relics in the Middle Ages*, London, 1979, shows vividly how important relics were considered to be and the lengths to which medieval people were prepared to go in order to obtain them.

The best one-volume account of crusades to the Holy Land is H–E. Mayer, *The Crusades*, 2nd edn, Oxford, 1986, which contains a valuable discussion of the doctrine of indulgences in chapter 2. A brief modern account of the later crusades has yet to be written. There are excellent monographs on individual crusades and particular areas of activity in K.M. Setton, gen. ed., *History of the Crusades*, vol. III, ed. H.W. Hazard, *The Fourteenth and Fifteenth Centuries*, Madison, 1975.

On p. 125 I cite the Life of St Odo of Cluny by John of Salerno, trans. G. Sitwell, *St Odo of Cluny*, London, 1958, p. 29.

Chapter 14   The Practice of the Christian Life

The works cited in chapters 7, 8, 11, 12, 13, all have relevance for this chapter. L.K. Little, *Religious Poverty and the Profit Economy in Medieval Europe,* London, 1978, discusses the important area of the relation between the mendicant Orders and the developing urban societies of the west.

The *Psychomachia* of Prudentius, which was influential in medieval understanding of the virtuous life, is translated in the Loeb Classical Library, by H.J. Thomson, *The Works of Prudentius,* 2 vols., 1949–53.

Chapter 15   Contacts with Other Religions

Historians of medieval Jewry in western Europe tend, understandably, to emphasize the growth of anti-semitism in that period and therefore to minimize the positive and peaceful aspects of Jewish–Christian relations. A work which attempts to treat official relations between the church and the Jews in a non-polemical way is E.A. Synan, *The Popes and the Jews in the Middle Ages,* London, 1965. I have been helped in my understanding of rare Christian conversions to Judaism by A.S. Abulafia, 'An eleventh-century exchange of letters between a Christian and a Jew', *Journal of Medieval History,* 7 (1981), pp. 153–74.

An important new study of relations between Christians and Muslims is that of B.Z. Kedar, *Crusade and Mission. European Approaches towards the Muslims,* Princeton, 1984. On the translation of the Koran and Muslim theological works, see J. Kritzeck, *Peter the Venerable and Islam,* Princeton, 1964. Helpful to an understanding of the gulf between western knowledge of Islam in the eleventh century and the portrayal of Islam in conventional polemic, J. France, 'The First Crusade and Islam', *The Muslim World,* 67 (1977), pp. 247–57. A great deal of work is being done on Muslims living under Christian rule in Aragon, much of it by R.I. Burns, e.g. *Islam under the Crusaders: Colonial Survival in the Thirteenth-Century Kingdom of Valencia,* Princeton, 1973. On the idiosyncratic ideals of Ramon Lull and their influence the most recent work is that of J.N. Hillgarth, *Ramon Lull and Lullism in Fourteenth-Century France.* Oxford, 1971.

There is no good treatment of western relations with and attitudes towards Buddhism in the Middle Ages, although the materials, I judge, exist for this if an orientalist were interested in writing about it. For western contacts with the orient see the brilliant work of J. Richard, *La Papauté et les Missions d'Orient au Moyen Age,* Rome, 1977. R.W. Southern devotes part of his lectures on *Western Views of Islam in the Middle Ages,* London, 1962, to contacts with Muslims in the Mongol empire, which are often neglected. The most readily available text of one of the medieval explorers of Asia is Marco Polo, *The Travels,* trans. R.E. Latham, Penguin Classics, 1958. On p. 145 I cite Benjamin of Tudela, *The Itinerary,* ed. and trans. M.N. Adler, London, 1907, pp. 5–6. On p. 150 I cite the opening words of *Barlaam and Ioasaph,* trans. G.R. Woodward, H. Mattingly, with intro. by D.M. Lang, Cambridge, 1967. On p. 152 I cite *The Book of the Estate of the Great Khan,* trans. H. Yule, ed. H. Cordier, *Cathay and the Way Thither,* III (Hakluyt Society, ser. 2, vol. 37, 1914), p. 94.

Chapter 16   Relations with the Eastern Churches

For readers who know nothing about the Eastern churches, T. Ware, *The Ortho-dox Church*, Harmondsworth, 1963, is a good introduction. For an introduction to the separated as well as the Orthodox eastern churches, D. Attwater, *The Christian Churches of the East*, 2 vols., new edn, London, 1961. For the Byzantine Church in the Middle Ages, J.M. Hussey, *The Orthodox Church in the Byzantine Empire*, Oxford, 1986. G. Every, *The Byzantine Patriarchate*, 2nd edn, London, 1962, takes into consideration the relations of the other three eastern patriarchates with the western church and does not concentrate solely on Constantinople. The same author's *Understanding Eastern Christianity*, London, 1980, contains much that is illuminating. All these works deal in part with the Eastern schism, but more detailed information is found in S. Runciman, *The Eastern Schism*, Oxford, 1955. The last attempt at oecumenical reunion is treated definitively in J. Gill, *The Council of Florence*, Cambridge, 1961.

For the influence of eastern Christians in western Europe, J–M. Sansterre, *Les Moines grecs et orientaux à Rome aux époques byzantine et carolingienne*, 2 vols, Brussels, 1980, is highly recommended. For the tenth and eleventh centuries B. Hamilton, *Monastic Reform, Catharism and the Crusades, 900–1300*, London, 1979, Essays I–VI.

On Prester John see the entertaining and scholarly work of C.F. Beckingham, *Between Christendom and Islam*, London, 1983, Essays I, II.

Chapter 17   Witchcraft, Ritual Magic and the Cult of the Magus

J.B. Russell, *Witchcraft in the Middle Ages*, London, 1972, is a systematic and sane treatment of a subject which too often attracts cranks. E. Peters, *The Magician, the Witch and the Law*, Hassocks, 1978, is a penetrating study of the way in which as Aristotelian views of the universe became more common in the later Middle Ages magic of all kinds came to be considered malefic by theologians and lawyers.

L. Thorndike, *A History of Magic and Experimental Science*, 8 vols., New York, 1947–58, as the title implies, gives a very full account of the way in which ritual magic formed part of the general understanding of the nature of the physical universe. F. Sherwood Taylor, *The Alchemists*, London, 1952, is a sensible, scientific inquiry into this topic, using terminology which a non-scientist will find comprehensible.

D.P. Walker, *The Ancient Theology*, London, 1972, the early chapters explain the origins of the belief that Christian principles were known to pagans in remote antiquity, a belief which was influential in the Italian Renaissance.

G.G. Scholem, *Major Trends in Jewish Mysticism*, Jerusalem, 1941, is an important study, *inter alia*, of the origins of the Cabala.

F. Yates, *Giordano Bruno and the Hermetic Tradition*, London, 1964, devotes half the book to the growth of the Hermetic tradition in fifteenth-century Florence.

On p. 164 I cite the Bishop's Canon in the translation of Russell, *Witchcraft*, pp. 76–7. On p. 166 I cite the *Malleus Maleficarum* in the translation of Montague Summers, London, 1928 and reprinted London, 1971. On p. 169 I cite Yates, *Giordano Bruno*, p. 111.

Chapter 18   A Tradition of Dissent

The whole field is surveyed by M. Lambert, *Medieval Heresy. Popular Movements from Bogomil to Hus*, London, 1977. The later Middle Ages are dealt with comprehensively by G. Leff, *Heresy in the Later Middle Ages, c.1250–1450*, 2 vols., Manchester, 1967.

On the period to *c.*1300, an invaluable source-book with commentary is provided by, W.L. Wakefield, A.P. Evans, ed. and trans., *Heresies of the High Middle Ages*, New York & London, 1969.

The origins of dualism are surveyed in S. Runciman, *The Medieval Manichee*, Cambridge, 1947, but although this is the most easily accessible work for English readers, few scholars would now accept the filiation between the various dualist movements which the author assumes. R.I. Moore, *The Origins of European Dissent*, 2nd edn, Oxford, 1985, an excellent and lively account of the early reforming movements and the beginnings of Catharism. Moore does not accept that dualists were present in the west in the eleventh century. A good full-length study of Cathars in English is much to be desired, in French it exists in J. Duvernoy, *Le Catharisme*, I. *La Religion des Cathares*, II. *L'Histoire des Cathares*, Paris, 1976, 1979.

J.A.V. Fine, *The Bosnian Church: a New Interpretation*, Boulder, 1975, argues that the established church of Bosnia in the later Middle Ages was schismatic Catholic not Cathar, but this view has found little general support.

A scholarly history of the Waldensians, J. Gonnet, A. Molnar, *Les Vaudois au Moyen Age*, Turin, 1974, and an examination of their absorption by the Calvinists and the rewriting of their history in E. Cameron, *The Reformation of the Heretics. The Waldenses of The Alps, 1480–1580*, Oxford, 1984.

For the Inquisition, B. Hamilton, *The Medieval Inquisition*, London, 1981, with bibliography.

For the origins of Hussitism see M. Spinka, *John Hus, a Biography*, 1968, a more accessible book for the general reader than the more specialized works of this Hussite scholar. An entertaining and valuable introduction to Wycliffe, K.B. McFarlane, *John Wycliffe and the Beginnings of English Nonconformity*, London, 1952. On the later history of the movement, J.A.F. Thomson, *The Later Lollards, 1414–1520*, Oxford, 1965.

The citation from the *Gospel According to the Mark of Silver* on p. 172 is taken from the translation by H. Waddell, *The Wandering Scholars*, Harmondsworth, 1954, p. 171, 6th edn.

Chapter 19   The Individual Quest for God

Much information is contained about solitaries in the general works about monasticism listed under chapter 3.

H. Waddell, *The Desert Fathers*, London, 1936, gives a translation of the Life of St Paul of Thebes.

H. Leyser, *Hermits and the New Monasticism*, London, 1984, has described the resurgence of eremitical communities in the central Middle Ages, a subject I have touched on in 'S. Pierre Damien et les mouvements monastiques de son temps', in *Monastic Reform . . .*, Essay VI.

P. Anson, *The Call of the Desert*, London, 1964, although written for the general reader, contains a wide range of information about medieval solitaries of all kinds.

Phillippe de Commynes, *Memoirs. The Reign of Louis XI, 1461–83*, trans. M. Jones, Penguin Classics, 1972, contains a vivid portrait of St Francis of Paola.

On p. 18 I cite Julian of Norwich, *Revelations of Divine Love*, trans. C. Wolters, Penguin Classics, 1966, p. 68.

Chapter 20   The Difficulties of Belief

The difficulties raised by Catharism are discussed in the works listed under chapter 18, and the problems of Biblical criticism in those listed under chapter 6.

The philosophical problems raised by the new Aristotle are discussed in a variety of works: E. Gilson, *History of Christian Philosophy in the Middle Ages*, London, 1955; D. Knowles, *The Evolution of Medieval Thought*, London, 1962; G. Leff, *Medieval Thought. St Augustine to Ockham*, Harmondsworth, 1958, is particularly illuminating in drawing attention to the indebtedness of Christian thinkers to Arabic and Jewish philosophers when wrestling with the relation between faith and reason.

D.E. Luscombe, *The School of Peter Abelard*, Cambridge, 1969, deals with the influence of Abelard on the scholastic thought and theological speculation of the twelfth century.

F.C. Copleston, *Aquinas*, Harmondsworth, 1955, is one among many studies of this great philosopher, but is written for the non-specialist by a specialist.

D.M. Nicol, *Church and Society in the Last Centuries of Byzantium*, Cambridge, 1979, explains the distinction between the Inner and Outer Learning in the Byzantine tradition, which influenced the west during the Italian Renaissance.

I have been greatly helped in writing this chapter by an unpublished paper by A. Murray, 'Was Religious Doubt regarded as a sin in the Middle Ages?', and I cite the passage from John Busch on p. 190 in Mr Murray's translation, in which I first read it, with his permission.

Index